T.L.S.

ESSAYS AND REVIEWS FROM

The Times Literary Supplement · 1973

12

T.L.S.

ESSAYS AND REVIEWS FROM

The Times Literary Supplement · 1973

12

London
OXFORD UNIVERSITY PRESS
New York   Toronto
1974

Oxford University Press, Ely House, London W1

GLASGOW NEW YORK TORONTO MELBOURNE WELLINGTON
CAPE TOWN IBADAN NAIROBI DAR ES SALAAM LUSAKA ADDIS ABABA
DELHI BOMBAY CALCUTTA MADRAS KARACHI LAHORE DACCA
KUALA LUMPUR SINGAPORE HONG KONG TOKYO

ISBN 0 19 211558 8

Printed in Great Britain by
Alden & Mowbray Ltd
at the Alden Press, Oxford

CONTENTS

1. COOL COUNSELS (28 September)   1

2. A PATRIOT FOR IRELAND (11 May)   12

3. POETRY IN 1973
    (*a*) THE LAST OF AUDEN (12 January)   19
    (*b*) BERRYMAN'S VALEDICTION (23 February)   25
    (*c*) LARKIN'S CHOICE (13 April)   36

4. WORKERS ABROAD (24 August)   46

5. FICTION OF 1973
    (*a*) IRIS MURDOCH: *The Black Prince* (23 February)   57
    (*b*) ANGUS WILSON: *As If By Magic* (1 June)   60
    (*c*) DAN JACOBSON: *The Wonder-Worker* (2 November)   64
    (*d*) LUDVÍK VACULÍK: *The Axe* and *The Guinea Pigs*
         (12 October)   66
    (*e*) THOMAS PYNCHON: *Gravity's Rainbow* (16 November)   70
    (*f*) BERYL BAINBRIDGE: *The Dressmaker* (28 September)   72

6. COMMUNING WITH REALITY (21 December)   74

7. THE NOT SO DARK AGES
    (*a*) ENGLAND MATURES (21 September)   85
    (*b*) THE ECONOMY EXPANDS (17 August)   94

8. THE THREE LADY Cs (27 April)   103

9. A HEGELIAN JESUS (20 July)   115

10. LORDS AND LADIES
    (*a*) SPONTANEOUSLY BYRONIC (19 October)   122
    (*b*) DARKLY SHAKESPEAREAN (27 April)   130

11. THE CLASSICAL HOUSMAN (9 February)   137

12. THE SF STORY (9 November)   144

13. RACE AND IQ (3 August)   154

14. AGAINST CONFORMITY
     (*a*) THE GAPING VOID (25 May)   165
     (*b*) THE HESSE CULT (31 August)   175

15. FICTION OF 1973
     (*g*) VLADIMIR NABOKOV: *Transparent Things* (4 May)   190
     (*h*) ANTHONY POWELL: *Temporary Kings* (22 June)   192
     (*i*) DAVID STOREY: *A Temporary Life* (21 September)   196
     (*j*) CLAUDE SIMON: *Triptyque* (23 March)   198
     (*k*) GRAHAM GREENE: *The Honorary Consul* (14 September)   200
     (*l*) YUKIO MISHIMA: *Runaway Horses* (30 November)   206

16. THE GREAT GRAMMATICUS (16 November)   210

17. THE CONFINES OF TRUTH
     (*a*) A SECOND DESCARTES? (30 November)   217
     (*b*) THE MATHEMATICAL HERITAGE (15 June)   224

NOTE

TLS 12 is a selection of review articles published in the *Times Literary Supplement* during 1973. These were among the longest and most substantial reviews of the year. They have been chosen so as to represent the aims and achievements of the *TLS*; its variety in terms of subject-matter, its astringency, its authoritativeness, and its lucidity. The subjects covered in *TLS 12* range from Harold Macmillan to Mathematics, with, in between: Literature, both English and foreign; History; Economics; Sociology; Science; Religion and Classics. There are three articles on Poetry, two of them standing as memorials to W. H. Auden and John Berryman; also reviews of twelve of the year's more durable novels. The index refers not only to the contents of the anthology but also to the more significant reviews published in the *TLS* during 1973.

I

COOL COUNSELS

THE FIVE EARLIER VOLUMES of Harold Macmillan's memoirs disappointed many readers by containing virtually nothing new. To the well-informed reader they were constantly irritating, partly because the few revelations were mostly trivial, and partly because there were no revelations at all on matters of moment, such as the crisis over the Suez Canal in 1956. Mr Macmillan's pose as the offhand amateur, to whom all these crises were unimportant and rather boring compared to the pleasures of pheasant shooting, reading Trollope, and enjoying an agreeable family life, was carried altogether too far. If that was all there was to the political career, it was reasonably argued, what was the point of writing an autobiography at all, especially one which seemed to become longer and more diffuse as Mr Macmillan became (in words which would have been unfamiliar at his old school) "shorter in wind, as in memory long"? It was with something like alarm and despondency that his final volume—if the sixth was indeed to be final—was awaited. But there was no need to worry, as it turns out: *At the End of the Day* is by far the best and most revealing of the lot. The wily old magician has pulled a fast one on his critics yet again.

This volume covers a shorter period of time than any of the others except its immediate predecessor. Both deal with the events of about two years, with some marginal overspill at each end. But there is no comparison between them in drama and importance. The title of the fifth volume—*Pointing the Way*—seemed designed to cover up some uncertainty of direction: it might as well have been called *Marking Time*. Mr Macmillan's last two years in office, by contrast, were as dramatic as any since the Second World War. They included one notable success, several intractable problems which are still with us today, and about half-a-dozen major crises. The success was the signature of the Partial Test-Ban Treaty in July, 1963—the last

---

HAROLD MACMILLAN: *At the End of the Day, 1961–1963*. 572 pp. Macmillan. £4.50.

1

important act of Mr Macmillan's term of office. The continuing problems differ from those of today only in their relatively less acute severity: abroad, the Middle East, South-East Asia, and Central Africa; at home, the search for an incomes policy, the emergence of "stagflation", the influx of coloured immigrants; and overall the need for international monetary reform. But towering above all these were the great crises of 1961–63: the Berlin Wall, the Cuba missiles, the negotiations with the European Communities, the security scandals, and the Profumo affair. As Mr Macmillan wrote with characteristic understatement, before the worst blows had fallen, "We have had a run of bad luck"; and, as he added with equally characteristic resignation, "Once this starts, everything seems to go wrong."

It is impossible not to admire the good-humoured stoicism and self-deprecating wit with which he faced his setbacks. Two qualities bore him up throughout: loyalty and a kind of relaxed irony. Loyalty is the sovereign virtue for Mr Macmillan. He would never let a colleague down, but he would not readily forgive a colleague who let him down: that was Mr Profumo's great offence. There are many examples in this volume. His decision to dismiss Selwyn Lloyd from the Treasury comes out clearly as the most painful of his political career and one of the few episodes which he frankly admits that he mismanaged. In the security crisis of 1962, he blames himself for allowing a junior Minister to resign, but congratulates himself that "I have been able to save the First Lord". What hurt him most about de Gaulle's veto on Britain's entry into the European Economic Community was the widespread suspicion that he had misled his "old friend" about his relations with the United States. There are constant references to his "devoted staff", ranging from housemaids to Permanent Under-Secretaries; and his devotion to them is strikingly paternal. The same feeling can be detected in his relations with the Queen, which were almost explicitly based on those of Melbourne and Disraeli with Victoria. More fortunate in his moment of history even than his predecessors, he was able to extend the same disarmingly gracious paternalism to President Kennedy as well. He must have enjoyed making the suggestion that the Queen and the President ought to write letters to each other.

Politics was for Mr Macmillan such a personal art that historians will find a significance in his treatment of each one of his contemporaries. Gaitskell and Wilson both come out in a more attractive light than in previous volumes, as the asperities of controversy grow milder in his old age. Adenauer is tiresome and ineffective, Diefenbaker unintelligible, Kennedy admirable in a crisis but apt to be led astray by bad influences like Robert McNamara and George Ball. Towards his younger colleagues he is fairly cool, though Edward Heath and Reginald Maudling earn good marks for trying. Mr Macmillan senses everywhere in the new generation a lack of imagination and vision. Even Kennedy, though "an extraordinarily quick and effective operator" on a specific problem, was too cautious: "on the wider issues, he seems rather lost". The same was evidently true of Mr Macmillan's own Cabinet, perhaps because of the influence of R. A. Butler. The relationship of the two men remains mysterious: Butler is constantly praised for hard work, diplomatic skill, academic brilliance, and so on; but he is also described as "a patient and unselfish political camel", and Mr Macmillan's quiet amusement whenever he comes a momentary cropper is scarcely concealed.

His treatment of Butler was always enigmatic and never wholly admirable. He is perhaps right in thinking that Butler feared to become Prime Minister—a judgment which is borne out by Butler's own memoirs—but there could be no question that he was the outstanding candidate in merit and seniority when Mr Macmillan had to retire. He had indeed been so for several years. Mr Macmillan recognized this when he explored the possibility of making Butler Deputy Prime Minister in 1961, but concluded that it was constitutionally impossible; he recognized it again when he appointed Butler to the unprecedented office of First Secretary of State (which he does not even mention in this volume). What could these things mean except that he regarded Butler as his natural successor? Yet he laments, as though he had anyone but himself to blame for it, that "I was not so happily placed as Churchill, whose successor had been designated for many years and against whom there could be no serious candidate". It seems that at heart Mr Macmillan never wanted Butler to succeed him. He gives as one reason the belief that Butler could not win the coming General Election, though most political observers would argue that Butler could have attracted the handful of floating voters who, in the event, tipped the scale against Sir Alec Douglas-Home. More probably he found Butler wanting by his own crucial test of loyalty. Memories of Munich and Suez, neither of which had been Butler's finest hour, still died hard.

Butler also had another defect, judged by Macmillan's criteria.

That relaxed irony which was a bond between the Prime Minister and President Kennedy was entirely missing from Butler's temperament. One of the most engaging anecdotes in this volume is of a meeting between Macmillan and Kennedy in 1963—the last time they ever met—to plan their strategy for the negotiations in Moscow on the Test-Ban Treaty. Having agreed everything in a private tête-à-tête, they felt obliged to stage a formal conference for the benefit of their staffs. Since there was no matter of substance left to discuss, Kennedy jokingly invited the Prime Minister's views on the appointment of a non-American Supreme Allied Commander in Europe, to the horror of the American officials present. Macmillan responded by suggesting the appointment of a Russian, in readiness for a war with Communist China. British officials took him so seriously that one of them was at pains to explain that the Prime Minister did not actually mean quite that. Butler, though by no means without a sense of humour, could never have indulged in such a charade. For one thing, he could never have been on the necessarily intimate terms with Kennedy. Nor could he ever have imitated Melbourne, as Macmillan could, in saying after a Cabinet meeting that it did not much matter what they all said so long as they all said the same thing.

Mr Macmillan's temperament was not an easy one to fit in with except for somebody with a closely similar background of education, society and experience. The pose of relaxation and detachment concealed a strong will and nervous intensity. He would often convey to subordinates that in a critical situation "the right action is no action at all"; but this was not always so, and it was a matter of judgment—*his* judgment—when it was right to act and when it was right simply to contemplate passing events. "It may be best to let things go on quietly for a bit", he would say, and act accordingly, even in the Cuba missiles crisis. But woe betide colleagues who took their cues too literally! Selwyn Lloyd was dismissed for failing to produce an incomes policy to follow the "pay pause". Peter Thorneycroft was sternly rebuked for lack of determination in pursuing the integration of the Service Ministries into the Ministry of Defence. Toward the end Mr Macmillan was infected by nervousness himself about the dynamism of the Labour Party under Mr Wilson's leadership, while "we are doing nothing". This was a sign that he was losing his grip, for in 1959 it was precisely by creating a feeling that nothing special needed to be done that he had won the general election. By 1963, the shock of the Profumo affair had already shown him that no more elections were to be won with slogans like "You've never had it so good!"

The fact that Mr Macmillan had plainly lost his grip by the late summer of 1963 makes it the more difficult to disentangle the drama of the succession. Almost the only thing that is quite plain is that no one—not even Macmillan himself—thought of Lord Home as a candidate until the eleventh hour. He reproduces a cartoon which makes the point with typical acuteness: five candidates trying on his clothes, none of them Lord Home. Beyond that it would perhaps be unfair to press the recollections of a sick man. Mr Macmillan tells the whole story with frankness so far as he knew it, but it has long since been made plain (for example, by Iain Macleod) that he could not have known it all. What is new is that Mr Macmillan had been seriously considering resignation for some weeks before he was taken ill, and had decided against it only within the last twenty-four hours. This fact makes it rather more reprehensible that he had made no contingency plan for the succession at all. Appealing some-what disingenuously to past history, he seems to suggest that it was none of his business. The Queen evidently did not agree with him, and seemed "very distressed", at least partly because of "all the difficulties about a successor in which the Crown will be much involved".

Mr Macmillan's appeal to history was characteristic, for he is equally at home with historians and historical figures. This volume begins with a long quotation from Arnold Toynbee, and more than once invokes parallels supplied by Macaulay or by historical novelists like Scott and Trollope. (Detective fiction is outside Mr Macmillan's ken, however, and this is used to explain why he was taken by surprise at the security scandals.) He was always trying to avoid the pitfalls of great predecessors, such as Peel, or to understand de Gaulle by reference to Napoleon and Louis XIV. Disraeli and Lord John Russell, Morley and Harcourt, the Abbé Sieyès and Talleyrand, and even Tiberius and Caius Gracchus are carefully scrutinized for illuminating precedents. More often than not the precedents are encouraging. For example, the Sino-Soviet dispute showed how history repeats itself:

Ideological agreement led no more on the Communist side to automatic cooperation than it did among the nations of Europe in the sixteenth and seventeenth centuries.

Mr Macmillan's selective reading of history through misted and rose-tinted spectacles goes some way towards accounting for his relaxed attitude in the face of crises. It was his downfall in the end, when he imagined that the press, in its campaign against him over security and Profumo, was going to suffer the same discomfiture as Titus Oates. But it served him in good stead through the international crises of his last two years, particularly the overlapping series in the autumn of 1962: the revolution in the Yemen, the Chinese attack on India, and the installation of Russian missiles in Cuba. In each case Macmillan's reactions were calm, shrewd, and little indebted to the orthodoxies of professional advice, as his own account shows cogently but without egoism. He never much liked experts. In the question of recognizing the new republican government of the Yemen he would have no truck with the diplomatic fiction that recognition does not confer approval, which everyone except diplomatists knows that it does; and he vigorously carried Kennedy with him in insisting on a bargain with the republicans before granting recognition. In the Chinese-Indian conflict, his instinct told him that the Communists intended no more than a limited advance to improve their frontier-line (for which, incidentally, they had at least an arguable case in international law); and again he was right. But most important of all was his role in the crisis over the missiles in Cuba, which can now be seen to have been not only Kennedy's but also Macmillan's finest hour.

For two reasons, the significance of the chapter called "On the Brink" could easily be missed. One is Mr Macmillan's characteristic method of narrative, which often suggests that it was an amusing lark, not without its awkward moments, but bound to come out right in the end provided one's own team all played the game in the right spirit. The other is that myths have grown up around the crisis which no attempt has previously been made to remove. It has come to be assumed that President Kennedy and his advisers managed the crisis entirely on their own, without consulting their allies beyond the occasional courtesy of keeping them informed; and that the British government in particular, so far from enjoying a "special relationship", was merely an impotent spectator. Mr Macmillan now shows, with documentary evidence which cannot be impugned, that the "special relationship" was never more special, not even in the heyday of Churchill and Roosevelt, than it was in October 1962. The triumphant vindication of his style of personal diplomacy has also inspired one of the best examples of his individual style of writing. It has been worth wading through six volumes of increasingly diffuse reminiscences for this succinct masterpiece.

Mr Macmillan was conscious from the first moment of his opportunity to write a definitive page of history. He took no risk that the world might little note nor long remember what he and the President said and did. Every conversation was recorded, and his diary kept up day by day. "The first day of the World Crisis!" he noted on October 22 with Churchillian enthusiasm. As a matter of fact, it had begun the evening before:

I was working quietly in my room in London on Sunday evening, 21 October, when about 10 p m I was handed by the duty clerk an urgent message from President Kennedy informing me that a serious crisis was rapidly developing between the United States and the Soviet Union.

Although Mr Macmillan does not condescend to mention it, that sentence demolishes with a single easy stroke the entire case of the critics who have belittled his role. For ten years they have been mocking the pretence that Britain played any part in the Cuba crisis. They can now read in the original texts that Mr Macmillan was not merely the first and only foreign statesman to be informed and consulted about the crisis, but that Kennedy was in daily contact with him to seek his advice, to the point where the management of it was little short of a joint Anglo-American operation. "The whole episode was like a battle", he writes; and justly adds: "We in Admiralty House felt as if we were in the battle HQ."

This conclusion emerges not merely—in fact, not at all—from the inflated egoism of an old man's memories. It emerges from the daily record of the "hot line" across the Atlantic. And it was entirely personal to Mr Macmillan, for the American ambassador in London added an immediate warning to the initial message:

The President particularly stressed that not only are the contents of the message confidential in the highest degree but that the fact that you are receiving a message at this time should on no account become known.

The consultation was exclusive and continuous throughout the crisis. It was initiated by the President and of course welcomed by the Prime Minister. But the latter made no attempt to press his advice or to solicit confidences: he had no need to. Day after day the two men spoke over what Mr Macmillan typically calls "the peculiar mechanism", always on the initiative of the President. The conversations were recorded, and copious extracts from them are published here for the first time. Never can a great historical crisis have been so fully documented; and never, too, can a man who was not nominally a participant have played such a crucial role in an international confrontation.

Mr Macmillan's story must be read as he wrote it. To summarize it is unnecessary, since the outcome is well known, and it would also be to rob it of its personal savour. It is a puzzle that he has given no hint of the truth before; but Mr Macmillan enjoys nothing better than being a puzzle. The reason cannot have lain in any mundane consideration of official secrets, for which almost all Prime Ministers have a robust contempt. Such considerations, if they applied at all, would apply today. No doubt the real reason lies in Mr Macmillan's sense of history. He did not mind being misunderstood and misrepresented because he knew that "great is truth and will prevail". That it did not prevail at once gave him the additional, ironic pleasure of a private joke. "Actually, our secrets were almost too well kept", he pretends to lament. The only mistake in the whole exercise, he suggests, was to send the crucial message to Khrushchev through diplomatic channels. Consequently it was slow to leak out and was not seen to have had its proper impact on Khrushchev's climb-down. "It almost seemed as if we had sent the telegram backing the horse *after* the race."

No one can teach Mr Macmillan how to write with his tongue in his cheek. He does so knowing that history must vindicate him. But history, he seems to have reasoned at the same time, is too serious a matter to be left to the historians, some of whom (like editors of *The Times*) he finds pretty exasperating.

So a new ploy had to be adopted without delay:

We are doing something to let the truth be known. . . . It will gradually seep through from Whitehall to London society and thence pretty generally. But it is rather a bore, and has some dangers. The British people must not feel themselves slighted.

The dangers were greater than he thought. "London society", as Mr Macmillan had once known it, did not exist any more. It had become something very different, as he was to learn from the Profumo affair the next year, when he had to admit that "I had not myself much knowledge of this new social world". Whatever steps were taken to "let the truth be known" were quite ineffective in London, where the derogatory myth was already becoming well established. They were more effective in Washington, where a good deal of anger was generated at the suggestion that American policy was unduly influenced by the British. No doubt they also had their effect in Paris, where de Gaulle could only be conscious that he had indeed, as was wrongly supposed to have been the case with Macmillan, played no part at all in the great drama. The French people, too, as he might well have written, "must not feel themselves slighted". It is understandable that he now regarded Britain as incorrigibly committed to the role of the United States's Trojan Horse. Exactly three months after the Cuba crisis ended, de Gaulle pronounced the famous "Non" which shut Britain out of the EEC for a decade.

Mr Macmillan's account of this other crucial episode is again illuminating but also tantalizing. It is less dramatic than the story of the Cuban crisis both because the issues were less apocalyptic and because the circumstances are already better known. But it is tantalizing because, even when Mr Macmillan has set down everything that he knows, the enigma of de Gaulle's performance remains unsolved. If he never meant to allow Britain into Europe, why did he allow the matter to be negotiated at all? If he did accept the possibility of Britain's membership in principle, why did he veto it just when the last of the technical difficulties were being removed? The most convincing point which Mr Macmillan makes is that the difficulty from de Gaulle's point of view lay in the essential similarity of the British and French attitudes to Europe. Both wanted a loosely organized *Europe des patries*, which both wanted to dominate. It was therefore impossible for both to be satisfied. But that was just as true at the beginning as at the end of the negotiations. It cannot therefore have been the decisive factor unless at some point de Gaulle changed his mind. Mr Macmillan is reluctant to accept that it was solely the "special relationship" between Britain and the United States which changed his mind. The reluctance is understandable, because the suggestion has been made that during his visit to France in December 1962 he misled de Gaulle about Britain's dealings with the United States on nuclear matters. It is not necessary to believe that unfair suggestion in order to conclude that de Gaulle was nevertheless deeply upset by the Nassau agreement, as well as disturbed by the Anglo-American cooperation in the Cuba crisis from which he was himself excluded.

The rebuff over the EEC did not affect Mr Macmillan's personal respect for de Gaulle, any more than the cancellation of his precious

Skybolt missile affected his personal respect for Kennedy. In the
latter case it could be argued that no British Prime Minister could
afford to nurse a grievance against any American President. But in
both cases there are better explanations. One is Mr Macmillan's
steady confidence that the verdict of history will vindicate him.
Another is his natural magnanimity. As Prime Minister, he was a
bad butcher; as a political controversialist, he is a bad hater. He
prefers to tease rather than abuse his opponents. He has charitable
words even for Mr Profumo. For those whom he cannot forgive, his
method of chastisement is a kind of pregnant anonymity. Sometimes
they can be identified, sometimes not. It is not hard to put a name to
the British Ambassador in Moscow whom he blames for the re-
cruitment of Vassall as a Russian spy, or to the American Treasury
official ("subsequently said to be a Communist agent") who
torpedoed Keynes's plan for an international monetary unit. It
would take more research to identify the former colleague ("one
of the most incompetent Ministers in office that I could recall")
who had suddenly become "a great authority on the subject of which
he had appeared almost ignorant when responsible", or the other
ex-Minister who "although still a bore and a complete failure at the
minor post to which I appointed him on trial, had acquired a new
authority below the gangway". By contrast, he has no hesitation
in naming the "agreeable but somewhat eccentric M.P.", Sir Harry
Legge-Bourke, who made a speech calling for his resignation, and
found himself a few days later, to his embarrassment, sitting next
to the Prime Minister in the Smoking Room. Naturally Mr Macmillan
stood him a drink: at least he was not a bore.

There is no question of Mr Macmillan's serene magnanimity.
His vindication by history will be another matter. Almost certainly
he will be recognized as the last British Prime Minister who success-
fully operated as if Britain were still a great power: his chapter on
the Cuba crisis alone virtually puts that beyond doubt. But he has
an even better claim, on which the last volume of his autobiography
lays little stress. In home affairs he was a Prime Minister of the same
stature as Neville Chamberlain and Clement Attlee; and he united
the nation as Baldwin had done, without succumbing to Baldwin's
fatal weakness. In his last two years Mr Macmillan's eyes were
fixed constantly on the international scene, as Churchill's had been
at the same stage of his career. A typical report on a Cabinet meeting
devotes only three lines to routine business, "chiefly schemes for

increasing pensions, insurance payments and other social benefits'',
before returning to the great world overseas. Only once or twice does
Mr Macmillan reveal his lifelong feelings on the internal state of the
nation: when he went to take part in a forlorn by-election in his old
constituency of Stockton, for instance, or when he sent Lord Hail-
sham to investigate the economic problems of the North-East, and
refused to allow his Chancellor of the Exchequer to contemplate
deflationary measures leading to unemployment. It is easy to forget
that his original reputation was made in domestic affairs, as an
early disciple of Keynes, and that he first became a national figure
by carrying out the pledge to build 300,000 houses in a year.

It is impossible yet to judge whether the domestic or the international Macmillan will enjoy the longer reputation, but there are
not many Prime Ministers of whom that doubt could even be
suggested. Watching his own performance, as he had been doing
with amused detachment for fifty years, Mr Macmillan himself would
probably hope for what he would casually call a bit of both. Whatever
his private feelings, his explicit claims for himself would be a
calculated underestimate. He would recognize that no major
historic change was completely comprised within his seven years as
Prime Minister—the second longest term in this century. Processes
which had already begun, both at home and abroad, continued
without getting out of hand. Until the last unlucky months, Mr
Macmillan seemed to be always in touch with them, if not always
in control. That is about as much as any modern Prime Minister
can expect. As a historian, evaluating himself as a politician, Mr
Macmillan could rate himself a qualified success. As a publisher,
evaluating himself as a writer, he could rate himself a very useful
addition to the list; and as any publisher would be delighted to note,
his latest book is by a long way his best so far.

2
A PATRIOT FOR IRELAND

ROGER CASEMENT, an Irishman, was hanged at Pentonville on August 3, 1916, as a traitor to the King of England. Ellis, the hangman, thought him "the bravest man it fell to my unhappy lot to execute". For half a century Casement's body lay in Pentonville jail. In 1953 Churchill told de Valera that it must lie there for ever: the law on the subject was "specific and binding". Twelve years later Harold Wilson was more generous. On February 23, 1965, Casement's remains were returned to Ireland. They were given a state funeral at Glasnevin. President de Valera had been ill and was told that he should not attend. He insisted that he must. At least, he was told, he must keep his head covered. De Valera replied: "Casement deserves better than that." Uncovered, he delivered the funeral oration.

Indeed Casement deserved better than that—better than the treatment he received during his lifetime and better than that accorded to him after his death. Even biographers sympathetic to Casement have been more interested in the authenticity of his private diaries than in his public achievements or, when they dealt with these, have presented him as an isolated, impractical figure— romantic, perhaps, but futile. At long last Brian Inglis has given Casement his due. This splendid book tells the story of a troubled soul who surmounted his troubles and rose to greatness—great as a noble character and greater still as the man who raised high the flag of Irish freedom and unity.

Mr Inglis brings great advantages to his task. Like Casement, he was brought up a Protestant and a Unionist, loyal to the British Crown. Like Casement, he came to put Ireland first and to mean by Ireland the united island. He understands Casement as no previous biographer has done. For Mr Inglis, Casement matters politically. He has seen through Casement's diaries and, though acknowledging them as genuine, emphasizes their unimportance for the study of

---

BRIAN INGLIS: *Roger Casement*. 448 pp. Hodder and Stoughton. £4.50.

Casement's career. Connoisseurs of official secrecy will be fascinated to learn that, while the diaries are now available to scholars, the Home Office files on Casement remain closed for 100 years. This concealment is easy to understand. The diaries were used quite irrelevantly to blacken Casement's character and send him to the gallows. We are still not allowed to know which British minister or civil servant hit on this repulsive idea. However we can make a good guess.

Casement's achievements were unexpected. He did not learn Irish patriotism at his mother's knee. He knew nothing of Wolfe Tone or of his later hero John Mitchel. He was hardly aware that there was an Irish language. He grew up in Ulster, a Protestant and a gentleman, regarding himself as a loyal British subject. He pursued an orthodox career in the British consular service. Here fate first took a hand. When stories reached Europe of the atrocities being committed in the Congo during Leopold's pursuit of Red Rubber, Casement, being the man on the spot, was sent to investigate. Casement discovered, to his own surprise, his hatred of human brutality and oppression. Casement was not alone in the Congo affair. E. D. Morel conducted the campaign in England and merited an equal tribute of admiration. But it was Casement's patient investigation, with its deadly array of facts, that made the campaign possible.

Mr Inglis tells the Congo story very much from Casement's side. The work of Leopold in the Congo has been studied in much greater detail by Belgian scholars, sometimes to the point of apology or even justification. Others will be content to echo the words of Cecil Rhodes, no mean judge, who said after meeting Leopold II: "Satan! I tell you that man is Satan!" At Leopold's orders thousands of natives were tortured or massacred. Vast areas of the country were depopulated. Few worse crimes were witnessed in modern history. It is little excuse that Belgium acquired some grandiose buildings from her share of the profits.

Unlike Morel, Casement was not a good organizer, nor was he at this time a good speaker. He relied more on the Foreign Office than on public opinion. Here he was disappointed. In earlier days British foreign secretaries and the Foreign Office had been themselves champions of human freedom. Palmerston, for instance, wrote more dispatches on the fight against the slave trade than on any other subject and declared that he would leave public life if Parliament cut off the money for the anti-slavery patrols.

In the twentieth century the Foreign Office went sour. In its eyes Casement was a nuisance, a consul who had exceeded his functions. The British Ambassador to Brussels wrote off the humanitarians as being "always prone to sentimentalism about slavery and other local customs to which the native populations were attached". Casement's report was emasculated and for a time withheld from publication. Lord Lansdowne, the Foreign Secretary, acquiesced. Better things might have been expected from Sir Edward Grey, his Liberal successor, particularly since he later described the Congo campaign as the greatest since Gladstone's against the Bulgarian atrocities. But, as Mr Inglis points out, Grey in his memoirs devoted only a few sentences to this campaign and many chapters to his devious diplomacy. Fitzmaurice, Grey's Under-Secretary, remarked: "It is not our interest to be having a row with Belgium also, if perchance we are having a row with Germany."

Casement did not have Morel's persistence. Also he needed new employment in his career in order to keep going financially. It was the Congo that first turned Casement against the British Government and made him distrust British policy. In a sense the Congo also led Casement to the cause of Irish independence. He returned to Ireland while waiting for a fresh appointment and there realized that the Irish people were in much the same situation as the natives of the Congo—ruled for good or ill by others, not allowed to rule themselves. Casement changed almost overnight from a loyal British subject into a potential rebel. This was more striking than it may seem in the light of later events. We know that Ireland was to become a republic. In the first decade of the present century this view was held only by a few Fenians in the obscure Irish Republican Brotherhood. The Home Rulers who dominated Irish politics regarded themselves as British. Their aim was autonomy, not independence. Casement was the first prominent figure who transformed the dreams of the IRB into a practical creed.

Casement said at the end of his life: "The best thing was the Congo." He himself contributed little to the final victory, when Leopold II was discredited and forced to transfer the Congo to Belgium. E. D. Morel received and deserved the principal credit for this. Mr Inglis might have added that the pursuit of Red Rubber, with all its horrors, became unnecessary once plantation rubber proved practicable and more profitable.

Casement, however, had a further encounter with the evil he had exposed in the Congo. This time the scandal was on the Putomayo in South America. Once more Casement was the man on the spot. Once more he investigated and produced a damning report. The response of British opinion was less emphatic. The same sort of campaign cannot be conducted twice, much as the Armenian massacres of the 1890s failed to provoke the stir that the Bulgarian atrocities had done twenty years earlier. E. D. Morel was now denouncing Grey's foreign policies. The British and American governments, though endorsing Casement's reports, were only concerned to hush up the scandal. Casement himself left South America and the British consular service.

The few years before the First World War were decisive for Casement's historical fame and for his own fate. Though knighted in 1911, he had ceased to regard himself as a British subject and had become an unequivocal Irish nationalist. He learnt to speak on the public platform. He counted as a political figure. Casement took up the almost unnoticed movement of Sinn Fein and transformed it into a practical cause. Ireland, he preached, should not seek concessions from Great Britain. She should declare her independence and act on it. Like Arthur Griffith, he pointed to the example of Hungary, with the curious personal link that his own father had saved Kossuth when threatened with extradition from Turkey.

Casement added a further point, not made by any other Irish leader. Irish independence, he believed, should be won in cooperation with Ulster, not against her. He even held that Ulster should lead the movement as she had done in previous centuries. Ulster's claim not to be incorporated in a Home Rule Ireland was exactly the same as Ireland's claim not to be incorporated in the United Kingdom. Casement often declared that he and Carson were fighting for the same cause and should appear on the same platform. It was English politicians, such as F. E. Smith, exploiting Ireland's difficulties for their own party advantage, whom he wanted to keep out.

Ulster provided a more practical analogy. If Ulster were permitted to buy arms in Germany and to seek German support, as the Unionists did, Ireland was entitled to do the same. As an independent country, Ireland should follow an independent policy. British maritime supremacy was no concern of hers, and the British must learn to live with a neutral Ireland. Casement's policy had its forerunners in the "Wild Geese" and later the Irish republicans who had sought French aid for Ireland's liberation.

All the same, he made a disastrous error. He thought that the Germans would take up the Irish cause for idealistic reasons, just as Masaryk counted on the support of British idealists for the liberation of the Czechs. There were enough British idealists to make Masaryk's line respectable and not a mere act of treason. There were no such idealists in Germany. When war broke out, Casement went to Germany and tried to recruit an Irish legion. The Germans, who preferred the British Empire to a free Ireland, regarded him as a nuisance. Casement became disillusioned, embittered. When reports reached him of a projected rising in Ireland, he travelled to Ireland in a German submarine in order to give warning that there would be no German aid and that, without it, a rising could not succeed.

This was the supreme irony of Casement's career. He was arrested and condemned to death for seeking to provoke rebellion when in fact he had come in order to ensure that the rising did not take place. Casement's trial makes sorry reading. He, an Irishman, was tried by an English Lord Chief Justice and an English jury. How, he asked the jury, would they like it if they had attempted a rising in England and had then been shipped off to Dublin for trial?

Casement wished to conduct his own case and simply to deny the authority over him of an English court. He was overruled. His counsel, Serjeant Sullivan, fought the case on a technicality, based on a statute of Edward III's reign. Naturally he lost. At one moment Sullivan ventured to hint that Casement had only done what F. E. Smith, the prosecuting Attorney-General, had done before him. When pulled up by Reading, the Lord Chief Justice—pilloried by Kipling as Gehazi—Sullivan broke down and withdrew from the case.

Casement was allowed to speak only after the jury had found him guilty. Mr Inglis does the great service of printing Casement's speech in full. It merits Wilfrid Blunt's verdict: "the finest document in patriotic literature, finer than anything in Plutarch or elsewhere in Pagan literature". It moved Blunt to "anger and delight that anything so perfect should have come from the mouth of a man of our time condemned to death". Years later, Nehru described the profound impression that the "extraordinarily moving and eloquent" statement made on him: "It seemed to point out exactly how a subject nation should feel."

Casement was condemned to death. There was an outcry in the United States, though President Wilson, himself of Ulster stock, passed by on the other side. It seemed that the trial would win neutral sympathies for Casement instead of discrediting him. Now was the time to produce the "black diaries"—private jottings of previous years which showed beyond reasonable doubt that Casement was a practising homosexual. The idea of discrediting Casement by means of the diaries seems to have originated with Ernley Blackwell, legal adviser to the Home Office. It was taken up by many others. Herbert Samuel, then Home Secretary, wrote: "Had Casement not been a man of atrocious moral character, the situation would have been even more difficult." Asquith asked Page, the American ambassador, whether he had heard about the diary. Page replied that he had seen it and had been given photographed copies of some of it. Asquith said: "Excellent, and you need not be particular about keeping it to yourself."

What was the relevance of the diaries even if they were genuine? None. No one had ever suspected Casement of homosexuality, and it never affected his policy or public conduct. For that matter, there were two practising homosexuals in the Cabinet which determined to blacken Casement. One of them later committed suicide; the other went into exile in order to escape prosecution. Asquith, however, passed no word of condemnation on either of them. Was it worse to run after boys than to develop senile passions for young girls and to be helpless with drink on the Treasury bench? Such was the state of Asquith, and it is held not to derogate from his conduct of affairs when Prime Minister. The loathsome story has no interest except as illustrating the desperate measures that an Imperial government will resort to when cornered.

Casement's death had quite other significance. It created the importance of Sinn Fein. The Easter Rising had been conducted by a few members of the IRB, not by Sinn Fein. Thanks to Casement, Sinn Fein got the credit for it. The independence of Ireland triumphed when Casement was hanged. He represented a second cause. He said in his last speech:

We aimed at winning the Ulster Volunteers to the cause of a United Ireland. We aimed at uniting all Irishmen in a natural and national bond of cohesion based on mutual self-respect. Our hope was a natural one and, if left to ourselves, not hard to accomplish. If external forces of destruction would but leave us alone, we were sure that Nature must bring us together.

Here is Casement's message for the present day. There is no Irish problem beyond solution. The problem that has racked Ireland for centuries is the British presence in Ireland. That problem can be solved only by British withdrawal.

3

POETRY IN 1973

(a) THE LAST OF AUDEN

"You don't need me to tell you what's going on:" writes W. H. Auden in his latest book's first piece, "the ochlocratic media, joint with under-the-dryer gossip, process and vent without intermission all to-day's ugly secrets. Imageable no longer, a featureless anonymous threat from behind, to-morrow has us gallowed shitless: if what is to happen occurs according to what Thucydides defined as 'human', we've had it, are in for a disaster that no four-letter words will tardy."

This passage is highly interesting prose, detectable only in its lexical intensity as the work of a poet: Hazlitt, right on this point as on so many others, long ago laid down the word about that giveaway proneness to local effect. An ochlocracy is mob rule; the *OED* last noticed "joint" being used that way in 1727; to gallow is an obsolete form of to gally, which is itself a way of saying to frighten that hasn't been heard for a long time anywhere except in a whaling station; "tardy" as a verb staggered on a few years past its moment of glory in *A Winter's Tale* to disappear in 1623. But let's start again.

In the title poem of his latest book, W. H. Auden writes:

> ... You don't need me to tell you what's
> going on: the ochlocratic media,
> joint with under-the-dryer gossip,
> process and vent without intermission
>
> all to-day's ugly secrets. Imageable
> no longer, a featureless anonymous
> threat from behind, to-morrow has us
> gallowed shitless: if what is to happen

(a) W. H. Auden: *Epistle to a Godson.* 72 pp. Faber and Faber. £1.40.
(b) John Berryman: *Delusions, Etc.* 69 pp. Faber and Faber. £1.50.
(c) *The Oxford Book of Twentieth-Century English Verse.* Chosen by Philip Larkin. 641 pp. Clarendon Press: Oxford University Press. £3.

> occurs according to what Thucydides
> defined as 'human', we've had it, are in for
> a disaster that no four-letter
> words will tardy. . . .

This passage is highly interesting poetry, but only within the confines of Auden's strictly prosaic later manner. Sentences wriggle intricately and at length down the syllabic grid.

> Blessed be all metrical rules that
>   forbid automatic responses,
>   force us to have second thoughts,
>   free from the fetters of Self.

The greatest modern verse technician, Auden long ago ran out of metrical rules needing more than a moment's effort to conform to. Technically, his later manner—which involves setting up a felt rhythmic progress inside an arbitrary syllabic convention—is really a way of restoring to the medium some of the resistance his virtuosity earlier wiped out. This technical mortification is closely allied with the ethical stand forbidding any irrationalities, all happy accidents. No automatic responses, no first thoughts. Helping to explain the omission of certain poems from his *Collected Shorter Poems 1927–1957*, Auden wrote in 1966:

A dishonest poem is one which expresses, no matter how well, feelings or beliefs which its author never felt or entertained. For example, I once expressed a desire for "New styles of architecture"; but I have never liked modern architecture. I prefer *old* styles, and one must be honest even about one's prejudices. Again, and much more shamefully, I once wrote:
>   History to the defeated
>   may say alas but cannot help nor pardon.

To say this is to equate goodness with success. It would have been bad enough if I had ever held this wicked doctrine, but that I should have stated it simply because it sounded to me rhetorically effective is quite inexcusable.

Glumly reconciling themselves to the loss of *September, 1939*, in its entirety and favourite fragments from other poems engraved in the consciousness of a generation, critics respectfully conceded Auden's right to take back what he had so freely given. It was interesting, though, that no strong movement arose to challenge Auden's assumption that these youthful poetic crimes were committed by the same self being dishonest, rather than a different self being honest. Auden was denying the pluralism of his own personality. It was his privilege to do so if he wanted to, but it was remarkable how tamely this crankily simplistic reinterpretation of his own creative selfhood was accepted.

More remarkable still, however, was the virtual silence which greeted the spectacle of a great modern talent disallowing the automatic response, proclaiming the virtues of knowing exactly what you mean against the vices of letting the poem find out what *it* wants to mean. Auden had apparently worked his way through to the last sentence of the *Tractatus Logico-Philosophicus*. "Wovon man nicht sprechen kann", Wittgenstein had written, "darüber muss man schweigen." What we cannot speak about we must pass over in silence. It was piquant to find the poet who above all others seemed to command the secret of modern magic occupying this position so very long after the philosopher who thought of it had moved out. Here was a man attacking the validity of his own seren-dipity, discrediting his own trick of setting up a bewitching resonance. Long before, combining with Louis MacNeice in preparing that seductive lash-up of a book *Letters from Iceland*, Auden had written:

> And the traveller hopes: "Let me be far from any
> Physician"; And the poets have names for the sea;

But on the way to press this was accidentally transformed into

> And the traveller hopes: "Let me be far from any
> Physician"; And the ports have names for the sea;

Noting straight away that "ports" suggested more than "poets", Auden let the slip stand. The names that ports have for the sea are likely to be functional as well as mythical, mistrustful as well as admiring, many-rooted rather than casually appropriate—in a word, serious. Or so we guess. Or so the unexpected ring of the word, its unpredictability in that context, leads us to conjecture—gives us *room* to conjecture. And this thinking-space, the parkland of imagina-tion that existed in Auden's earlier manner, was what marked it out— and what he annihilated in forming his later manner. There have been artists who possessed some of Auden's magic and who went on to lose it, but it is hard to think of anyone who deliberately suppressed it. All conscious artists feel the urge to refine what is unique in their work, but few interpret this call to refine as a command to eliminate. Unless we are dealing with a self-destructive enthusiast —and Auden on the face of it can scarcely be categorized as one of those—then we are up against that most disciplined of all artistic adventurers, the man who gets sick of his own winning streak.

Pick up a photostat of the 1928 *Poems* and read it through (it takes about twenty minutes): was there ever a more capacious young talent? It goes beyond precocity.

> We saw in Spring
> The frozen buzzard
> Flipped down the weir and carried out to sea.
> Before the trees threw shadows down in challenge
> To snoring midges.
> Before the autumn came
> To focus stars more sharply in the sky
> In Spring we saw
> The bulb pillow
> Raising the skull,
> Thrusting a crocus through clenched teeth.

Hindsight lends us prescience, but it is permissible to claim that merely on the basis of this passage's first three lines we would have pronounced the writer capable of virtually anything. The way the turn from the second line into the third kinetically matches the whole stated action is perfect and obviously instinctive—what other men occasionally achieve was all there as a gift.

> The sprinkler on the lawn
> Weaves a cool vertigo, and stumps are drawn; . . .

Elated by the effortless lyricism of a coup like this, we need to remember not just Auden's age, but the time. Yeats had not yet finished forming the compact musicality of his last phase, and the authoritative clarities of the first of Eliot's Quartets were still years away. Auden got this sonic drive absolutely from out of the blue. The plainest statement he could make seemed to come out as poetry:

> Nor was that final, for about that time
> Gannets blown over northward, going home . . .

It was a Shakespearean gift, not just in magnitude but in its unsettling—and unsettling especially to its possessor—characteristic of making anything said sound truer than true. In all of English poetry it is difficult to think of any other poet who turned out permanent work so early—and whose work seemed so tense with the obligation to be permanent. In his distinguished essay on Auden, John Bayley penetratingly pointed out that it was not in Auden's creative stance ever to admit to being young. What has not yet suffici-

ently been noticed is that it was not in the nature of Auden's talent
to win sympathy by fumbling towards an effect—to claim the privi-
leges of the not yet weathered, or traffic in the pathos of an art in
search of its object. Instant accomplishment denied him a creative
adolescence.

As always in Auden, ethics and techniques were bound up together.
Barely out of his teens, he was already trying to discipline, rather
than exploit, the artistic equivalent of a Midas touch. It is for this
reason that the *Scrutiny* group's later limiting judgments and dismis-
sals of Auden were wrong-headed as well as insensitive: they were
branding as permanently undergraduate the one major modern
gift which had never been content with its own cleverness for a
moment. They missed the drama of Auden's career in the 1930s and
1940s, never realizing that the early obscurity and the later bookish-
ness were both ways of distancing, rather than striving after, effect.
The moral struggle in Auden was fought out between what was
possible to his gift and what he thought allowable to it: the moralists,
looking for struggles of a different kind, saw in his work nothing
but its declarative self-assurance. The more he worked for ironic
poise, the more they detected incorrigible playfulness. Subsequent
critical systems, had they been applied, would not have fared much
better. Suppose, for example, that our standards of the desirable in
poetry are based on the accurate registration of worldly things. We
would think, in that case, that a man who had come from the frozen
buzzards of 1928 to the etymological fossicking of 1972 had moved
from the apex of an art to the base. But suppose the ability to send
frozen birds flipping over the mind's weir came too easily to be gone
on with? What then?

> Doom is dark and deeper than any sea-dingle.
> Upon what man it fall
> In spring, day-wishing flowers appearing,
> Avalanche sliding, white snow from rock-face,
> That he should leave his house,
> No cloud-soft hand can hold him, restraint by women;
> But ever that man goes
> Through place-keepers, through forest trees,
> A stranger to strangers over undried sea,
> Houses for fishes, suffocating water,
> Or lonely on fell as chat,
> By pot-holed becks
> A bird stone-haunting, an unquiet bird.

Quoted from the first public edition of *Poems*, this stanza was the
kind of thing which made Auden the hero of the young intelligentsia.
Noteworthy, though, is the way in which the enchanting declarative
evocation discussed above is painstakingly avoided. The stanza's
rhythmic progress is as dazzlingly erratic as a skyrocket toppled from
its bottle. The switchback syntax, the Hardyesque hyphenated com-
pounds—they pack things tight, and the reader is never once allowed
to draw an inattentive breath. One of the many triumphs of Auden's
first public volume was that this difficult verse came to be regarded
as equally characteristic with the simpler felicities that were everywhere apparent.

> Beams from your car may cross a bedroom wall,
> They wake no sleeper: you may hear the wind
> Arriving driven from the ignorant sea
> To hurt itself on pane, on bark of elm
> Where sap unbaffled rises, being spring; . . .

Merely to mention the headlight beams crossing the wall was
enough to create them for the reader's dazzled eye. But Auden's
maturity had already arrived: he was well aware that such moments
were not to be thought of as the high points of poetry—rather as the
rest points. Take, for example, these lines from "Prologue", the
opening poem of his 1936 collection *Look, Stranger!*

> And make us as Newton was, who in his garden watching
> The apple falling towards England, became aware
> Between himself and her of an eternal tie.

The apple falling towards England is superb, but poetry which had
such effects as a *raison d'être* would be a menace. This very instance
has in fact come under critical attack—an accusation of decadence
has been levelled. But it should be obvious that Auden had no
intention of allowing such facility to become fatal. Set against it
were the inhibitors; syntactical, grammatical, lexical. And with them
they brought ambiguity, resonance, areas of doubt and discovery—
all the things his later poetry was to lose. The suggestiveness of
Auden's poetry lay in the tension between his primal lyricism and
the means employed to discipline it. The suggestiveness couldn't
survive if either term went missing. And eventually it was the lyricism
that went.

Looking through the individual collections of Auden's poems, each
in succession strikes us as transitional. On each occasion there seems

to be a further move towards paraphrasable clarity. Even at the height of his bookish phase (in, say, *New Year Letter*) Auden is still being more narrowly clear than he was before. Gradually, as we read on to the end, we see what kind of progress this has been. It has been a movement away from excitement and towards satisfaction.

Epistle to a Godson is like *About the House* and *City Without Walls* in being utterly without the excitement we recognize as Audenesque. And yet it, like them, gives a peculiar satisfaction: the patriarch grunts, having seen much and come a long way. The book is flat champagne, but it's still champagne. Part of Auden's genius was to know the necessity of chastening his talent, ensuring that his poetry would be something more enduring than mere magic. The resource and energy he devoted to containing and condensing his natural lyricism provide one of the great dramas in modern literary history. Pick up *Look, Stranger!* or *Another Time*—they read like thrillers. Every poem instantly establishes its formal separateness from all the others. Through Auden's work we trace not just themes but different ways of getting something unforgettably said: the poem's workings are in the forefront of attention. Finally the contrast between the early and the late manners is itself part of the drama. To understand Auden fully, we need to understand how a man with the capacity to say anything should want to escape from the oppression of meaning too much. Late Auden is the completion of a technical evolution in which technique has always been thought of as an instrument of self-denial. What Auden means by the fetters of Self is the tyranny of an ungoverned talent, and his late poetry is a completed testament to the self-control which he saw the necessity for from the very start—the most commendable precocity of all.

(b) BERRYMAN'S VALEDICTION

JOHN BERRYMAN'S POETRY ripened from dignified impersonality to comic egoism, and declined from that into sober self-exploitation. It is the work of the middle period that holds and rewards its reader best. But to create that union of mask and exposé, the poet had to come to terms with the dismal facts of his early life.

Berryman's parents were devout Roman Catholics living in a small town in Oklahoma. From the age of five John used to serve at mass for a priest he adored, and he went to a Catholic school. But his father, a prosperous banker named John Allyn Smith, often and baselessly accused his wife of wishing to leave him. The couple had two sons, John and a younger child, Jefferson. It looks as if the father preferred John; he went fishing and shooting with the boy, and sometimes took him along on military manoeuvres—for Mr Smith was an officer in the National Guard. The mother, a schoolteacher, seems to have preferred the younger, less volatile son.

When John was ten years old, the family moved to Tampa, Florida, on the Gulf of Mexico. Here the piety survived while the matrimonial agitation grew. Mr Smith now began threatening to take one of his sons, swim out to sea, and drown himself with the boy. Finally, the father shot himself outside the window of John's room.

Mrs Smith then moved her family to New York, where she was courted by another banker, John Angus McAlpin Berryman, whom her elder son feared and disliked. She married Mr Berryman and he adopted the boys, who took his name. Meanwhile, John gave up Catholicism and began writing. When he was fourteen, he left home to go to an Episcopal school in Connecticut. Here he came to like the chaplain and Episcopalianism, but spent four unhappy years at odds with the other boys and thinking constantly of suicide. Once he lay down on the tracks before a train and had to be pulled off.

Only when he reached Columbia University did Berryman meet a fatherly mentor who suited him as a lifetime model. This was Mark Van Doren, the distinguished scholar and teacher who also had a reputation as a poet. At Columbia, Berryman lost his religious faith, attended all Van Doren's classes; and evidently decided to follow his master's example; for poetry, teaching, and scholarship became the lines of his own career. He now wrote poems about death and learnt to admire first Auden, then Yeats. On taking his degree, he won a fellowship that sent him to Clare, Cambridge. In England, Berryman launched himself as a man of letters. He met Dylan Thomas and had tea with Yeats. He wrote more poetry and projected a critical life of Shakespeare. Returning to the United States in 1938, he found his way into the literary circles of the *Partisan Review*, the *Kenyon Review*, and the liberal weeklies. Delmore Schwartz, even more dazzling in conversation than in print, became the closest of his friends.

For the next sixteen years Berryman showed much ambition but did not distinguish himself in a memorable way from other poets of his generation. He taught at various universities and published poems in visible places. He composed a powerful sonnet sequence but kept it in his desk. He wrote good criticism and a few short stories. He also produced a superb biographical study of Stephen Crane.

Only in the work on Crane, glowing with psychological insight and deeply sympathetic with its subject, do Berryman's real preoccupations obtrude themselves. His sense of guilt over his father's death had encased him in a melancholy that turned him to alcohol. It was probably disillusionment with his mother that made him into a frantic Don Juan, inclined to humiliate every woman he might seduce. His feelings towards his brother were transformed into a rivalry with other young poets, screened by quasi-fraternal affection. His rootlessness—the abrupt changes in his home, his religion, his name—brought out a troubled awareness of the gap between the social person and the private self.

Excluded from the early poems was the hesitant inarticulateness of the worried beginner trying to find his feet on strange and challenging ground. As a talker Berryman held listeners with irreverent anecdotes and comic outbursts; as a poet he strove to sound dignified and meditative. Over his disorderly cycle of melancholy, alcohol and sex he maintained a literary façade that grew thinner and thinner. "The Lovers", a story he published in 1945, suggests the uneasiness Berryman felt at the fraudulence of his act.

Yet the early poems disclose some qualities that mark all his verse. Bewitched by Auden, Berryman preferred rhymed, stanzaic forms to free verse. To frame or start many of the poems, he used public facts—international crises, social disorders, the miscellaneous news of the day; and there are subtle particularities of time and place in the designs. For all his impersonality, the disembodied poet intervenes constantly between his subject and the reader. Often, a deliberately ruptured syntax quarrels with the unbroken surface of style, suggesting an inarticulate self behind the literary character. To see the more transitory features of the poems Berryman wrote before 1946, one need not look far, because he summarized them, half-deliberately, in a sketch of Auden's early work: "ominous, flat, and social; elliptical and indistinctly allusive; casual in tone and form, frightening in import".

Berryman married in 1942 (on Dylan Thomas's birthday, the day before his own) a bright, patient woman. But the melancholy, heavy drinking, and sexual gamesmanship went on. At Princeton in the spring of 1946 he fell in love with a bibulous younger woman who beat him at his own sport. She had a husband and child; so the affair turned into a chain of deceits, separations, furtive meetings, and—for the poet—scorching guilt. Berryman's chronic need to suffer pain became acute in sexual passion; the woman who lured him and hurt him would hold him. Before autumn his mistress decided she could live without the poet, and abandoned Berryman to his "helpless and devoted wife".

The hysterical sonnets in which he recorded this affair exhibit the chaos of his hidden personality. Their energy, furiously breaking over the pattern of the Italian rhyme scheme, almost justifies the rupture of syntax which the poet indulges in. But the hodge-podge language and jumble of images reduce the total effect to grotesquerie. What Berryman gained from the experiment was the discovery that his inner character made a stronger centre for a poem than the one he cultivated as an author. He also began to appreciate the grace of inarticulateness as a disarming style for conveying the nature of his protagonist: weak, corrupt, and self-absorbed.

Suppressing the sonnets (which were not published for twenty years), Berryman continued to write impersonal poems, with the influence of Robert Lowell added to that of Auden and Yeats. One group called "Nervous Songs" made use of his panics and introspective gloom. In them the poet tried to re-create the consciousness of several neurotic types. All of them are obscure, morbid self-examinations by anxious persons. Since Berryman could only imagine other people as aspects of himself, the element of dramatic monologue fails. Yet these poems fix some of his old virtues and establish new ones. He keeps the exhilarating dialectic of the sonnets, in which the poet speaks from sharply contrasted points of view, replies to himself or his mistress, and suddenly drops one tone for its opposite. Each poem has three stanzas of six pentameter lines rhymed unpredictably. The form is looser than the sonnet but rigid enough to make significant barriers to the waves of feeling. Dedicated to his brother, the "Nervous Songs" suggest Berryman's feeling that he had now produced something not matched by his rivals.

The outcome of his Princeton love affair darkened the poet's suicidal gloom, and he turned to psychoanalysis. For the rest of his life he had to spend long periods in private or group therapy, or in a hospital; and finally he joined Alcoholics Anonymous. But with all this care he still deteriorated, and during his last months the Minneapolis police used to pick him up and take him to a "detoxification centre". If the knowledge he wrung from so much sorrow could not at last preserve him, Berryman was able to apply it to scholarship in a profoundly rewarding way; and his Freudian study of Stephen Crane appeared in 1950. Meanwhile, it seems, he had conferred on Robert Lowell the part of the younger brother whom he wished to excel. After Lowell brought out *The Mills of the Kavanaughs*, Berryman completed a poem matching its design. The two works are stanzaic and of comparable lengths. Both of them are humourless meditations in which a wife considers her relation to her husband while the poet's voice moves in and out of the frame. American history and problems of religious faith supply the intellectual substance of both.

Berryman's *Homage to Mistress Bradstreet* includes two peculiarly strenuous passages. In one, ending the first third of the poem, the young Puritan bride tries to express the pain she feels in giving birth to a child. In the other, much longer passage, filling the middle third, the poet imagines himself communing with her spirit and in effect seducing her.

It is entirely in Berryman's character that he should have Anne Bradstreet speak of the miseries and isolation of colonial life, dwell on the agony of an accouchement, and undergo a seduction of her spirit by that of the poet. His imagination of women tends always to the idea of a lonely girl who desires him and whom he may love and leave because otherwise she will leave him. His idea of love tends to voluptuousness, not tenderness, and not a passion for an irreplaceable person. Because he liked to compare writing to parturition and poems to children, Berryman could easily supply the voice of a wife who writes didactic verse while producing eight children. Because he believed the creator of high art must serve an apprenticeship to pain, there is hardly any limit to the suffering he can inflict on Anne Bradstreet. Infatuated with his own creation, he cries, "I miss you Anne". Absent from other joys, she says "I *want* to take you for my lover".

The stanza form is difficult, involving four different line lengths and an intricate rhyme scheme. To fit his words in, Berryman disrupts his syntax even more arbitrarily here than in his sonnets. His conceits and language are again frantic with incongruity. If the poem received unusual attention, the reason is that a shocking mixture of religiosity with sexuality will attract intelligent readers if it is served in exalted language. The rapt solemnity of the poet's posture discouraged a frivolous response to his vagaries. The obscurity of the poem, its air of historical learning, its quasi-sublimity of tone, all protected it from the judgment it might have drawn.

Within the bizarre design of *Homage to Mistress Bradstreet* one finds valuable devices. If Berryman chose a difficult stanza, he employed it flexibly, varying rhyme scheme and line length. One sees the possibility of a form complex in itself and so handled as to offer interesting variations. The give and take between author and protagonist, the quick changes of voice and viewpoint—especially in the middle section of the poem—recapture the life-giving dialectic of the sonnets. The blurring of identities, sometimes leaving us unsure of the speaker, reminds us of Berryman's brooding over selfhood. A thoughtful reader cannot escape the impression that the poet is often talking to and indeed consoling himself: "I am a man of griefs and fits/trying to be my friend."

About the time the poem was published as a book, Berryman's first marriage ended in divorce; and though he married again in 1956, he was divorced once more, only to marry a third time in 1961. Meanwhile, he worked on another long poem, or collection of poems, ultimately known as *Dream Songs.*

The speaker of these poems is called Henry, a name given Berryman by his second wife in a routine domestic joke. In his book on Crane, he had examined the novelist's addiction to this name and observed that it belongs, among other characters, to the main figure of a long story called "The Monster", which Berryman analysed and praised at length. Crane deals in that story with the relation between a doctor and his Negro hostler, Henry Johnson. The doctor's little boy is fond of Henry, turning to him for comfort when he is in disgrace. Henry prides himself on his good looks, stylish clothes, and effectiveness with ladies. When the doctor's house catches fire, Henry in effect rescues the little boy. But while doing so, he collapses, his face is destroyed by acid, and his mind is unhinged. Though he survives, he becomes a crazy, if harmless, monster with no face. He terrifies everyone who sees him and must live finally wearing a veil, cut off from almost all companionship, singing incoherently to himself. The doctor alone can and will look after him. In a savage irony, the doctor's faithfulness to his son's rescuer ruins his medical practice and brings down social ostracism.

Crane pays attention to the hostler's speech. Henry Johnson is fluent and elaborately polite; but he talks in the deepest Southern accent, with no regard for grammar. Outside the doctor's home he makes two speaking appearances, both scenes of courtship. In the first, the young lady is thrilled by his elegance and conversation; she keeps him for hours. In the second, when he is the escaped monster, she flees, leaving him to mumble repetitiously into the void, sentences like, "I jes' drap in ter ax you 'bout er daince".

As an undergraduate, Berryman had told a fellow student named Brooks Johnson, who hated Negroes, that he himself had "some coon blood". One assumes that Crane's story excited Berryman's fears about the division of his own life between the eloquent public figure and the inarticulate, hidden self, the fear that alcohol and skirt-craziness might turn him into a monster, the fear that his love would destroy those who hoped to rescue him. Berryman's Henry is a white man in blackface who speaks at times the dialect of Crane's monster; and the poet presents Henry with the same blend of farce and pathos that Crane uses for Henry Johnson.

But Henry is only one of the poet's masks in *Dream Songs*. The drama of Berryman's work is often taken from that of the old minstrel show. In this there were two end men, Mr Bones and Mr Tambo, who responded to questions put by the middle man or interlocutor. Just as Mr Tambo played the tambourine, so his opposite number played the bones, or flat sticks used as rhythmical clappers. It is as impulsive Mr Bones that Henry bandies questions with a shrewder self. The sound of "bone" is almost a condensation of "Berryman"; and two Shakespearian allusions probably enrich the name. In *A Midsummer Night's Dream*, Titania, bewitched, asks Bottom, wearing the ass's head, whether he will hear music; and Bottom calls for "the tongs and the bones". In *2 Henry IV* Doll Tearsheet curses the skinny beadle who is dragging her to punishment, and calls him "Goodman death, goodman bones". Berryman knew Shakespeare too well to miss these references. But even without them it is clear that the death-loving music-maker Bones wants answers from the poet's more reflective faculty, the voice of chastened wisdom. "Come away, Mr Bones", says the middle man. Among these forces hovers the poet who sings to himself of love and despair, whose veil conceals his ugly void, and whose ugliness hides his nobility.

As the *Dream Songs* proceed, the machinery of the minstrel show often rusts in idleness. But the motifs connected with Henry dominate the work. When Berryman analysed Crane's story, he lingered on the theme of rescue; and it is obvious that he found great power in the doctrine that whoever preserves another man from ruin is likely to be destroyed for his zeal. In *Dream Songs* Henry appeals for rescue to a number of figures, male and female; but he also fears they will harm themselves if they help him. "Cling to me", he says, "and I promise you'll drown too." He yearns to succour those who need him; he feels guilty for failing allies like Delmore Schwartz. He writes a string of elegies for poets who were not preserved. He wishes he had rescued his own father, and that his father had rescued him. Above all, he disarms the reader, who must pity, love, forgive, and save this martyred poet.

Lowell published *Life Studies* while Berryman was writing the *Dream Songs*; and Lowell's habit of undercutting his own despair with a humorous, ironic commentary probably influenced his friend's work. But long before he read *Life Studies*, Berryman admired Pound's *Cantos*. He had been struck by Pound's use of masks and once described the subject of the *Cantos* as "the life of the modern poet", which is nearly the description he gave of his own subject. An older model still was *Song of Myself*. Whitman frames his cheerful egoism in disarming humour. He makes a drama out of self-observation; for he is "both in and out of the game and watching and wondering at it"; and in *Calamus* he warns any followers, "I am not what you supposed. . . . The way is suspicious, the result uncertain, perhaps destructive."

There are signs that Berryman hoped to impose order on his work not only by a web of recurrent motifs and the drama of self-consciousness but also more mechanically. The number seven finds its way into the scheme. *Dream Songs* is 7,000 lines long, divided into seven books, of which I-III were published separately as *77 Dream Songs*. The number of poems in Book IV, Books V-VII, and the entire collection is also divisible by seven; and these sections are not insignificant. The middle book, IV, is a descent into hell; here the poet speaks as a buried, decaying corpse but surfaces at the end of the book. One thinks of Book VI of the *Aeneid*, also marking a halfway point. Berryman's father's suicide is dealt with in the first poem of Book I, the penultimate poem of Book III, the last poem of Book V, and the penultimate poem of Book VII, in which the poet imagines himself returning to Oklahoma, digging his father up, and destroying with an axe the "start" of his own tragedy.

If one looks for coherence in *Dream Songs*, the metrical form may satisfy the need best. It is derived from the form Berryman had used in his "Nervous Songs". Each poem has three stanzas of six iambic lines. The pattern they approach is that the third and last lines of the stanza should have three beats, the others five. Rhyme is normal. The tendency is for the third line to rhyme with the last and for the rest to pair off either in couplets, or alternately: abcabc, or aabccb. But the pattern is handled freely. Often the lines are an odd length or do not rhyme. When the form is most regular, the poem is likely to be weak.

The charm of this form is that the short lines both enclose and connect. They define and link the tercets and stanzas within each poem; they also tie the poems to one another. Sometimes the poet seizes the opportunity for a dialectic of strophe, anti-strophe, epode. Berryman has no skill as a rhymester. Yet the unpredictable absence and appearance of rhyme works; for it gives an ironic bounce to bleak peasages.

None of these elements will account for the appeal of the best *Dream Songs*. It is true that as one advances through 7,000 lines, one gathers information and learns habits that make the shape or meaning of the separate poems clearer. But the unity of the work is no greater than that of a sonnet sequence. In fact, the design of *Dream Songs* involves a return to that of Berryman's sonnets, with the focus shifted from the figure of the mistress to the sensibility of the poet.

Here, of course, the imagined dialogues are not between different persons. Neither are they, as in "Nervous Songs" and *Homage to Mistress Bradstreet*, embedded in a dramatic monologue. What had been the frame in those poems moves to the centre of *Dream Songs*: the dialectic is internalized. At the same time, by the device of naming the protagonist Henry or Bones, and speaking of him in the third person, Berryman transcends his egocentricity. Not the poet's self but his attitudes towards himself become the theme. The mask replaces the speaker. This fact opens the way for the splendid virtue of the *Dream Songs*, their irony, sometimes comic, sometimes grim:

You couldn't bear to grow old, but we grow old.
Our differences accumulate. Our skin
tightens or droops: it alters.
Take courage, things are not what they have been
and they will never again. Hot hearts grow cold,
the rush to the surface falters,

secretive grows the disappearing soul
learned & uncertain, young again
but not in the same way:
Heraclitus had a wise word here to say,
which I forget.

By assigning his despair to Henry and Mr Bones, Berryman puts it outside himself; it is now tame and approachable, something to play with and ridicule. Even when the despair is explicitly suicidal, one feels (wrongly, alas) that the poet can control it and put it to work:

My eyes with which I see so easily
will become closed. My friendly heart will stop.
I won't sit up.
Nose me, soon you won't like it——ee——
worse than a pesthouse; and my thought all gone
& the vanish of the sun.

The vanish of the moon, which Henry loved
on charming nights when Henry young was moved
by delicate ladies
with ripped-off panties, mouths open to kiss.
They say the coffin closes without a sound
& is lowered underground!

As Henry, the poet can drop his civilized speech along with the anxiety that civilization breeds. He develops an expressive style out of the inarticulateness that fascinated him and that belongs to our time; and through it he not only disarms us but shares the wordlessness of readers who distrust elegance and fluency. The inarticulateness of the misnamed monster talks for those who see monsters taking over the world, and who have found no coherent language to express their horror.

A rainy Sunday morning, on vacation
as well as Fellowship, he could not rest:
bitterly he shook his head.
—Mr Bones, the Lord will bring us to a nation
where everybody only rest.—I confess
that notion bores me dead,

for there's no occupation there, save God,
if that, and long experience of His works
has not taught me his love.

There was nothing to keep Berryman from going on with the *Dream Songs*. Two appeared in his posthumous volume; and a thousand more might have come out in his lifetime. Henry might have grown into a public figure like Mr Dooley, airing his moods and opinions from day to day before an audience that had learnt what to expect. In the way of general ideas and moral insights Berryman has little that is fresh to offer. Neither is he a phrase-maker, nor a magician with words. It is emblematic that a childhood disease should have weakened his hearing, because his ear for rhythm is undistinguished. For all his talent and learning, Berryman could not come near the intellectual style of Auden or the middle-aged Lowell. Once he had circulated the most sensational facts of his private life, his richest treasure was the ironic drama of Henry's diary.

So it strikes one as a hero's mistake that Berryman should have turned his back on this invention and chosen a simpler exploitation of auto-analysis for his last two books. Both these collections are carefully organized. In *Love & Fame* one moves from part to part in a visible direction. Sexual passion gives way to literary ambition, which is overtaken by spiritual darkness; and at last the poet turns to God with a set of prayers. In *Delusions, Etc.* (published posthumously), Berryman hugs his faith revived. From his new belvedere his old rationalism seems hard to tell from delusion; and he knows his faith must seem foolish to his old readers. After prayers of doubt about his right to mercy, the poet celebrates artists who suffered ordeals like his own and met difficult deaths. Imminent mortality then makes him eager to use death, to bring the remainder of his life into harmony with faith. In a further group of poems he defiantly accepts his uniqueness and perhaps the need for a death of his own. And so a closing set of prayers show him ready, disbelieving in hell and accepting death as salvation or nothing. The book amounts on some pages to a suicide note: "I've *had* it. I can't wait." Yet the final poem remains affirmative: "Aware to the dry throat of the wide hell in the world . . ./mockt in abysm by one shallow wife,/with the ponder both of priesthood & of State/heavy upon me, yea/all the black same I dance my blue head off!"

The coherence of the last books cannot replace the pleasures of the *Dream Songs*: their deliberate humour and indirection; viewpoints that never stand still, a tone that hops from aspiration to bathos. In the last poems, the strongest humour seems unintentional; it would be cruel to deal seriously with their serious argument; their inarticulateness is painfully artless. Having discovered that his sensibility could bewitch us, Berryman made the error of growing solemn about it; and the reader's attention must move back from the poet's attitude to his mind. Speaking in the first person, without Henry to screen him, Berryman challenges comparison with the most brilliant poets alive. But his thoughts, as bare thoughts, neither please nor fascinate. The last books have an intense but narrowly documentary appeal. Those who are attached to the poet will read them for the scandalous information they supply about his life, for the pathetic account of his journey homeward to religious faith, for the brave valediction of a man who chose his own way to die.

(*c*) LARKIN'S CHOICE

AN ANTHOLOGY of the scope and consequence of the new *Oxford Book of Twentieth-Century English Verse*, edited by Philip Larkin, is bound to raise dust far beyond any reasonable area of controversy. Time will tell what the public makes of it: meanwhile its denouncers and applauders are going to be those professional poets and critics who have a watching brief on contemporary verse. Just about every name omitted, and even more each name included, will seem to the brokers of our heritage a shameful selling-short or a ridiculous marking-up. Yet, as the reviews roll in, Mr Larkin might like to console himself with the thought that his critics know the world he is charting so well that their reactions must partake more of *amour propre* than zeal for the public good. He has as little to fear from them as the proprietor of a Free House from a chain of Tied Houses.

Not that his is an impeccable anthology, but many of its short-comings are due to the nature of anthologies themselves, and it is hardly fair to look to his slightest choice (there are 625 pages and 584 individual poems) for commitment to the dogmatic duty of judging English poetry at its restless mid-century point. Anthologies cannot fairly distil the best poems of an age: so often the best poems are very long or are the sum of many imperfect smaller parts. Instead, like sampler records issued by firms with wide-ranging catalogues of fine artists' recordings, they can guide the interested consumer in his own further investigation. The more powerful an anthology, the more dangerous its influence can be. To know any anthology well is still to know only a little bit of many minds. Each anthology therefore is much less than the sum of its parts.

In this one, more than 200 poets have been assembled. Does Mr Larkin believe that each of them is significant? The answer must obviously be no. Then does he mean that each poem printed is good of its kind, and that he has been careful to select those kinds which are most worth preserving, and to ensure that no form of categorizing should prevent major figures from being properly represented or outstandingly fine poems from getting in? This time the answer is yes, since he says so in hardly any more words in the introduction. Why then has the book been received with an outcry in the first fortnight since its publication? Because, whether he likes it or not, Mr Larkin's admirers and detractors have elevated him into a polemical figure— not because of his powers as an anthologist but because of his eminence as a poet.

He could hardly be so good a poet if he did not have strong views, and those views are generally anti-Modernist. But what must be surprising everyone is the form his anti-Modernism has taken— an overwhelming of the indispensable innovators, Eliot, Lawrence and Auden, by a mass of documentary verse writers varying from the interesting (May Wedderburn Cannan on Rouen in the First World War) to the insipid (Francis Brett Young, Gilbert Frankau, Wilfrid Gibson, Herbert Asquith and Muriel Stuart). It is the poets who are in who make this a strange anthology rather than those who are left out.

It could be argued that until he reaches the post-Second World War poets, Mr Larkin's only serious omission is David Jones— Pound being American by his terms of reference. Yet Charles Sorley is as good a poet as Rupert Brooke and Ivor Gurney, and Arthur Symons did not die until 1944. If Symons's best work was done before the turn of the century, so was a good deal of Hardy's. More disturbing is the representation of the key poets of the anthology; Mr Larkin has often chosen idiosyncratically, as he should have done, but he has also undertaken a quiet revolution within the canon of accepted talent.

Detailed criticism of his taste can wait until later in this review.

Some attempt must be made now to describe the tone and feeling of the book, while recognizing that such things are impalpable and highly personal. It is an individual, even polemical, selection masquerading as a parade of the spirit of the age. Thus it falls between two well-favoured stools, being neither an embattled anthology such as Michael Roberts's *Faber Book of Modern Verse* and Kenneth Allott's *Penguin Book of Contemporary Verse*, nor a scholarly compilation like so many of the other Oxford Books, chosen on historical lines. At times it feels as if it belongs to each of these categories, yet it tries to avoid paying the price of allegiance to either.

One book it never echoes is its famous precursor, W. B. Yeats's *Oxford Book of Modern Verse*. Mr Larkin supplies a two-page introduction of almost forensic scrupulousness where Yeats offers forty-two pages of rambling prejudice. Yeats's certainties are on the same absolute scale—Dorothy Wellesley (and she isn't all bad, as Mr Larkin demonstrates by choosing the same poem which Yeats praises so fulsomely, "Horses"), W. J. Turner, Oliver St John Gogarty, Edith Sitwell and Margot Ruddock: the elderly seer prides himself on his patrician certainty. He excludes Andrew Young, Wilfred Owen and Edwin Muir with the same oracular assurance, and his choice of the poems of Hardy, Hopkins, Housman, Edward Thomas and D. H. Lawrence is decidedly shallow. But he does, as generations of wondering readers have admitted, know his mind. Mr Larkin invites us to fossick for his. The key disclaimer in his introduction is of truly *Catch 22* comprehensiveness:

In the end I found that my material fell into three groups: poems representing aspects of the talents of poets judged either by the age or by myself to be worthy of inclusion, poems judged by me to be worthy of inclusion without reference to their authors, and poems judged by me to carry with them something of the century in which they were written.

After that, the deluge, with everybody in the Ark. No wonder the reviewers who have cavilled most have been poets—they don't know where they are with him. His book looks like the biggest Pantheon in the world—and what sort of Pantheon is that?

Some declare Mr Larkin's performance to be straightforward treason—the English disease of preferring amateurism to professionalism, Congreve's wanting to be taken for a gentleman rather than a writer. But the English have always been like this (Sir Walter Raleigh and the Earl of Rochester didn't write badly for men without a self-conscious calling to poetry), and the American habit of parading one's vocation can lead to mistaking the intention for the performance.

It is probably fairer to ascribe the disquiet shown by the anthology's critics to a recognition of Mr Larkin's own equivocal attitudes. Other than an hostility to Modernism, either official (i.e., Franco-American) or homegrown, his selection shows two notable leanings or quirks of taste. He dislikes obscurity in poetry and he is romantically patriotic. He can find no space for independent experimenters such as Christopher Middleton and Roy Fisher, yet there are many poems included which seem to have little justification beyond their being concerned with the spirit of England, either at war or in communion with herself—Chesterton's "Rolling English Road", Brooke's "The Soldier" and "Grantchester", and Lawrence Binyon's "For the Fallen" among them. But it must be admitted that this Englishness is also the anthology's strongest point. It emerges in Mr Larkin's careful and original selection from Hardy, it dictates the space allotted to Sir John Betjeman and it accounts for the high proportion of poems of place and circumstance. It can be felt in the poems of Charlotte Mew (a first-class choice from an unfairly neglected poet), in the Shropshire bias of the Housman quota, in John Davidson and W. H. Davies, in D. H. Lawrence's "The Collier's Wife", in the generous allocation given to Stevie Smith, in Gavin Ewart's, Charles Causley's and Hugh Popham's poems of life in the forces in the Second World War, and in the imaginative selection from Kingsley Amis.

Some commentators have suggested the anthology could be read as social history: if so, it is social history with a strong romantic bias. This bias, which might be called "The way we lived then", is more pervasive even than the fondness for light verse, though that, in itself, helps tilt the anthology away from any recognition that the twentieth century has been a time of crisis in poetry. It is interesting to observe how Mr Larkin acclimatizes poets such as Eliot, Basil Bunting, Hugh MacDiarmid and Dylan Thomas by setting them among so many devoted chapter-and-versifiers. If we do not notice Modernism, he seems to be saying, perhaps it will go away.

Early rumours suggested that the anthology might deserve the title, *The Oxford Book of Thomas Hardy's Verse*, but in the event Hardy is allotted twenty-six pages, which places him second to Eliot, with twenty-nine. The choice is very good and sets the tone for

the book—a concern for the facts of a case encouraging an amplitude
of emotion which the facts give rise to. As Hardy puts it in some
lines from "In Tenebris":

> The stout upstanders say, All's well with us: ruers have
>   nought to rue!
> And what the potent say so oft, can it fail to be somewhat
>   true?
> Breezily go they, breezily come; their dust smokes around
>   their career,
> Till I think I am one born out of due time, who has no
>   calling here.
> ....
> Let him in whose ears the low-voiced Best is killed by the
>   clash of the First,
> Who holds that if way to the Better there be, it exacts a full
>   look at the Worst,
> Who feels that delight is a delicate growth cramped by
>   crookedness, custom, and fear,
> Get him up and be gone as one shaped awry; he disturbs
>   the order here.

Is it reading too much into these lines to set them at the head of
this book as poet's and anthologist's rebuke to both evolutionary
hope and excitable innovation? Besides "In Tenebris", Mr Larkin
includes "The Ruined Maid", "After a Journey", "The Newcomer's
Wife", "An Ancient to Ancients", and a beautiful but unfamiliar
poem, "The Sunshade". One might ask for "The Last Signal",
"Before Life and After" and "Afterwards", but twenty-seven poems,
though inevitably not the ideal anthology one has been carrying in
one's head for decades, is enough to justify the present-day reappraisal of Hardy as the father of modern British poetry, and one
of the supreme poets of the past 200 years.

Mr Larkin includes Robert Bridges's *tour-de-force* of facetiousness
and metric, "Poor Poll", which is a relief after the boredom of
"London Snow" and the extraordinary spelling and diction of the
extract from "The Testament of Beauty". In John Davidson's
"Thirty Bob a Week", much admired by T. S. Eliot, pre-echoes
of Mr Bleaney and the Toads can be heard. And that remarkable
vision by a trapped Victorian city-dweller of a Highland "altogether
elsewhere", "A Runnable Stag", is happily in as well. Mr Larkin
has found poems by John Meade Falkner which are much better
than novelists' verses usually are, and a piece of rhyming doggerel by

E. Nesbit which is like an inventory of his own attitudes. The only remarkable thing about Eden Phillpotts is his lifespan—at ninety-eight, he lived longer than any other contributor to the anthology. Few people could quarrel with Kipling's representation, though here Mr Larkin has chosen rather too many well-known anthology pieces. Exactly the same is true of the selection from Yeats, though it must be admitted that the best Yeats almost chooses itself. Belloc and J. M. Synge emerge poorly. One or two of the *Cautionary Tales* might have been included, bearing in mind Mr Larkin's affection for light verse; and some of Synge's Irish curses would have been more representative of him.

Here the anthology arrives at the Georgians, where Mr Larkin seems to have done his most thorough research, unearthing several forgotten names and discovering verses by famous men with a Sunday talent for poetry. It is here also that he has been most tolerant of weak writing. It is extraordinarily hard today to be fair to a poem like Ralph Hodgson's "The Bull", yet if one reads it in the light of Mr Larkin's implied reassessment, it does have Smart-and-Blake-like qualities. Due to good selection, the poems of W. H. Davies appear stronger than they probably are. The choice of Edward Thomas's poems is very fair, except for the unaccountable absence of "Old Man", and John Masefield's brilliant "Reynard the Fox" is well represented.

At this point, bad poems by Alfred Noyes, Herbert Palmer, Herbert Asquith and John Drinkwater appear. Soon after comes Francis Brett Young's "Seascape", an anecdote tricked out in spurious blank verse remembered from Tennyson and Shakespeare, and Gilbert Frankau's sub-Kipling "Gun Teams". The number of flops in this part of the book is not as considerable as some reviewers have suggested, but set beside the harsh judging which cuts down so many young poets at the end of the anthology, it does look provocative. Mr Larkin is known to think that the present is always overestimated. He appears to have chosen instead to overestimate that part of the past farthest from contemporary taste. However salutary the lesson may be for fashionable minds, it has not improved his book. Printing Sir John Squire's "The Stockyard" is a more attractive kind of eccentricity. This sincere, accurate and impassioned description of the Chicago slaughterhouses is very upsetting to read, but, unfortunately, a shameful voice inside one says, is it any more than well-written indignation and guilt, is it really poetry? To ask this question is to provoke the biggest doubt the whole anthology gives rise to. A concern for truth, a dismissal of humbug and pretension, an attempt at a miniature social history, a polemic against fashion—these are all aspects of the book. But a loyalty to poetry in whatever shape and form it took during the century— this, which should have been Mr Larkin's aim, has been shouldered aside. Not for the first time, a fine poet is seen to prefer extra-poetical criteria when judging other men's work.

"Kangaroo" and "Mountain Lion" by D. H. Lawrence are worth their space, but it is a pity that none of the tortoise poems are in. Lawrence's animal poems are so much the most sensitive and original things he wrote that they show up the rest of his work as inflated and overreaching. More space might have been allotted him on historical grounds, as the only successful practitioner of free verse in these islands up until the 1960s. Moving on, one resents the niggardly representation of Andrew Young but applauds the choice from Siegfried Sassoon, especially the inclusion of strange and successful poems such as "Sporting Acquaintances" and "Two Old Ladies". Edith Sitwell, who is a presiding genius of Yeats's book, is cut down by Mr Larkin—very properly, though putting in only one poem from *Façade* and none from *Gold Coast Customs* is hardly fair if one is going to print a long extract from her later tinsel-and-apocalypse manner.

Apart from "La figlia che piange", the selection from Eliot is sensible. It is good to get some of the choruses from *Murder in the Cathedral*, whose psalmic splendour shows Eliot's writing at its best. Mr Larkin's taste for unfashionable good sense inclines him to admire such amateur poems as G. D. H. Cole's "Civil Riot". After reading this account of the anger and despair of the 1930s, one begins to see his point that there are other considerations when compiling an anthology besides poetic merit:

> So I'm not
> Passing judgment, only saying
> What I saw
> When some men I know and like,
> After seven months on strike,
> Got the wrong side of the law,
> ....
>
> Got beaten up and battered
> Plenty and to spare.

Oh, I don't suppose it mattered;
But I happened to be there.

Mr Larkin will always be on the side of those who were there and
cared enough to record their feelings. In the same way, he will
applaud scrupulous resisters of current enthusiasms, like A. P.
Herbert, whose "Less Nonsense", a document of the days of
Soviet-worship before the Second Front, is nevertheless only
tolerable polemical verse and has no place in an anthology like this.
The extract from Hugh MacDiarmid's "Lament for the Great
Music" is impressive but illustrates the ineffectiveness of anthologies.
The reader is left up in the air with no recourse but to seek out
MacDiarmid's works themselves.

It is entirely admirable that we are given Wilfred Owen's "Insensibility" and not "Strange Meeting". Together with *The Waste Land*,
"Insensibility" is one of the two finest poems in the book. Owen's
fellow-sufferer in the First World War, Robert Graves, seems not to
have engaged Mr Larkin's deeper interest, since the selection from
his ever-revised canon is safe and rather flavourless. On the other
hand, the quiver of poems by Edmund Blunden is brilliantly sorted.
One would have to go far to find a more effective coup in Englishry
than this passage from "Almswomen".

> How happy go the rich fair-weather days
> When on the roadside folk stare in amaze
> At such a honeycomb of fruit and flowers
> As mellows round their threshold; what long hours
> They gloat upon their steepling hollyhocks,
> Bee's balsam, feathery southernwood and stocks,
> Fiery dragon's mouths, great mallow leaves
> For salves, and lemon-plants in bushy sheaves,
> Shagged Esau's-hands with five green finger-tips.
> Such old sweet names are ever on their lips.

The late Noël Coward is represented by "The Boy Actor", which
is a pity. He would have shown up better in his Cole Porter vein,
with, say, "The Stately Homes of England" or "There are Bad
Times just around the Corner". Near Coward shines a single poem
(and the complaint that far too many poets are represented by a
single work is a just one) by F. Pratt Green, the sort of fugitive
pleasure which anthologies can restore to circulation. It is entitled
"The Old Couple" and this is the last stanza:

Too old for loving now, but not for love,
The old couple lie, several feet apart,
Their chesty breathing like a muted duet
On wind instruments, trying to think of
Things to hang on to, such as the tinkle
That a budgerigar makes when it shifts
Its feather weight from one leg to another,
The way, on windy nights, linoleum lifts.

Naturally, the Betjeman selection is good and original. "Ireland with Emily" is a little-known piece of virtuosity by the Laureate which should now join "The Subaltern's Lovesong" and the rest in the popular pantheon.

Overall, Mr Larkin tends to like Louis MacNeice and W. H. Auden at their least grand. He swerves from their seriousness and prefers their masterly levity. To put in the whole of the background commentary to Grierson's GPO film, *Night Mail*, is carrying documentary care for the England of the 1930s too far. Mr Larkin is not responsible for Auden's barbarous revisions, but it still hurts to read part three of "In Memory of W. B. Yeats" shorn of its stanza about Kipling and Claudel. "The Fall of Rome" and "Goodbye to the Mezzogiorno" are both welcome, and "Up There", the attic poem from *About the House*, is an interesting choice, since it uses the material, if not the attitudes, of a typical Larkin poem. Except for "Mythology", the selection from Lawrence Durrell is poor. "Poggio" is a tired anthology piece, like a marginal annotation to the *Alexandria Quartet*. "General Uncebunke" or that sovereign of the Mediterranean poems, "On First Looking into Loeb's Horace", would have been preferable. It was an original, if not necessarily an effective, idea to quote the long verse passage from one of Dylan Thomas's letters to Vernon Watkins. Mr Larkin treats Keith Douglas with an almost Yeats-like indifference. "Vergissmeinnicht" is in, but not "How to Kill" or "Behaviour of Fish in an Egyptian Tea Garden". Except for his touchstones—Hardy, Betjeman and Stevie Smith—he approaches the major poets of the age with suspicion, while lavishing attention on neglected minor versifiers.

Once the 1950s and 1960s are reached, the anthology becomes much more unreliable. Perhaps the year 1965, when Mr Larkin started work, is the key to his method of sorting, but the incidence of single-poem representation goes up and so does the frequency of choices coming from first and second collections. There are redeeming moments—the poems of Derek Walcott and Rosemary Tonks being brilliantly chosen; but anyone wanting to know what has happened since 1950 would be better advised to read A. Alvarez's *The New Poetry* or Edward Lucie-Smith's *British Poetry since 1945* (both Penguins).

Part of this notice has been devoted to a reviewer's most tempting side-issue—composing an alternative anthology to the one under examination. But the reasons for this are clear: we have been offered a monument which is composed of hundreds of broken pieces. If some of the fault is Mr Larkin's, the greater part lies in the nature of anthologies, Oxford official ones in particular. Time has done the work of the editors of the earlier Oxford Books of Verse for them, but Mr Larkin has had to cope with his responsibility to present-day feelings as well as with his own taste. Reading his anthology will pain some poets, but it will probably please many people. Yet there is no gainsaying a feeling that it is not one of the great anthologies. While not preposterous like Yeats's, it manages to be eccentric and institutional at once, and leaves the reader with a confused picture of English verse in this century.

4

WORKERS ABROAD

IT IS UNLIKELY that a migrant worker would be in a position to review *Immigrant Workers and Class Structure in Western Europe* for the *TLS*. Yet the main usefulness of the book lies in its information about the experience of such workers. It is the most wide-ranging and best-investigated study yet made on the subject. Despite their academic style, Stephen Castles and Godula Kosack have seen with their own eyes and not only worked in libraries. The book's political theories are less striking than its information. The study concentrates on the lives of immigrant workers in four countries: Germany, France, Switzerland and Britain. Britain is the case apart. Outside Britain, most migrant workers are temporary migrants, who travel singly without their families, and who often do not speak the language of the "host country". Chronic unemployment and poverty have forced them to migrate. The relatively high wages offered in north-west Europe suggest to them the hope of eventually saving enough money to return home and set up themselves and their families securely above the starvation line.

All the quotations which follow are, unless otherwise stated, from the book under review.

"The social history of industrialization is that of mass movements from country to town." The large-scale migration of nine million workers from southern Europe and North Africa to north-west Europe during the past fifteen years is the last dramatic phase of a process that began two centuries ago with the industrial revolution. Many of the workers' subjective experiences have remained surprisingly comparable, and, within the subject, different historical times coexist, packed densely and painfully together, often acquiring

STEPHEN CASTLES and GODULA KOSACK: *Immigrant Workers and Class Structure in Western Europe*. 514 pp. Oxford University Press for the Institute of Race Relations. £5.50.

a suspended timelessness; behind the sociological findings and statistics, the dimensions of the migrant worker's experience are mostly those of dream alternating with nightmare.

If you decide to try to migrate as a worker—and it is by no means certain that you will be accepted: those who become migrant workers are considered the fortunate ones—if you do try to migrate as a worker, legally or illegally, the chances are that you come from a village or small town where there are no factories, and where there is nothing to prepare you for the reality of life in a large industrial city. "The immigrant worker, coming to Western Europe for the first time, may never have seen a factory before, let alone have worked in one. He has probably lived all his life in a peasant community, using traditional production methods and pre-industrial technology. The hours and rhythms of work have been determined by the seasons and by the natural needs of plants and animals."

You have probably spoken to friends or friends of friends who have already made the journey and experienced the foreign city. They will have told you of the fabulous opportunities to be found there. If you are shrewd, you will guess that they are exaggerating and boasting: you will have seen that when they talk of the foreign city, their pride is at stake. But since you believe that you are more hard-working, shrewder and stronger than they you will assume that, whereas they have to exaggerate their success, you will achieve the success you need.

Before you leave, if you are going the legal way, you usually undergo a medical examination. Hundreds of men are examined at the same time. You feel confident because many of the others are very evidently unfit. (Some of them are quite simply too small.) They make you hold up your arms, reach to your toes, work your fingers, and the doctors touch you to feel your strength the way a buyer does when he is deciding whether or not to purchase a horse or a bull. "Immigrants to all Western European countries are subject to medical control before they are allowed to enter. This has two purposes: first to ensure that the immigrants are free from infectious diseases or communicable parasites; secondly, that the workers are physically capable of doing the type of work for which they are recruited."

When they ask you to prove that you can read, you hesitate several times and perhaps you jump a line by mistake. But you know you can read and you have already ignored the touts outside the labour office who are offering you (for a price) the secret of what you will have to read—along with specimens of guaranteed healthy urine which some are foolish enough to buy and to try to substitute for their own in case their own is not up to standard. "In countries like Portugal and Greece a considerable proportion of the population is illiterate. The majority of migrants come from the poorest classes. Their educational standards are therefore likely to be even lower than the national average for the countries concerned. Illiteracy is only part of the problem of general basic education which immigrants have. A large number of people count as literate although they are merely able to write their names."

If you have said you are a skilled worker, they may test your skill. Build a brick wall there on the office floor, they say to a village mason. He has twenty bricks, but he is so nervous he begins at the wrong end, and they say he is not a mason. He is—but the foreigners don't know it.

The moment comes when you have to say goodbye to your family. Some in the village. Others accompany you to the station in the big town. They are proud that you are going. They are awaiting your new wages. You are going to rescue them from the poverty of a lifetime. But when it comes to saying goodbye at the railway station through a metal grille you can only put your fingers through because they do not allow relatives on the platform—when it comes to this, you see your wife or your mother and you think: Will I ever see them again? Who knows whether a parting is the last parting? You answer to yourself: Only God in his wisdom.

In almost all cases the migrant absorbs at least superficially some of the norms and values of the host society. In particular, he becomes part of the system of norms, values and deprivations of a consumer society within a matter of a year or two. After about one year, most polyannual migrants realize that short-term participation in a high-wage economy does not once and for all eliminate their deprivation back home, however spartan their conduct in their country of employment. They decide to extend their stay abroad in the expectation of really amassing the big wage packets they have been hoping for and then returning home and starting a new life. By this time, however, a polyannual migrant has become subject to new deprivations, namely, those of the lower working class in the receiving country. Some of these deprivations are entirely new in the sense that he had never experienced them before entering a consumer society (e g, he is made to want cameras, record players, tape recorders, electric shavers, and so on). (W. R. Böhning, *The Migration of Workers in the United Kingdom and the European Community*, 1972.)

How long you are going to stay away does not depend on you. It depends on the contract you have signed as an act of faith, your job, your health, and the country you are going to. The first time, you won't be allowed to stay more than a year, and during that year it is almost impossible to change your job. Then you come back and try again. The same hope, the same medical examination, the same parting. It is easier to stay in France, but in France, one way or another, most of the situations you find yourself in are illegal. In any of the foreign countries, if you want to stay as long as possible, you need to keep quiet, work hard, never complain and be seen only when there is work to be done.

The policies of governments and employers often contribute to keeping immigrant workers in low occupational positions. Firstly, restrictions on length of stay are likely to prevent immigrant workers from achieving promotion. These restrictions go under the guise of protecting the domestic labour market. For many employers and officials, "the great value of the employment of foreigners lies in the fact that we thus have a mobile labour potential at our disposal". This is the opinion of Ulrich Freiherr v. Gienanth, a leading representative of the German Employers' Federation. The idea is that foreigners should be used as the regulators of the labour market: in times of labour shortage they should be brought in; if there is a recession, they should simply be dismissed and expelled from the country with no consideration of their needs. This is only possible if the foreign workers are prevented from taking up key positions in the production process and if they are prevented from settling permanently.

When you cross the frontier you cross into a world where almost every word, whether spoken or written, is meaningless to you. At first you try to guess. But then you discover that you cannot afford to guess wrong. All the words addressed to you, or written for your benefit, are orders or prohibitions. It is safer not to guess, but to wait until they are made clear. You yourself can never speak to the foreigner. And your inability to speak proves your inferiority. You can nod your head. Otherwise you can only talk to your friends who are mostly as bewildered as you. The ones who have been before, and they are the ones who have been quieter than the rest since the journey started, try to teach you a few words. But it is not a question of words. After several weeks you try to ask for coffee. What the word *coffee* means is that *you* are asking for some coffee and *you* should not be. What the word *she* means is that *you* are a randy dog. When you use words, you are like a dog barking.

It must be remembered that the overwhelming majority of immigrant workers do not speak the language of the new country, nor do they learn it quickly, for reasons connected both with their basic education and with their position in society. Ignorance of the language affects the position of the immigrant at work in various ways. . . . He tends to get either completely unskilled jobs which can easily be demonstrated by the foreman, or repetitive semi-skilled jobs, in which he is instructed once and then left at for long periods. . . . Ignorance of the language cuts the immigrant off from his workmates. It hinders the growth of friendship and understanding between them, and makes it more difficult to bring the immigrants into the trade unions. Small misunderstandings about work practices or personal matters may therefore develop into major problems.

Later, when you start work, you are told to put that thing here. One of them shows you how. When you have done it right ten times he leaves you to get on with it. You do it 100,000 times. In your language there are no words for the thing you are putting with the other thing. Sometimes it seems that what you are doing and where you are do not even exist in your language.

Many Italians, who are used to regarding wild birds as a delicacy on the menu at home, may be surprised when they find themselves arrested for hunting birds. As a Swiss newspaper writes: "If the Swiss or Italian authorities had at courses or in leaflets drawn the foreign workers' attention to the fact that cats, dogs, swans, singing birds and hedgehogs do not belong on the dinner table in our country, we should have been saved a good deal of exasperation." This is certainly a point worth considering. If prospective immigrants were provided with adequate information not only on the laws of the new country but also on its norms and customs, particularly with regard to sexual behaviour, this might prevent many misunderstandings. An immigrant cannot be expected to know *a priori* that pigs and chickens may be eaten but swans and hedgehogs may not. Nor can he know at first that Western European women have greater sexual freedom than Southern European women. However, one should not hope too much from mere explanation, for norms which have been engrained since childhood are not easily displaced.

Your work is repetitive, hard, unhealthy and dirty. The work you do is a stigma. You not only suffer it, you also suffer the inferiority of which it is the mark. You never see one of their workers doing the same work as you do.

Immigrant workers . . . are usually employed in occupations rejected by indigenous workers. In a situation of full employment, the nationals of the country concerned have taken advantage of opportunities for moving into better-paying, more pleasant jobs, usually in the white-collar or skilled sectors. The immigrants have been left in the jobs deserted by the others. . . . Immigrant workers tend to be heavily concentrated in certain industries or occupations, such as building, engineering, textiles and clothing, catering, domestic service. These are the sectors which have either the lowest pay or the worst working conditions. . . . In France the older established European immigrant groups—Italians, Spaniards, Poles— tend to have rather higher socio-economic status than the Portuguese and North Africans. In Switzerland it is the Italians and Spaniards who are worst off, compared with those from Germany, France or Austria. In Germany, the lowest positions are occupied by Southern Europeans and Turks. . . .

You send about a third of your wages home each month.

The second major benefit to the sending countries results from the flow of funds remitted by the migrants to their families and relatives back home. These flows have grown very rapidly—even faster than migration itself—in recent years. In Yugoslavia and Turkey, for example, remittance flows—currently totalling about $500 million and $600 million a year, respectively—are now their major source of foreign exchange. The current annual flow of remittances from all migrants in Europe to their home countries is over $2.5 billion, which is, as a comparison well in excess of the total value of actual lending disbursed world-wide by the World Bank Group each year. (Ian M. Hume, "Migrant Workers in Europe", *Finance and Development*, March 1973.)

You dream continually of making as much money in as short a time as possible. You work overtime whenever you can. You work at the quickest rate possible if you are on piecework. You see their workers watching you and they have special words for you which make them laugh. If they know you carry a knife they may stop. The faster you work, the more hostile they become. But they are not in a hurry. They go home every night.

The immigration of manual workers to Western Europe has been described as colonization in reverse. The immigrants are given the jobs that no one else will do. This encourages the indigenous population to take on a colonialist mentality, regarding it as the inevitable destiny of the new- comers to carry out all the menial tasks. Immigration helps to give large sections of the indigenous working class the consciousness of a "labour aristocracy" which supports or acquiesces in the exploitation of another section of the working class. In this way immigration helps to stabilize the capitalist order, not only economically but also politically.

You never make the necessary savings in the time you had hoped. You always have to stay longer, return more times than you imagined. Your hopes are continually deferred. You don't see your children grow up. Instead you dream of their working with you when you have saved enough to buy a business or a tractor.

The usual goal of small peasants who migrate is to save enough to pay their debts and improve their farm on return. Rural workers hope to buy land or to set up small retail or construction businesses in order to become more independent. P. Vigorelli studied the occupation of migrants who had returned to Italy, and came to the following conclusions: "The majority of returnees do not lean towards working in industry and rather look for work in the tertiary occupations if they have gained experience in this field while abroad, and if they have been able to save up the necessary capital to carry out an autonomous occupation."

If you have no papers you have no political or trade union rights at all. If you have the correct papers and permits you have rights up to the point where they do not hinder your employer. After that you have no rights again.

In Germany the Foreigners' Law of 1965 is officially regarded as a liberalization. The right of political activity is, however, severely restricted by Section 2 of Paragraph 6, which states: "The political activity of foreigners can be restricted or forbidden, if the prevention of disturbances of public safety and order or of detriment to the political process in the German Federal Republic, or other important interests of the German Federal Republic require it." This rule is so vague that it permits the authorities to ban whatever activities they wish.

After a long while you discover something unexpected. You are treated like dogs, but just because of that, if there is a crowd of you together, people fear you. They are not sure whether the crowd is not a pack of dogs with rabies—it might be.

This almost hysterical fear of action by immigrant workers is not confined to Germany; as this example shows: "At the Citroen car assembly plant on the outskirts of Brussels, a group of Spanish, Italian and other foreign workers went on strike in December 1969 over a minor incident when one of them was moved on a production line. At once the local police appeared on the scene (at the request of Citroen or of the local mayor, no one can say) with riot helmets and fire hoses, as though dealing with an uprising, not a minor strike."

If you are a politico, you fight and you get deported with a police dossier; you cannot depend on any trade union help. If you are not— and why should you be?—you try to avoid trouble. You are not working for socialism, you are working to save enough money to prove that you are human. Meanwhile, the Communists are no more interested in you, and your bunkfull of problems, than are the capitalists who have imported you.

Migration involves the transfer of a valuable economic resource—human labour—from the poor to the rich countries. The workers who migrate may have been unemployed in the country of origin, but this does not alter the fact that the community has invested considerable sums in their upbringing. Economists sometimes speak of "emigration as capital export", similar to the export of other factors of production. . . . This being so, it is relevant to try to calculate the cost of a migrant for his country of origin. Most workers migrate around the age of 20, just when they reach the peak of their working capacity. The costs we are concerned with are those of feeding, clothing, and housing a person and providing health and educational and other services, until he reaches working age. . . . C. Caporale gives a cost equivalent to 8.7 years of labour for bringing up a person until he reaches working age. . . . A. Fontani quotes estimates of the *Istituto Italiano per la Protezione Sociale*, which puts the cost of raising a worker at 150,000 lire per year. By the time a worker reaches the age of 20 the nation will have paid more than 3 million lire for his upbringing. This . . . is roughly equivalent to $5,000.

Your family are thousands of kilometres away and you do not tell them what it is like, for they would despise you for tolerating it. Meanwhile you work and wait. And the waiting is the worst. On Sundays you can weep. A day without work brings you no nearer the dreamt-of end: it is a day in purgatory. On weekdays the worst time is between finishing work and falling asleep. But you are tired and so it is not so bad as the weekend. When you look round the room at the other men, you see the same thing on all their faces, young and old equally. The faces of men who live without women have a special look: not so much a look of hunger as an appearance of neglect.

Being deprived of normal family life, either because they have left their families at home or because they have migrated before getting married, they find it difficult to have a satisfactory sex life. Prejudice from the local population makes casual relationships with indigenous women difficult. Equally, the need to save money prevents many men from having an affair which means taking a woman out, buying presents, etc. For the same reason, the higher class prostitutes are unavailable to them. Thus in Germany, for example: "private brothels for foreign workers have been found; venereal diseases are increasing again". One such "private foreigners' brothel" operating in a company-owned workers' hostel has been described in a German magazine: "Once a week a German pimp appears with an Italian prostitute in an Opel car with reclining seats. The time for each person is carefully measured: five minutes as a rule, and anyone who can't make it in that period can buy a few minutes more for 10 Marks. Custom is keen and there is a queue waiting along the fence."

You live in one of two different kinds of lodgings. Either you live in lodgings owned by your employers or you go out and find your own. Both kinds are bad. If you live in accommodation supplied by your employers, you pay back to them, for your bed and your food, some of the wages they have paid you. (Currently there are about 7.5 Swiss francs to the pound.)

Two or three hundred Italian and Spanish seasonal workers were housed in wooden huts by the building firm which employed them, with three or four men to each room. In some of the rooms there was not even space for a bed for each man, so that mattresses had to be rolled out on the floor at night. All cooking was done in the rooms on two-burner calor gas stoves; heating was also by calor gas, but was inadequate. The windows were not windproof, the roofs and walls allowed damp to penetrate. . . . The rent was 65 Swiss francs per month for each worker, and was deducted directly from the wage packets. The employer had a monthly income of 240 Swiss francs per room and around 15,000 Swiss francs for the whole set of wooden huts.

Not only do you pay your employer, but you are subject to the same kind of orders as at work. Your suitcase, for instance. Your locked suitcase is the only private space you have had since you left the village. About a twentieth of a square metre. But you are forbidden to keep it near where you sleep. All suitcases have to be stored away. Everywhere you feel yourself surrounded by invisible barbed wire.

Discipline has become a fetish for many people dealing with immigrant workers, and regulations like those generally used in Germany are formulated and applied in a way more appropriate to a boarding school or a borstal than a workers' hostel. For instance, paragraph 2 of the German regulations forbids entry to any persons not employed in the works, in particular to women and children. It is not only single workers who are prevented from having normal social and sexual relationships in this way. Married men and women, whose spouses are living in separate workers' hostels, are only able to meet them in parks and cafés. Women have on occasions been expelled from hostels because their husbands have stayed the night.

You can try to live freely outside the barbed wire. You can find your own accommodation. It has to be cheap if you are going to be able to save. You have already learnt that if you cannot afford to pay much you are more liable to be cheated; only the rich and the starving are not cheated.

A newspaper describes two houses in Zurich in which 140 Italians were housed paying 75 Swiss francs per month: "The rooms are 'furnished' with four beds each, four cheap cupboards, a table and two or three chairs.

During the winter each tenant has to pay an additional 6 francs for heating: 90 francs for the four rooms. When the workers take up residence they have to deposit 30 francs as security and they are not given a receipt for this. The monthly yield on these small buildings dating from 1925: 10,500 francs, plus 840 francs for heating.... The two houses are in urgent need of repair. The kitchen and the lavatories are in a deplorable state. When the rent was raised from 65 to 75 francs per bed the workers complained to the rent tribunal. The owners then agreed to take out one bed from each room but only provided there was a supplementary increase in rent 'to meet the deficit'. The rent tribunal finally suggested a compromise: an increase of 7 francs in the rent and the possibility for the owners to impose a supplementary increase during the course of the year."

Tired, waiting, cheated, you go to bed in the hope of forgetting where you are. Your sleep is like your locked suitcase—it contains all you brought with you.

A type of accommodation almost exclusively for immigrant workers and their families is the so-called *hôtel meublé* or *hôtel garni*. They are somewhat cheaper than normal tourist hotels, but the facilities offered are generally very poor indeed. For many Africans or Portuguese a place in such an *hôtel* is the only alternative to putting up a hovel of their own on some wasteland on the outskirts of the cities. . . . In an *hôtel* room intended for one double bed there are ten beds. In the erstwhile office of the *hôtel*: four beds. Usually the beds are bunks, with a distance of at most 50cm between them. Sometimes this amount of space is only found every second bed. In the cellars the palliasses on the upper bunks are only 50cm from the ceiling. When the beds are not in bunk form they are arranged in groups of six, sometimes covering the entire outer rim of the room. They can only be got into via the foot.

How does it end? You do not know. Some give up. There are millions more to take their place. Some achieve a fraction of what they had hoped. Some go mad and are put in institutions. Many fall ill, especially with tuberculosis and peptic ulcers. Gradually you get used to it.

Migration is seen by the ruling class in both the sending and receiving countries as an important factor for stabilizing the existing political system. A leading representative of the German Employers' Association has emphasized this point: "Need and poverty, which are usually connected with unemployment, lead to political radicalization, and we see that particularly in the Mediterranean countries the people are still receptive towards radical slogans. In the long run it cannot be a matter of indifference to us if one day there are bases for the Red Fleet on the Adriatic and airfields for the Red Air Force on the plain of the Po. Italy still has the biggest Communist party in Western Europe. I think we can only eliminate this danger by improving the social and economic structures in the

countries of the Mediterranean area. One way of improving these structures is that in the first place we give the people from this area the chance
of finding work and hence also corresponding earning opportunities in
the highly industrialized countries of Western Europe."

You find yourself laughing. You distinguish between the bad and
the very bad. You go to the railway station to meet the new arrivals
from your country. The hall of the station becomes the least foreign
place you know. The winters are worse than the summers. In the
summer your bosses go for holidays to your country. Their wives
come back with the shawls or sandals you once dreamt of buying
for your wife or sister. But at least the summers are warm. You
change and you adapt. You buy city things to take back home. To
show that it has been worth it. And after a number of years, one
time when you go home for your short holiday, you suspect that
you no longer belong there either. Who are you then?

5

FICTION OF 1973

(a) IRIS MURDOCH

The Black Prince

THE TITLE refers, of course, not to Edward III's warrior son but to Hamlet, whom Iris Murdoch's narrator at one euphoric moment describes as "the tormented empty sinful consciousness of man seared by the bright light of art, the god's flayed victim dancing the dance of creation". And it may as well be said at once that the reviewer considers *The Black Prince* to be Miss Murdoch's *Hamlet*—a novel in which she comes to grips with the crucial questions that have preoccupied her ever since *Under the Net*, and in which, more passionately, densely and eloquently than in any previous book, she restates her philosophical position, in the form of a question: "Can there be a *natural*, as it were Shakespearean felicity in the moral life?"

As long ago as 1960, in an article for the *Yale Review*, Miss Murdoch offered various definitions of the artist's role, of the complex tensions involved in his duty to form ("the temptation of love and its peril, whether in art or life: to round off a situation, sum up a character . . . art has *got* to have form, whereas life need not") and his moral obligation to include "reality with all its odd contingent ways". She said then that the artist is "indeed the analogon of

---

(*a*) IRIS MURDOCH: *The Black Prince*. 364 pp. Chatto and Windus. £2.50.

(*b*) ANGUS WILSON: *As If By Magic*. 415 pp. Secker and Warburg. £2.50.

(*c*) DAN JACOBSON: *The Wonder-Worker*. 191 pp. Weidenfeld and Nicolson. £2.25.

(*d*) LUDVÍK VACULÍK: *The Axe*. Translated by Marian Sling. 222 pp. Deutsch. £2.50. *The Guinea Pigs*. Translated by KÁČA POLÁČKOVÁ. 167 pp. New York: Third Press. $7.95.

(*e*) THOMAS PYNCHON: *Gravity's Rainbow*. 760 pp. Cape. £3.95 (paperback, £1.95).

(*f*) BERYL BAINBRIDGE: *The Dressmaker*. 152 pp. Duckworth. £2.35.

the good man . . . the lover who, nothing himself, lets others be through him." And in her latest novel she has, both symbolically (by constantly reminding us of *Hamlet*) and dramatically (by means of a Hamlet-artist narrator), crystallized these monumental statements into a remarkable fictional shape.

Bradley Pearson, we learn from the device of an "Editor's" foreword, has been persuaded to write the story of his unhappy love. Art has been his doom; his aim has been to obey its dictates of truth, however pathetically (as he later says) this may reveal a lack of the dignity contingent on a "character" in a work of art. He is, at the start of the story, a fifty-eight-year-old retired tax inspector living a cosy bachelor life off Charlotte Street, planning to disappear to rural seclusion and write his Great Book. One of Miss Murdoch's splendid skills is to plunge at once into tantalizing situations. Bradley's doorbell rings to announce the catastrophic news, brought by her shambling parasitic brother Francis, that Christian, the ex-wife he had put out of mind, has returned from America a rich, and clearly predatory, widow.

The telephone simultaneously summons him to the bedside of Rachel, wife of his old friend Arnold Baffin, and Francis (who plays throughout the familiar Murdochian role of unlovable confidant, intruder catalyst, Sancho Panza *sensuel*) shares Bradley's discovery that Arnold, famous best-selling novelist and ideal husband, has just beaten up a desperate vindictive wife. It is in this distressed and disorientated state that Bradley, in a characteristically Murdoch scene, encounters Arnold and Rachel's only daughter Julian, at first taking her for a boy as she symbolically scatters shredded love-letters to the Bloomsbury traffic: he agrees to coach her on *Hamlet*.

It will not have taken the habitual reader long to predict what follows this traumatic day's events. Rachel seduces Bradley, Arnold falls in love with the dashing Christian, Francis panders and suggests that Bradley has always been in love with Arnold. And, of course, Bradley falls in love with twenty-year-old Julian. It has happened before, and not only in many of Miss Murdoch's novels, that an elderly man succumbs as though bewitched to a young *ingénue*. But for Bradley this love is, we are to accept, the artist's fate; Julian the unattainable is not a muse (though he can at last verbalize his convictions about art, truth, Shakespeare); she is not, although she has been a schoolgirl Hamlet and provokes him to rape when she dons black velvet complete with skull, the incarnation of his literary lodestar; she *is*, he comes too late to realize, the book he knows he must write, the book is "her deification".

Not, of course, that his recollection in tranquillity happens during the hectic events of the novel. Bradley observes, in one of the elliptical philosophical passages which here flow naturally from the action, that human wickedness is usually "the product of a semi-deliberate inattention, a sort of swooning relationship to time". And he compares this to the artist's knowledge of "the space between the stage where the work is too unformed to have committed itself and the stage where it is too late to improve it . . .". At such a moment of "swooning", Bradley allows Rachel to think he is hers; tells his love to Julian; refuses his drugged and despairing sister's plea for attention; hides his knowledge of her suicide from Julian; and finally falls into the trap that jealous murder has set, thus losing his freedom and his love forever.

Yet, in spite of melodramatic tragedy blacker than Miss Murdoch has previously allowed, we are surely intended to focus not on the causality of Bradley's tale of love and death but on its justification as a statement about virtue (which of course Miss Murdoch sees as no less a concern of art than of living). For instance, is Bradley the self-deluding egoist of the "postscripts" by the other protagonists? Is he another Accidental Man, propelled (as he himself believes at times) by the "insubstantial shadow" of some "black Eros" who predestines love and plunges him into knowledge and doom? Or is he, alone and justified only by his own words, the artist whose every act is an agonized inching towards truth?

It is unlikely that Miss Murdoch's answers are intended to be more than tentative—that has always been one fascination of her novels. *The Black Prince* is grimmer and more bookish than most but it is also full of the very comic stuff, what Bradley calls "the foul contingency", of life, all that irony he tries ineffectively to exclude. He is, for instance, obliged at one moment to lend the dirty socks, stuffed in his pocket after an undignified exit from Rachel's bed, to her barefoot daughter in the boutique from which he wants to buy her a pair of purple boots. Being a puritan, and easily disgusted, he is constantly confronted with middle-aged, pudgy, pink and pear-shaped ladies needing affection; he is nearly sick in the Royal Opera House; he is embarrassed by his (phallic) pleasure in the Post Office Tower. He—or his creator—has some excellent jokes at the expense of reviewers castigating the too-prolific novelist.

Not all the devices quite come off, and the Chinese boxes of truth within the "truth" of Bradley's apologia do not seem necessary. You cannot disarm criticism by letting characters say they don't find other characters (such as Julian or Arnold) very convincing. Miss Murdoch herself has disclaimed the conscious intention of being "a philosophical novelist" and highly values the naturalistic pre-occupation with "various individuals"; yet she must surely now recognize that what gives her work its own individuality—here in its most thematic form—is her courage in tangling us all, and her various individuals, with the philosopher's cerebrations. This time, the cerebrations are given both voice and shape in her narrator, who, as he says of Shakespeare writing *Hamlet*, "makes the crisis of his own identity into the very central stuff of his art".

(*b*) ANGUS WILSON

As If By Magic

WHERE ARE THEY NOW, the sniffing ladies in mangy toques adorned with violets? The ex-army bores, a bit pushed for gee-gee money? The secret drinkers, bitchy little blackmailers and huge, flabby, poodle-stroking mothers? Perhaps such distressed and distressing gentlefolk may still be seen lurking in tired Home Counties parlours, or grumbling at the new washable-vinyl wall-paper in the guest-house dining-room; but wherever they are, Angus Wilson, once their champion, has abandoned them to their pink gins and quiet extinction.

Not that the Wilson world is suddenly purged of its oafs, hypocrites and henna-haired theatricals. Indeed, this new novel displays such an extravagant range of half-human oddities that Mr Wilson has wisely chosen not to preface it with the once-traditional cast-list, which would surely have encouraged in the reader an unhealthy premature disbelief. What thread of sense, after all, could possibly link a verbose and bogus Austrian guru, operating in Goa; a pair of waffling Singhalese trendies, trying to make a Hampstead out of Colombo; an apoplectic neo-Fascist tycoon with a fancy for the occult; and, in Borneo, a leering freemasonry of colonial pederasts, caught in mid-orgy?

The answer really is that Mr Wilson himself is the only true link. It is his "chaffing" (a favourite word), his mimicry, his non-stop mynah-bird act that keep the book together, at grave cost to his characters' independent vitality, their "reality". But before we face the large and troubled question of Mr Wilson's perpetually allusive narrative presence, we must examine his central characters, the two chosen vessels whose voyages make *As If By Magic* Mr Wilson's first extended exercise in literary globe-trotting.

The two in question are Hamo Langmuir, incipiently middle-aged plant geneticist, and his hippy god-daughter Alexandra Grant. As another character remarks: "By their names you can tell them." Miss A. Grant is a student; and Hamo—well, it looks for a while as though Mr Wilson will resist the temptation, but he eventually arranges for an Indian newspaper to commit the typographical blunder necessary to change "Hamo" to the insulting but none the less accurate "Homo". The love that once dared not speak its name has become highly vociferous in the six years since Mr Wilson last brought forth a novel, and he has clearly enjoyed making Langmuir an openly, even engagingly hedonistic, homosexual; though it must be said that earlier novels, particularly *Hemlock and After*, benefited by the furtive tension imposed by the old repressive law. It is a tension that is sadly missing here.

The book's first section rather toilingly sets up the parallel journeys of the two half-related souls, Alexandra and Hamo, searcher and researcher: the girl departing with a strange mime-troupe to a hippy colony on the Moroccan coast, and the scientist on a world tour of inspection to check on the practical progress of his brain-child "Magic", a new high-yield rice that is transforming the agronomic structures of developing countries all over the world. It is Hamo's gradual discovery of the disruptive influence of "Magic", its power to worsen still further the economic imbalances operating in the most distressed, "hopeless" areas, that gives impetus to the process of self-realization soon under way within him: a stock-taking process all Mr Wilson's major figures, from Bernard Sands to Sylvia Calvert, have undergone.

Hamo not only stands at the moral centre of the novel but falls about conspicuously in aid of its comedy, a wildly erratic and brutally ironic comedy of sexual frustration. Throughout his travels, his devotion to another magic, the powerful thrill of lust, sends him in ungainly pursuit of servant-youths luckless enough to conform to the enchanted formula:"Chest 30 inches, Waist 24 inches, Hips 35 inches. . . ." Thwarted every time, he manages simultaneously to outrage the social sensibilities of his hosts and bring misery to the objects of his masturbatory desires. One lad is drowned while attempting to save Hamo from that very fate; and in Goa, another, presented by Hamo with a pair of binoculars ("magic glasses"—Mr Wilson never misses an opportunity of spreading the symbolism) is stoned to death for making voyeuristic use of the apparatus. Hamo's sexual and politico-scientific culpabilities, suddenly united in this fatally misguided gesture of giving, drive him to scrap his conventionally framed report and write to London to insist instead on radical changes in research-planning, with a new emphasis, "however quixotic", on the human aspect of the work. Hamo sails out to present these new convictions to a rioting Goan mob, by whom he is very savagely slain.

So much is basically acceptable in its design. The pathetic string-bean Hamo, a sterile mutant on a mission of fertility, is much the most successful feature of the novel. The Alexandra episodes, clogged and charmless by comparison, are not even very reliably accurate; one gets the feeling here that Mr Wilson has tried to think his way into an unfelt empathy with the young and perplexed, only to come up with mystifications and unhelpful ambiguities. Alexandra's experiments with the "magic" (again) triangle of herself, Ned and Rodrigo, fellow-mummers in the mime-troupe, make turgid reading, especially when they drag in D. H. Lawrence to facilitate some tedious literary role-playing. One might have blamed the obsessive tinkering with the "Birkin-Gerald-Ursula tripling" on Alexandra's histrionic personality and Eng Lit training, if this urge to live out lit crit points were not already such a familiar tic of Mr Wilson's. Sometimes, admittedly, he has made a neat, if rather precious, use of it as shorthand in the formulation of instant judgments. "I'm a natural Emma", someone would blithely remark; and there would be "Dornford Yates jaunts", "W. H. Davies people", "Quilpish humour" and so on. It is interesting to note, incidentally, how closely this habit of labelling is related to the jaunty camp of the following, from *The Wrong Set*: "In his jade green linen shirt, white silk tie with green spots and olive green daks, he looked very English intellectual, very Pirates of Penzance."

Mr Wilson seems not to fear that the evocation of literary antecedents at vital moments will puncture the sense of "the totality of life" he is so eager to generate and sustain. But there are several points in the present novel when his own literary inclinations seem to precede and overwhelm the human instincts of a character; and at such times it becomes disastrously clear that the personage in question owes his first allegiance not to the realities, or even fantasy-realities, operative in Mr Wilson's created world but to the self-indulgently exposed mechanics of his imagination. Thus Alexandra, attempting to save her guru from the Goan rioters, finds herself rescued by Charles Dickens:

Then suddenly a memory of Little Dorrit, of Mr Pancks exposing the old fraud Casby to the tenants of Bleeding Heart Yard by cutting off his patriarchal locks, came back to her. She pulled the beige hat from off Swami's head, trusting that the absurdity of his appearance would make her laugh and that her laughter would prove infectious.

Alexandra spends the last page of the novel trying not to see herself as Jane Austen's Mrs Bennet, and cursing English literature for infecting her mind with such mimetic notions—but it is difficult to hold her responsible for them in the first place when they proceed so shamelessly from Mr Wilson's well-advertised literary preferences. An earlier moment of crisis, with the runaway Alexandra confronting her pursuing parents in a Northern hotel, is similarly encumbered with the bookish quotation-mania. "She walked straight down to the bar. She chose a quotation", says Mr Wilson, as if figures entering rooms unexpectedly were obliged to do *something* of the sort, "that she knew would enrage Him" (her father). This Café Royal gesture, the delicate selection of a wounding literary barb, is simply not proper to the occasion. Even worse is the performance of the dandified Rodrigo, whose ammunition is pathetically feeble as quotable mottoes go: "Oh, shut up, for God's sake", he cries, scolding Alexandra. "I don't know whether to quote adulterous Aunt Rosemary to you—'Inquests are terribly bad form', or my mother, 'It never does to be bitter'." The answer is that Mr Wilson should have kept Rodrigo's mouth shut.

These vexing mannerisms would not be so noticeable if the narrative did not so frequently dip and swoop from apparent normality to parody, to fantasy and back again, obliging the reader to keep exhaustingly alert to authorial hints at changes in tone and direction. This "levels of reality" business is a recurring question in discussions of Angus Wilson's work (his book *The Wild Garden* drew attention to an extreme polarity between the views of Frank Kermode and Raymond Williams on the matter), and *As If By Magic* is going to excite new debate; for it seems that Mr Wilson, as he grows older, is increasingly prepared to afflict his reader with a puzzlement amounting almost to a sense of exclusion. He has never been in favour of utter clarity, but rather of "disseminating the moral proposition so completely in a mass of living experience that it is never directly sensed as you read but only apprehended at the end as a result of the life you have shared". A laudable scheme; but at least two large set-pieces in the present novel are so thoroughly difficult to "share" that one is tempted to dismiss them wholesale.

The first is a forty-five page discussion involving Alexandra, her parents, Hamo, Ned and Rodrigo, during which Mr Wilson reaches a new peak of miscalculated hyper-allusiveness (Alexandra's novelist father even adopts the guise of the hero of a current children's television programme, *Hector's House*, which will send the scholars of AD 2001 scurrying to the video-library); the whole thing is suddenly halted with a slap and a kiss, preposterous melodrama. The second glaring lapse is the Borneo orgy, as weirdly perfumed a piece of private pornography as this author has allowed himself, and as bad in its gloating way as the coy captions in Hamo's sex mags.

A perfunctory epilogue points up the grand old liberal morals we have numbly distilled out of Hamo's fate. But we are left in confusion; surprised by Angus Wilson's ambition and jolted by his vigour, but disappointed by the splurging waywardness of the new work. It is his noisiest performance so far and his least assured.

(c) DAN JACOBSON

The Wonder-Worker

DAN JACOBSON'S NEW BOOK is a dry, ingenious fable about what it is like to be mad—to float free of human limitations and entanglements, to be imprisoned in a private dream of power. The narrative is out of joint. The hero's personal history has somehow got folded over and scissored, so that when it is opened out it reveals not one man but two, one writing the other's life. They exist side by side—character catching eerie glimpses of author out of the corner of his eye, author struggling to keep character in his place. Meeting, becoming whole, is what they must avoid. It would mean all the pain of consciousness, of feeling and thinking and remembering.

This way, split off, neither is quite real, neither is vulnerable or guilty. It is this feat *The Wonder-Worker* explores: the trick of ceasing to be human, of denying the muddle of living: "I know what I'm doing. Writing down descriptions of places I have never visited, people I have never met, deeds I have never done, I am a free man. . . ." The processes of growth and decay, his own past and future, have come to seem mere organic fidgetings in a world essentially—ideally—dead.

And so this author describes his character's brief foray into humanity with ironic detachment, from the moment of his conception ("Timothy" is foisted upon a bemused and unenthusiastic couple holidaying in the Isle of Wight) to his lonely apotheosis. His father's fumbling ineptitudes, his mother's regular Friday afternoon infidelities, his desperate schoolboy love for noisy, cruel Susie, all serve to teach Timothy the true nature of the world. It is not a home, though it pretends to be, it has nothing to do with men and women: it is a place of *things*, a maze of planes and textures and facets that have their own inscrutable order. When he looks at his mother or the girl he loves, what he sees is the gold or copper of hair, the flecked, stony mosaic of eyes, the ivory of teeth—

The gates of matter opened for him. He was taken into garden after garden of eternal rigidity and symmetry, whose repose he did not disturb, for with his entry their repose became his own.

Like other merciless visionaries before him, he cannot stand the feeble, independent noises people make, they have to be silenced. When he has performed that horrible act of reverence, and left his world calm, tidy and dead, "Timothy" is free. With a final, inspirational twist he walks back into his author's dream for good.

It is a neat, nasty tale, told with much panache. The style Mr Jacobson has found for his two-dimensional man is crisp and clever; the structure is meticulously worked out. Yet, for all this undoubted skill, *The Wonder-Worker* is disappointing. Mr Jacobson doesn't conjure the mortuary glee of the authentic Gothic—the mechanism he has invented doesn't seem to move him, one cannot quite believe in his complicity with his awful hero. Perhaps this is because his is characteristically a patient, not a violent imagination; he is not close enough—not convincingly close—to the dangerous edge of things, where imagined perfection turns into totalitarian nightmare. The result is that, strangely indeed for him, one senses

a lack of real *interest* in what's going on, a faintly weary professionalism. It all fits rather too readily into a contemporary convention—
self-conscious, acrobatic, crystalline. Though *The Wonder-Worker*
represents a new departure for Mr Jacobson, sadly it's a move away
from originality into a kind of pastiche.

(d) LUDVÍK VACULÍK

The Axe and The Guinea Pigs

IN A RECENT INTERVIEW with a Western journalist, Ludvík Vaculík
complained that he had become so allergic to the number 2,000 that
it upset him merely to be told that somebody had travelled 2,000
kilometres. One can only sympathize with him: however remarkable
a document of the 1968 reform movement the *2,000 Words* manifesto
may have been, it has nearly eclipsed his other work, whether political
journalism and reportage or fiction. Thus it is with a considerable
delay that we are provided with an English translation of his novel
The Axe, which, when it was first published in 1967, was hailed,
together with Milan Kundera's *The Joke*, as a sign that Czech
prose could once again be judged by European standards.

Yet, whatever the author's own feelings, it is difficult not to
associate the narrator in this novel with the man who has acquired
such a wide reputation for his forthrightness in public matters. The
same emphasis on ethical norms, on justice, truth and honour as the
fundamentals of a humanely arranged society, on the inviolability
of conscience and on the value of the individual, the same marks of
an original and independent mind which made the manifesto famous
can be found in the novel.

The story, told in the first person, is of a Prague journalist who
has just reached the halfway point in his life. After many years of
absence, he returns for a visit to his native village in eastern Moravia,
near the Slovak border. Here, calling on relatives and talking to
local people, far from the hectic city atmosphere, he rediscovers
his roots. The present blends with reminiscences of both the recent
and a much earlier past, often in the middle of a dialogue, without
any warning to the reader that a shift in time is to take place: people
and things appear both as they are and as they used to be and the
contrasts are revealing:

"We'll have to regulate the stream again", Dad said, and as he spoke, the fish vanished; "and straighten that path", and the line of apple trees toppled to the ground; "and one day, maybe, we'll lay a branch line on the other side to the factory", he said, and a hideous embankment of slag bulged over the mill-race.

"Many tasks await us", he frowned, "and we have many enemies", he said, and Mother died.

It is his dead father whom the narrator recalls most frequently, and who emerges as the second principal character. A carpenter driven by poverty in the 1930s to take a job in faraway Persia, he was a man standing with his feet in the mud of everyday life, but with his head in the stars. A self-educated, stubborn visionary, hoping for a better world, he would have been a religious reformer in another age; instead, he invested his faith in the dream of socialism. After the war, he lived to see not the realization of his dream but its debasement. Having accepted a local executive post, he was in many cases obliged by party discipline to act at variance with his character. The frustration ate away his moral strength, alienated him from his family, and finally broke him. The son can at least draw on his father's experience: faced with a similar conflict between his conscience and his alleged duty, he can resolve the dilemma in favour of loyalty to his self.

Outlining the story in such terms does not, however, do the book justice. For *The Axe* is not a political novel, but rather a ballad, in which the character of the father stands out as having almost mythical dimensions. It is no coincidence that Vaculík has set his story on the slopes of the Carpathian mountains, where it is still possible to live in close contact with nature and where traces of an earlier humanity survive despite the onslaught of what goes under the description of modern civilization; the section of the novel dealing with the son's problems in Prague seems rather flat in comparison.

The countryman in Vaculík obviously detests the faceless monster which changes villages into dormitory towns from which people are taken by bus to nearby factories, but what he is really after is the erosion of the more spiritual aspects of a particular way of life. A strong believer in basic human virtues, he has a low opinion of the rot that is spreading from the West:

When I was born, I mounted a hill and surveyed the scene. And it struck me at once that in the direction of Moravia and Bohemia I observed nothing that boded any good. That's the truth, even as a boy I had the idea that there was absolutely nothing over there to dream about. Today I am discovering the truth of that. For the people themselves lack the stuff of dreams. My childhood instinct was correct. One should not be so anxious to discover what people elsewhere possess and what they are doing. One should not be continually comparing oneself with others and always reckoning the disparities to one's disadvantage. And why struggle so hard to keep up with this or that when, for the most part, it's heading for the arsehole.

And therefore: ape America if you want, you Czech copycats!

Because: what have you to offer, anyhow, you monopolistic numskulls?

The humour of this passage is not at all exceptional; though it is written by a disillusioned and angry man, sarcasm, self-irony and plain comedy abound in *The Axe* as part of the homely wisdom with which it is infused. Czech critics have pointed to another quality in Vaculík's novel, which regrettably cannot be imparted by any translation: his use of the Valachian dialect as a way of reviving a language stifled by clichés. He reduces it to its rudiments—odd word order and the occasional regionalisms—but on the Czech ear it makes the immediate impression west country speech may have on the Londoner: that of people who live closer to the soil and are somehow truer to themselves and more trustworthy.

But Vaculík's admiration for traditional ways does not make him a man merely anxious to bring back the past, nor is *The Axe* simply a piece of social criticism relating to Communist rule in Czechoslovakia. It is set in the author's homeland, but his passionate defence of man's right to preserve his integrity against disruptive pressures and his warning that a true sense of values is being diluted in the name of conjectural welfare apply universally.

While *The Axe* tells of the corruption of a dream, *The Guinea Pigs* deals with a nightmare. It begins with a sentence which no reviewer could resist quoting: "There are more than a million people living in the city of Prague whom I'd just as soon not name here." Instead, the narrator introduces his family of four, and goes on to describe how they acquired a cat, which they later had to give up, since cats don't like being kept in city flats, how they then bought a guinea-pig, which is a more suitable animal, and so on, frequently addressing his readers as "dear children" and explaining the less familiar terms to them.

A children's story, then? Of a very queer kind. Into a cheerful, amusing tale protrude glimpses of a strange and haunting world. The father of the family works in a bank, where it is considered normal for employees to steal money. Only the unlucky have it taken away from them at the door by security guards; no one knows, however, what happens to the confiscated money and rumours abound. The guinea-pigs mate, die, and assume a great importance for the father, who conducts experiments with them at night after he has finished with his mysterious sums. Unexplained and inexplicable events take place both at home and in the bank; the father, who has a funny way with words, such as occasionally calling the State Bank the State Gang, is very much concerned about a *hypothesis* that the confiscated money may ruin the economy; to learn more about financial matters, he reads "an outstanding study written by an American economist of the early nineteenth-century by the name of E. A. Poe", called "A Descent into the Maelstrom". The story continues like this to an equally strange ending. Throughout, there is an uncanny sense of something being terribly wrong, of an irrationality that people no longer question but accept as natural.

Parts of *The Guinea Pigs* remain incomprehensible, and are seemingly intended to be so, yet this is possibly one of the best novels to have come from Eastern Europe since the war. But what does it all mean? The key to the riddle lies in the date when the novel was written. What it describes is the state of mind, not only of its author, but of a whole nation: for this is Czechoslovakia after the Soviet invasion. Here we do not just have the gradual destruction of a way of life, the erosion of ideals and profanation of values as in *The Axe*. In *The Guinea Pigs* we witness the total collapse of every aspect of humanity: words have lost their meaning, reality is adjusted to suit theory, life is not only absurd, it is utterly nonsensical, and people turn into fearful little animals. What starts out as a cheerful story, ends in the darkest, almost metaphysical horror; there is no faith left, no hope—in anything. Kafka, too, lived in Prague. . . .

Both novels have found good translators, familiar with the subject-matter from their own experience. While the American publishers of *The Guinea Pigs* (which has never appeared in Czechoslovakia) have been content to leave the Czech names as they were, the English production of *The Axe* employs some rather bizarre transliterations. This seems unnecessary nowadays; it is not only wrong linguistically, but also inconsistent, so that we find *Drahushe*, *Dechin* (in place of Drahuše, Děčín) side by side with *Dvořák*. What next? President Pompeedoo?

(e) THOMAS PYNCHON

Gravity's Rainbow

IMAGINE A LIMBO, where death has come, but not the end—a breathless, frenzied, sickening, yet somehow moronically *cheerful* interval that seems to go on forever. That is about as close as one can come to a brief description of *Gravity's Rainbow*. Though it is monstrously long and over-populated, it all takes place in one prolonged moment —the no-man's land between war and peace in Europe in 1944–45, the unnatural pause between the landing of a V-2 on London and the sound of its descent. Into this ominous gap crowd innumerable, motley, period characters, bringing with them all their mental baggage: songs, films, fantasies, plots and counter-plots that stretch away to the corners of the shrinking globe. The V-2's menacing flight over-arches them all, not to bring order into their lives (or the book) but to light up the chaos. Thomas Pynchon's fictions of order do not progress: this book inherits the paranoia of *The Crying of Lot 49* (1966) and the coincidental cataclysms of *V* (1963). After V-1, V-2: by some underground route, not unlike one of his own plots, Mr Pynchon has managed to coincide with himself, returning to his fascinated reconstruction of the true, buried history of World War Two.

That history can be read everywhere, if you know how to look: in "scraps of lost paper, graffiti on the broken walls where facing has been shot away to reveal the brick underneath—broken in specific shapes that also may be read . . .". In a madhouse in England "there's a long-term schiz . . . who believes that *he* is World War II". Is that a clue, or did it all start when the American Food and Drug people "took the cocaine out of Coca-Cola, which gave us an alcoholic and death-oriented generation of Yanks ideally equipped to fight WW II"? Or perhaps ICI are behind it, or the war is a giant laboratory or test-pad? The worst thing, though, is that the war has got inside, that instincts themselves are attuned to death. The map that Slothrop, the American hero, makes of his sexual adventures in London, turns out to correspond with rocket hits, except that Slothrop always makes it a few days earlier; his bemused, bawdy progress through Europe takes him through a series of comic-book metamorphoses—Plasticman, Rocketman, Pigman (pig as in Gadarene swine)—approaching ever more closely to pure mechanism; and of course THEY (British Intelligence is it, or who?) are always at his back, taking notes, adjusting the stimuli (now a Dutch blonde, now a Catholic movie star), using his penis like a dowsing-rod to track down the rocket.

Slothrop's predicament is only the most thorough example of the fate overtaking every one of the cast: their desires have been re-arranged just as surely as the reflexes of Pavlov's dogs. And someone, it's rumoured, has invented an erectile plastic. But as all the separate plans, private nightmares, optings-out and mistaken intentions converge, it becomes clear that no one's in charge. There is no conspiracy—or rather, everyone's in it; the master-plan is really only the coincidence of hundreds of sub-plots.

Mr Pynchon is often accused of knowing too well what he's about —of having a neat theoretic solution at hand that makes the length and detail of the novel redundant. Actually, almost the reverse is true: significances are dirt cheap round here; they are as much a part of the intransigent stuff of life and death as groans or belches. The sinister plots that oppress the characters of *Gravity's Rainbow* are their own. All the lives, all the deaths, press upon the hero's particular life like a force from outside, yet he himself is a part of the pressure on those others. Each act is irrevocable, soon—now —it will always have happened like this and no other way. Your free actions are stolen from you; as you do it, it clicks into place, part of history, and you've performed the ritual prat-fall once more.

And so this massive book resolves itself, with comic despair, into a concatenation of episodes, rich in illusionist detail tripping over into frantic farce. It's very hard to read—impossible, it has to be said, to read continuously—not because of density or obscurity, but because it's so nearly devoid of hierarchy or perspective:

There is a movie going on, under the rug. On the floor, 24 hours a day, pull back the rug sure enough there's that damn movie!

Every character is in the foreground, even memories take the form of total recall. You couldn't find a more democratic novel: it positively prevents you from classifying, summarizing, subsuming the past in the present; you're bound to read it as though it's all happening now. Perhaps that is why it doesn't seem to make much sense to compare *Gravity's Rainbow* (as one enthusiastic American review quoted on the jacket does) to *Moby Dick* and *Ulysses*. Those books leave the reader with an immense amount of inventing to do on his

own account; this one just *is*, like the movie under the rug. Mr
Pynchon's marvellous inventiveness is almost entirely without
nuance, without resonance: the characters, the situations, the words
are fixed, comic quantities. You may laugh, or cry, roll in the aisles
or leave the cinema—whatever you do, you're still a helpless
spectator.

(*f*) BERYL BAINBRIDGE

The Dressmaker

Our current national preoccupation with all the kitsch trappings of
the 1930s and 1940s will provide future historians with some melancholy reflections on alienation. Fun for the young; and for those who
lived through the upheaval of society, a wistful reassurance that in
those days we had a role, that the country fit for heroes seemed to
everyone worth fighting for. All the more surprising, and salutary,
therefore, to find a young novelist evoking with ruthless realism
the darkest days of 1944—and, a million miles away from heroics,
adumbrating in one grim little tale the cataclysm that war created
in working-class society.

At once, with the cracked mirror, the sofa upholstered in LMS
material, the strips of asbestos pasted across the window, the jug
of water poured on the coals, Beryl Bainbridge has us there, in a
poky Liverpool terrace house still lit by gas, watching Nellie the
dressmaker sweep up broken glass, take out her teeth, and—one
more crisis survived—get her hysterical niece Rita and foolish sister
Margo up the lino stairs to the warm oblivion of a shared bed.
But it is already clear from Miss Bainbridge's chilling hints that the
crisis isn't another raid. Not until the final pages does she reveal
why Rita is hysterical or why Nellie, the pillar of puritanical spin-
sterish respectability, needed that secret glass of Christmas port.

The story is cruelly bare. Nellie has mothered pale skimpy Rita as
her own dear departed mother would have wished—and everything
in Nellie's life is done under mother's steely eye from Heaven—
as well as keeping house for roving sister Margo (still indecently
ready for Mr Right, off among coarse munitions workers, tipsy when
she gets the chance) and sighing over brother Jack, a squeamish
butcher. No harm in letting the child go to a party up the road—

indeed, pretty bouncing Valerie, one of her best customers, has won even Nellie's indulgent affection. But Rita's instant and slyly concealed infatuation with the lanky GI who held her hand comes as a nasty shock. Seldom, as the reader sees, can passion have survived so pathetic a relationship—blank-eyed with boredom, the American only answers Rita's agonized attempt to find a romantic setting among the rain-sodden municipal gardens by saying that "it ain't nothing like home". Warned by Nellie against everything to do with her body, Rita's prissy frigidity bewilders and angers him. She forgives his illiteracy, even the gleam in his eye as scrawny Auntie Margo flirts over Sunday tea—as Miss Bainbridge bleakly says, "If there had been less space in her life before his coming, he would not have taken up so much room."

The end is nasty, brutish and hardly credible, had we not been made gradually aware just how fragile is Nellie's apparently monolithic placidity. To survive not merely a lifetime's unrelieved daily struggle against poverty, to cling to "standards" when all around the transatlantic invaders are buying favours with their petrol and oranges and ham, to know that treasured possessions may survive Hitler but that no one any longer cares—this is Nellie's burden of stress, and although she is a frightening, perhaps pathological, character, Miss Bainbridge gives her Zolaesque tragic status. It is also Rita's story—the story of bewildered adolescence, twisting a sodden handkerchief in the ladies, where brasher girls rub sand on their legs to simulate stockings and seem not wicked, as her dad says, to chase the Yanks, but simply hungry for love like herself.

To have disinterred so many nasty things in the woodshed and yet evoked a workaday image of Liverpudlian optimism and resilience, in so few claustrophobic pages, is a remarkable achievement. Miss Bainbridge's imagination pushes her towards nightmare, and her eye for detail is macabre; but because she writes with taut, matter-of-fact simplicity this seems as authentic as any contemporary image the camera has preserved of that mercifully vanished past.

6

COMMUNING WITH REALITY

"THERE HAVE AS YET BEEN very few women thinkers and artists", Rebecca West wrote in 1931; "that is to say, women who have not adopted masculine values as the basis of their work." She could think of only six: Madame de la Fayette, Madame de Sévigné, Jane Austen, Colette, Willa Cather, Virginia Woolf. Not many women have appeared in the years since then that one would want to add to Dame Rebecca's list, for the terms she set are severe: to be both a thinker and an artist, and to escape the limitations and distortions that follow when a gifted woman adapts her talents to the world of men.

The point that Dame Rebecca was making was not that woman artists should be explicitly and exclusively feminine, but rather that they should be free to realize their gifts without considering the roles that social definitions of gender impose. Thus in an essay on Clemence Dane she distinguished between a novelist who is female, and a woman novelist, of which she took Miss Dane to be an example—

which is to say that she has not allowed herself to be merely a mirror in which to reflect life; before treating her material she has treated herself. She has created herself in the form in which the man-governed modern world, so far as it can be ascertained from its art, thinks woman ought to be created. In other words, she moulds herself in the likeness of the heroine of standard fiction.

(This was written in 1928, before Germaine Greer was born.) For Dame Rebecca, the ideal creative condition for a woman is to be beyond roles—to be a mirror of reality itself. Virginia Woolf was saying much the same thing, at the same time, in *A Room of One's Own*, when she described the "androgynous mind", and offered as a definition that "it is resonant and porous; that it transmits emotion

---

PETER WOLFE: *Rebecca West: Artist and Thinker*. 166 pp. Carbondale, Illinois: Southern Illinois University Press (Feffer and Simons). £3.

without impediment; that it is naturally creative, incandescent and undivided".

Whether one takes Dame Rebecca's definition or Virginia Woolf's one must conclude that the greatest living example of a woman who has achieved that state, who has been both a thinker and an artist, and who has managed over some sixty years to express a spacious sense of reality, is Rebecca West. Indeed, one might propose that her achievement is not to be located in this book or in that one, but in the whole—that her books combine to make one created work of art, the mind of Rebecca West. There is support for this view in the fact that the name by which she is known is itself a persona taken from a work of art. When a writer chooses another name for his writing self, he is doing more than inventing a pseudonym: he is naming, and in a sense creating, his imaginative identity. Hence George Orwell—a commonplace Christian name and an English river—together name the plain-speaking Englishman that Eric Blair chose to be in his work. And Rebecca West is another such: the brilliant and rebellious Ibsen heroine is chosen to replace Cicily Fairfield (a name that in itself seems almost too good an example of English gentility). To choose that name was to claim the ideas and the radical posture of Ibsen, and particularly his ideas about women, as one's own public identity. The choice suggests an exceptional woman, willing her life to be an example of woman's situation.

One must feel some discomfort in the fact that an appreciation of so considerable a talent as Dame Rebecca's should start, inevitably, with the problems arising from her sex. In the case of some other woman writers this might be avoidable; but Dame Rebecca has made the subject a continuing theme of her work and of her life. There is scarcely a book of hers that does not have in it a feminist character (often thrust in anyhow, simply to make a speech against corsets), or a feminist idea. And her own career as a successful professional writer has demonstrated both the problem of being a woman artist, and the solution to it.

In the years before the First World War, when Rebecca West was a young girl in London, making a place in journalism, she was an active Suffragist, and her early work shows the feminist spirit of that time very clearly. Her first book, *Henry James* (1916), is at its best when it deals with James's female characters: Daisy Miller, Claire de Cintré, Isabel Archer, Nanda Brookenham: all those cherished Jamesian sensibilities are treated severely, irreverently, and wittily. James had refused, she concludes, "to dramatize in his imagination anything concerning women save their failures and successes as sexual beings". One is at first astonished that James, of all writers, should be convicted of being just another insensitive male, as though he were Hemingway or Norman Mailer, but the case is well and cleverly made. It is surely the first book that could be called feminist literary criticism.

Dame Rebecca's second book, the delicate and beautiful *Return of the Soldier* (1918), is feminist in another way. It is a rare kind of book, a woman's war novel, in which the madness and destruction of man's war are refracted in the crystal of a woman's enclosed, private life. From it emerges the antithesis that continues throughout Dame Rebecca's work, between the will-to-die, which is male and creates poverty, war, and the ruin of civilizations, and the will-to-live, which is female, and bears and nourishes. *The Return of the Soldier* is a small masterpiece; but it is more nearly a "woman's novel", in the sense that *Pointed Roofs* and *Mrs Dalloway* are woman's novels, than anything else Dame Rebecca wrote, and one can understand why she chose not to continue in this manner, after such a bright beginning. For it comes too close to being *merely* a woman's novel, and so confirming the notions about women that exist in a man-governed modern world. Perhaps one might say that, though it was feminist, it was not androgynous enough.

Those first two books anticipate the later work in other ways than by their feminism: the critical book is witty, stylish, and full of self-assurance and high spirits; the novel holds implicit in it Dame Rebecca's mature sense of the world and human values. The world of the novel is a difficult one for sensitive persons to survive in: it is full of pain and suffering, frustration and betrayal, it will not adapt itself to human needs. In that world the greatest human value is realism—to know things as they are. At the end of the novel the heroine thinks:

There is a draught that we must drink or not be fully human . . . I knew that one must know the truth. I knew quite well that when one is adult one must raise to one's lips the wine of the truth, heedless that it is not sweet like milk but draws the mouth with its strength, and celebrate communion with reality, or else walk for ever queer and small like a dwarf.

Communion with reality is a large ambition, and one that must lead a woman away from her private world, to politics and art and history, to law and religion and crime. It is the course that Dame Rebecca has followed, extending and deepening her account of reality until few modern writers can match her range, or her steady moral seriousness.

In the books of the following decade or so, one can see Dame Rebecca reaching out toward larger subjects. In the 1920s there were two novels, both now forgotten: *The Judge* (1922), a long melodramatic story of sex, guilt, and power, interesting for the autobiographical beginning in Edinburgh, and for remarks about the nature of man-woman relations, but imaginatively lifeless; and *Harriet Hume* (1929), subtitled "A London Fantasy", written, Dame Rebecca said, to find out why she loved London. Neither melodrama nor fantasy was the right form for Dame Rebecca's mind to expand in, and these are her least successful novels.

Two critical books of the same period—*The Strange Necessity* (1928) and *Ending in Earnest* (1931)—are collections of essays and reviews that indicate the growth of Dame Rebecca's reputation as a journalist. Each book contains one extended essay, and both of these are important to an account of the development of her thought. In *The Strange Necessity* the title essay addresses questions that are to recur in her work, questions as central to her thought as questions of gender: "Why does art matter?" she asks, "And why does it matter so much? What is this strange necessity?" The answer derives from her view of man as divided between the will to live and the will to die: art is necessary because it sustains life.

The essay is interesting for the strength and subtlety of its argument, but it is perhaps most interesting for the shape that the argument takes. It begins like an essay by Virginia Woolf, mixing an account of a stroll in the city with thoughts about literature, making it all seem informal and easy, and consciously charming, and very womanly. But it moves on to a level of intellectual toughness and knowledge where Virginia Woolf could never have followed, drawing upon psychology and physiology, and making skilful use of Pavlov's *Conditioned Reflexes*. It is as though Dame Rebecca were acting out her liberation from the stereotypes of her sex, and showing us how a free mind might play upon ideas.

Her conviction of the moral necessity of art also underlies Dame Rebecca's elegiac essay on D. H. Lawrence in *Ending in Earnest*. It is not surprising that she should admire Lawrence, for he was a writer much like herself—a moralist, a preacher against death, an artist who could not confine his imagination within conventional literary forms. "One will rejoice", she wrote, "that our age produced one artist who had the earnestness of the patristic writers, who like them could know no peace till he had discovered what made men lust after death." She might have been writing about herself.

By 1930, Dame Rebecca's version of reality was virtually complete in its broad outlines. Her world was a dualistic world, in which good and evil, life and death battle eternally, an uncertain world, where man wanders unsupported and unknowing. His enemy is within him: the will-to-die that hates life, the need to be cruel and to suffer. His hope is in his capacity for knowledge, for communion with reality, and for the imperishable order of art. Out of art, reason, and tradition man might construct the Just City; but that goal is obstructed by the spirit that denies.

That understanding of the world is clear, but it had not yet found imaginative expression. The literary forms Dame Rebecca worked in were still those of the woman novelist—the novel and the literary essay; and in the novel she was still hunting for a personal voice. One has no sense of increasing skill and assurance in the fiction she wrote during the 1930s, neither in the stories of *The Harsh Voice* (1935) nor in the novel, *The Thinking Reed* (1936). The two books are different in manner from each other, and from the earlier fiction, and the differences suggest uncertainty, and nervous experiment. One might well have concluded in 1936 that Dame Rebecca was not a novelist and would never be one.

But three years earlier she had taken a step that was to free her from restraining literary convention: she had agreed to write a short life of Saint Augustine. The assignment was an odd one for a literary journalist to take on, but it was a wise one: it led Dame Rebecca to history, religion and psychology and it engaged her mind with a great mind and a body of thought that touched her own deeply, and shaped her thinking for the rest of her career.

Dame Rebecca's Augustine is an archetype of modern man, both in his psychological nature and in his political situation. Psychologically he is introspective and life-denying, disgusted by physical existence, and especially by sex, guilty, and convinced of the need to expiate his guilt by suffering. Politically, he is civilized man, possessed of a tradition and a culture but uncertain of its present value and threatened by anti-culture, the barbarian at the gate. His importance is that he made himself an archetype by imposing his nature upon the doctrine of the Church, and thus creating Western man in his own image; he gave his authority to man's desire for guilt and punishment, for cruelty and suffering. For Dame Rebecca, we are all the heirs of Augustine's problems: "Every phrase I read of his", she later wrote, "sounds in my ears like the sentence of my doom and the doom of my age."

One aspect of that doom has to do with art. Augustine's true vocation, in Dame Rebecca's view, was for imaginative writing; he denied that vocation, and, though he made an art of his denial in the *Confessions*, he bequeathed to posterity a complex of life-denying and art-denying ideas that still determine the content of our literature and our attitudes toward it. Dame Rebecca seizes this opportunity for further speculations on the psychology of art, and on art's friends and enemies. The argument follows closely from "The Strange Necessity", and one can see Dame Rebecca extending her command of reality by taking her theory and fleshing it with details drawn from the history of religion. The process is like that of a landscape painter, who has his scene sketched, and is now filling the canvas, building and adding details, but not altering the form. By writing the life of Augustine, in the terms she had chosen, Dame Rebecca had clarified and particularized her vision. She was ready to write her masterpiece.

And what an odd masterpiece *Black Lamb and Grey Falcon* is! Superficially it is a travel book about a trip to the Balkans in 1937. But it includes so much more, is at once so comprehensive and so personal, that it has no genre, unless one invents one, calling it an epic testament, and placing it with the other great literary oddities of that odd genre—with Robert Burton's *Anatomy of Melancholy*, T. E. Lawrence's *Seven Pillars of Wisdom*, James Agee's *Let Us Now Praise Famous Men*. It is a narrative of a journey, and a long meditation on the patterns of Western history; it is a book of Balkan portraits, and a theory of the relations between East and West in Europe; and it is a book about its own time, a moving response to the contemporary political, moral and spiritual condition of Europe. Dame Rebecca's intention, she wrote, was "to put on paper what a typical Englishwoman felt and thought in the late nineteen-thirties when, already convinced of the inevitability of the second Anglo-German war, she had been able to follow the dark waters of that event back to its source".

The sources are in fact many: the Roman Empire and its decline,

Augustine, Napoleon, and behind them all man's divided nature, living and creative, but in love with cruelty and death. It is a dark book, for a dark time. The barbarians are at the gate again, and in the past—as the book shows us—barbarism has triumphed, because men have willed it so. "If human beings were to continue to be what they are", Dame Rebecca sombrely concludes, "to act as they have acted in the phases of history covered by this book, then it would be good for all of us to die." But she is not without hope, and the principal source of hope, as in her earlier work, is in art: "Art gives us hope that history may change its spots and man become honourable."

The book itself is that—a major example of the art that gives us hope. In its pages are combined all the gifts that earlier Dame Rebecca had distributed among many books: the vivid characterizations and descriptions; the powerful analyses of history and politics; the wit; the passages of meditative and lyric beauty. In "The Strange Necessity" Dame Rebecca quoted approvingly a remark by George Santayana that one might start with any work of art or natural object and infer the whole universe; *Black Lamb and Grey Falcon* starts with a visit to a minor Balkan state and ends by giving order and meaning to past and present, to religion, art, morals and politics, to the people of the Balkans and their troubled land. It is an extraordinary achievement.

The historical importance of *Black Lamb* is, or should be, very great, for it is a supreme effort, by a mind at the height of its powers, to understand the catastrophe of the Second World War as it came on; it stands at the end of the 1930s like a massive baroque cenotaph. The importance for Dame Rebecca is also great and obvious; in this one book she cast aside entirely the restrictions of "woman writer" and revealed the true range of her mind. It is, in its majestic scale, an answer to the notion that the proper scale of a woman's imagination should be a "little bit (two inches wide) of Ivory".

Rebecca West's greatest period of creativity began with *Black Lamb*, and one can see now how the books that follow depend on it and derive from it. The two books of trials, *The Meaning of Treason* (1949) and *A Train of Powder* (1955) relate to *Black Lamb* in two ways: they extend Dame Rebecca's "world" into the realm of law, and they complete her meditation on the meaning of modern history. Law must obviously be a crucial concept to one who sees the world divided between civilization and barbarism, for law is the wall that men build against disorder. Treason is a wilful breaching of that wall, and fascism is a denial that a wall can exist, and so of course Dame Rebecca would be fascinated by the case of Lord Haw-Haw, and the judgments at Nuremberg, and would see those trials as political tragedies. Her accounts of the trials are, in a sense, journalism, but they are journalism raised to a high level of art and thought, with the richness of understanding that makes *Black Lamb* a great book. Character and setting are created with extraordinary vividness, action and dialogue are as convincing as in a novel. Yet they are scrupulously factual, and because they are factual (as *Black Lamb* also is), they perform an important moral function.

Dame Rebecca writes: it is the presentation of the facts that matters:

The facts that, put together, are the face of the age . . . for if people do not have the face of the age set clear before them they begin to imagine it; and fantasy, if it is not disciplined by the intellect and kept in faith with reality by the instinct of art, dwells among the wishes and fears of childhood, and so sees life either as simply answering any prayer or as endlessly emitting nightmare monsters from a womb-like cave.

The face of the age in these cases is the face of a traitor, a Nazi, a murderer, a lynch-mob. But one must confront that face for the sake of reality, and once more it is art that comes to our aid. Dame Rebecca's art takes us beyond the facts, to the questions they raise: what in men leads them to betray their fellows? What are the foundations of stability and chaos in human societies? What defences can men build against the strain of evil in themselves? These are moral questions, and these three "factual" books—*Black Lamb* and the two books of trials—are moral books; but they are also artful and imaginative. Here Dame Rebecca has found her true form, in which art and fact meet, and keep faith with reality.

Of Dame Rebecca's three most recent books, two are novels, one an ambitious critical study. *The Fountain Overflows* (1957) is about the condition of childhood, as *Black Lamb* is about the condition of Serbs and Croats—that is, childhood is the metaphor for a view of the world. The particular childhood here is very like Dame Rebecca's own, and the book has considerable biographical interest. But as a novel it is flawed by the insistent, intruding intelligence of the author, turning recollection into ideas about music or about childhood itself, or sometimes, dealing with fictional parents and siblings in what seems a personal, resentful way. It is, in short, not fully realized as fiction, and, though one reads it with pleasure at the author's bright company, it will not quite do as a novel.

The Fountain Overflows seems, in retrospect, a regression, back from the large authority of the previous studies to the restraints of the earlier fiction. The book that followed it, *The Court and the Castle*, recovers that authority. It is her most considerable work of criticism, a brilliant, expansive, stimulating, eccentric book. One can get at its curious nature best, perhaps, by glossing the subtitle: "A Study of the Interactions of Political and Religious Ideas in Imaginative Literature". One knows, of course, that Dame Rebecca began her journalistic career as a political writer, and that she has always had an acute political sense; that quality is everywhere evident in her best books. It is also apparent that her sense of the nature of man and his world is a religious one. But how do these sets of ideas interact? To a religious mind, man's moral state is a constant, but political ideologies are transient; politics therefore ought to follow from religion, and to take pragmatic rather than ideological forms. In Dame Rebecca's case this certainly seems to be true. Her religion, as it appears in her books, is mainly a concern with the existence of evil; given the reality of evil, ideas about the uses of power and about the structures of society follow, but they do not coalesce in a political system. She has, one might say, political wisdom but not a political ideology. Given the persistence of evil, it is appropriate that her study of the interactions of political and religious ideas should begin with Augustine and end with Kafka; for they share an eternal problem.

It is difficult to define in a word the peculiar note of authority that Rebecca West's criticism has, but perhaps the best term is episcopal: she writes like a fourth-century African bishop, praising the righteous, condemning heretics, explaining doctrine, confident always of the rightness of her judgments and of their firm moral bases. She is easy with terms like Manichaean and Pelagian, and can use them as metaphors for literary situations; and the language is significant, for in her world heresies do exist, and they matter. A woman admirer of Dame Rebecca once described her, wryly, as a "female Patriarch", and that phrase does indeed describe her critical posture.

The Birds Fall Down (1966) is her last novel, and her finest: indeed it is excellent enough to bear comparison with the great political novels, with *The Possessed* and *Under Western Eyes*. Like those novels, it is concerned with the international political spasm that began in nineteenth-century Russia and spread across Europe; or, rather, it is concerned with the victims of that spasm. For there is not much political theory in the novel, only the deeply imagined thoughts and actions of persons caught in the stress of political motives: a young girl, an old Russian count, an anarchist, a double agent. It is Dame Rebecca's most completely imagined novel, perhaps because it is the one that is farthest from the particulars of her own experience. It alone should assure her of a place in the history of English fiction.

In *Black Lamb* Dame Rebecca records—or perhaps invents—an interview with a German girl, a university student who has come seeking material for a thesis on Dame Rebecca's works. The girl is lumpishly, Germanically pedantic, and Dame Rebecca winces at the prospect of becoming her dissertation:

> I explained that I was a writer wholly unsuitable for her purpose . . . that I had never used my writing to make a continuous disclosure of my own personality to others, but to discover for my own edification what I knew about various subjects which I found to be important to me. . . .

Her work, she concludes, "could not fuse to make a picture of a writer, since the interstices were too wide".

This is an acute observation, and it remains true: Dame Rebecca's work has not fused in the minds of critics, and she has no secure literary status—the interstices between her books, between *Black Lamb* and *The Return of the Soldier*, between *The Meaning of Treason* and *Saint Augustine*, are too wide: she is too difficult to define. Surprisingly, she does not seem even to have gained a following among the partisans of women's liberation, though one would think that in the True Church of Women she well deserves a Lady Chapel. Perhaps she would have fared better if she had continued as she began, as a novelist who also wrote essays. *The Return of the Soldier*, *Harriet Hume*, and *Letter to a Grandfather* prove that she could do the Virginia Woolf manner well enough to win a place among woman novelists of sensibility. But what she told the German girl is obviously true: she wrote for another reason, to discover what she knew. In the end it is the inquiring mind that we know, and not the personality, or the sensibility. Or the gender, for to discover what she knows, a woman must stretch beyond woman's matters. That fine, strong androgynous mind that we meet in her books is her achievement; knowing it, we could not wish that her work were anything except what it is.

It is astonishing, in these days of critical overkill, that Peter Wolfe's little book is the only one yet written on Rebecca West. But perhaps the problems that he has had with his subject explain why others have not attempted the job. Professor Wolfe is a professor of English Literature, and he has brought his Eng-Lit methods and expectations to a subject that does not easily submit to those presumptions. For Rebecca West cannot be dealt with in the academic language of novel-criticism: to call her fiction Jamesian is simply irrelevant, and to find resemblances to T. S. Eliot and Graham Greene and Virginia Woolf is to blur what is original. The best thing in the book is the first chapter, which puts Dame Rebecca's Augustinianism in reasonable order, and relates it to her views on art and love; anyone interested in Dame Rebecca will find these pages useful. But from there on the book slides into summaries and academic trivialities, and one might apply to it what Professor Wolfe has to say about *The Return of the Soldier* (which he misunderstands and underrates): "Because Rebecca West's grasp of fictional method is more academic than instinctive, the book's technique and subject do not jell." One ought not to dismiss too harshly the first attempt at a difficult critical task; but it is nevertheless the case that the book does not jell. A full appreciation of Dame Rebecca's achievement is still to come. But it will come; she will have her proper place among thinkers and artists, one day.

7

THE NOT SO DARK AGES

(a) ENGLAND MATURES

A QUARTER OF A CENTURY AGO David Douglas undertook the editorship of two ambitious projects at the invitation of Messrs Eyre and Spottiswoode. The one was a series of thirteen weighty volumes of "English Historical Documents" from 500 to 1914, the other an almost equally weighty collection of the lives of fourteen English monarchs. Both series, despite ancestral voices prophesying disaster, have made good, largely owing to the good judgment and staying-power of Professor Douglas. The series of Documents is nearing completion and the medieval volumes, at least, have proved permanently useful to every kind of student from A-level to the professorial chair. The list of monarchs, which includes William Rufus, Edward VI and George II, while excluding four Henrys, two Charleses, and three Georges, has already inspired at least three biographies of the highest class, apart from the present one. Professor Douglas himself has played a captain's part in both innings, so to say, with his Documents on the twelfth century and his life of William the Conqueror. W. L. Warren's life of Henry II, whatever criticisms may be made, is unquestionably a worthy member of the series, and will remain for many years an essential work of reference for its period.

Most historians would agree that, in a list of the half-dozen monarchs before 1837 who have done most to shape the course of

---

(a) W. L. WARREN: *Henry II.* 693 pp plus 26 plates. Eyre Methuen. £7.95.

(b) GEORGES DUBY: *Guerriers et paysans VII-XIIe siècle.* Premier essor de l'économie européenne. 308 pp. Paris: Gallimard. 40fr. *Hommes et structures du moyen âge.* 424 pp. Paris: Mouton. 36fr.

MAURICE LOMBARD: *Espaces et réseaux du haut moyen âge.* 229 pp. Paris: Mouton. 28fr.

M. M. POSTAN: *Essays on Medieval Agriculture and General Problems of the Medieval Economy.* 302 pp. £4.80. *Medieval Trade and Finance.* 382 pp. £5. Cambridge University Press.

English history, Henry II would deserve inclusion. Alfred, William I, Edward I, Henry VIII and Elizabeth I would be competitors, and earlier generations would have put either Henry V or William III before Henry II, but in the past hundred years he has forged ahead of his rivals. Two of the greatest of English medieval historians, Stubbs and Maitland, have been mainly responsible for this estimate. Stubbs, by his editions of contemporary historians, and his classical selection of constitutional and legal texts, placed Henry firmly as "one of the most conspicuous actors in the drama of English history" and (in a characteristic phrase) "one of the conscious creators of English greatness". Stubbs saw Henry truly as the one who, with whatever motives, asserted the authority of the king and the rule of law and the benefits of centralized and efficient administration in a land threatened by feudal anarchy. He regarded Henry's reign, however, through late Victorian spectacles, as a crucial moment in the growth of English constitutional liberty.

It was left to Maitland, the lawyer, less politically and emotionally involved, to isolate the new legal processes and technical formulas of Henry's assizes. These made possible a rational application of the old laws of England to an expanding and maturing country, together with the emergence and perfecting of the Common Law and the royal courts, which were devised for passing needs, but destined to find permanent and ever-increasing employment.

Inspired by these two great historians, numerous scholars and editors of competence have printed the original documents, to which Stubbs and Maitland, and only a few others, had previously had access. Among these are the Pipe Rolls, revealing the receipts and disbursements of the Exchequer, the annual accounts of the sheriffs, and the early volumes of the Selden Society. All this has turned attention from the well-worn paths of the Becket controversy and directed it to the work of Henry's ministers at the exchequer and on eyre.

Dr Warren faced a formidable task. The amount of source material for the reign of Henry II is abundant, and disparate in character, yet all the letters, records, chronicles, biographies, charters and the rest leave certain topics, and certain periods, including some critical years, still in the dark. Neither Henry nor his principal servants, apart from Richard FitzNigel, tell us what they are doing or why they are doing it. We have ultimately to work backwards from the fact to the motive as well as we can.

Then there is the vast extent of territory over which Henry exercised at least some form of control, from the Pyrenees to central Ireland and the Scottish border. For almost all the military and diplomatic activity (apart from the Becket affair) for almost forty years, historians are dependent on chroniclers domiciled in England and with no direct inside knowledge of government. The best that can be done is to excavate a framework of fact and fill this out with half-seen purposes and effects.

Add to this the Becket controversy, with its own voluminous but narcissistic literature, which cuts across the normal interests of Henry's designs, and creates the illusion that the world stood still to watch the outcome. We have only to contrast all this with the straightforward life-story of William the Conqueror or Edward I, where the king's activities can be carried through as the focus of all else, to see how great the difficulties are with Henry II. Even Dr Warren has not been wholly successful in controlling these difficulties. Perhaps they cannot be mastered at any level between the brief survey and the purely factual and chronological detail of Eyton's *Itinerary* of the king and his court.

As it is, readers who are not familiar with the period will find the first 200 pages and part of the last eighty heavy going. This is due not to any fault of the narrator, but to the seemingly haphazard sequence of detailed doings in various lands, with a king who spent the greater part of his time across the Channel, and crossed the narrow water twenty-eight times. But in between these indigestible portions, there is a central core of 400 pages dealing with the two great and significant interests of the reign: the governance of England, and the relations between Henry and Thomas Becket. Here even the reader unfamiliar with the period will find himself carried along with the flood.

The achievement of Henry—or, more correctly, the achievement of Henry and his trusted ministers—was to get a legal and administrative grip on the whole population of the country. This grip was far from painless, but it was not that of a tyrant or of a faceless bureaucracy, but of a system of finance and justice which was, within its context, rational and workable, and which enlisted the cooperation of all the solid constituents of the realm. The key elements were the royal Exchequer and the royal justices in eyre and on the bench at Westminster.

The Exchequer, originally the group of clerks staffing the royal chapel and acting as the king's scribes, had assumed its financial importance under Bishop Roger of Salisbury in the days of Henry I. It decayed in Stephen's reign, but was revived when Henry II called Bishop Nigel of Ely, Roger's nephew and disciple, out of retirement to rehabilitate the machinery. It was Nigel's son, Richard, who produced what Maitland called "one of the most wonderful things of Henry's wonderful reign", the *Dialogue of the Exchequer*, explaining the technique and the procedure of the office in which the barons of the Exchequer did their work. Through their agency the king was able to control the sources of his income from the royal estates up and down the country, which were managed by the sheriffs of each county who farmed them—that is, who contracted for them with the Exchequer at a fixed annual rate—and who collected any special taxes imposed and the various debts, private or feudal, owing to the Crown by individuals. The statement of all this, the nearest equivalent to a balance sheet, appears in the yearly Pipe Rolls, that remarkable sequence of annual audits, intact from 1155, which tells us so much of the financial life of medieval England.

The royal justices in eyre, who were in regular perambulation through the shires, were at first mainly charged with hearing claims to property from those dispossessed or disinherited in the troubles of Stephen's reign and subsequent broils; their tools were the royal writ and the evidence of a local jury. Hitherto an aggrieved landowner could, at great expense of time and money, obtain a writ—that is, a brief order—from the king to the sheriff to do him justice. The sheriff might prevaricate; the king might depart for Aquitaine and forget. Under the reformed system the plaintiff could purchase a writ from the chancery ordering the sheriff, writ in hand, to restore the property conditionally to the plaintiff, summon a local jury to meet the king's justices (a "jury of recognition") to pronounce on the fact of previous possession. At this meeting the king's writ (known from this as a "returnable writ") was handed by the sheriff to the justices, who decided the possessorial suit, with compensation for the plaintiff if equitable, leaving either party to apply to the royal court for a decision on the basic rights between the two claimants. In this further trial, if it occurred, the decision—hitherto left to the ordeal by battle, fire or water—was replaced, if the plaintiff so requested, by a verdict based on the judgment of twelve knights of the shire acting as a jury. The same procedure was applied to cases of disputed inheritance and disputes over right of advowson to benefices. Normally, it ensured a reasonably swift and rational decision on the facts of the case, and encouraged a peaceful settlement or compromise before the second trial by jury took place.

Criminal justice was reformed later in the reign. Hitherto detection and prosecution of crime had been either an affair of communal hue and cry, or a private suit at the manorial or shire court. Now it was gradually taken up into the routine of the justices in eyre. A jury of elected worthies of each locality (a "jury of presentment") was charged with delating anyone suspected of crime. Those against whom the justices' opinion supported the jury's charge were then put to the ordeal, but very soon it became usual for the jury to be asked for their verdict on the guilt, as well as on the suspicion, attaching to the defendant, and, when the Fourth Lateran Council in 1215 banned the ordeal, this task of the jury became standard.

These two examples, which do not stand alone, show a remarkable advance in rational and efficient control both of property rights and crime, from purely local and haphazard methods to a system of regular and civilized procedure. The historian inevitably asks two questions. What was the motive of these innovations, and who was chiefly responsible for the invention and application of this simple and effective procedure?

It seems clear that the purpose was not primarily to promote justice or to benefit the king's subjects, but to secure royal control over property and its owners, to secure peace and order and, it should be added, to realize the profits of fines. *Magnum emolumentum justitia*. The royal courts were a financial asset. The second question is not so easily answered. Bracton, writing almost a century later, tells us that the *chef d'oeuvre* of the system, the returnable writ of *novel disseisin* (= recent dispossession) described above, was the product of many sleepless nights on the part of the king and his ministers. Many students of the period will feel that the systematic advances towards rationalization, taken in England in years when the king was here, there, and everywhere, fighting off either Becket or his family, must have been debated and executed primarily and principally by the brilliant group of men who served Henry at the Exchequer and in the courts: Richard FitzNigel, Richard of Ilchester, Master Thomas Brown, Richard de Lucy, John of Oxford, and the rest. They were the Roundell Palmers, the Cardwells, the Trevelyans and the Morants of their age. They were often abused and maligned by their "opposite numbers" among the clerks of Becket's entourage, such as John of Salisbury and Herbert of Bosham, some of whom nevertheless passed easily, with William FitzStephen, across the frontier into the ranks of the sheriffs and justices. They went their rounds in eyre and confuted devious or bumbling sheriffs at the Exchequer, with a keen enjoyment of their professional expertise, while Henry was hunting or fighting. But the king had a fine mind, when he chose to apply it. We know that he used to watch with interest the manoeuvres at the Exchequer, and we can see him presiding at great cases in the king's court. He certainly appreciated and approved what was done in his name.

Stubbs, almost a century ago, saw as a principal result of all these reforms the death-knell of feudalism. Dr Warren contests this, pointing out that on the Continent Henry's authority depended on his feudal homage and jurisdiction and that at home his relations with his barons, and theirs with their labour force, were conditioned by feudal ties. He adds that Henry was no friend of the borough or commune, and had no new ideas of non-feudal dues—apart from the new "tallage" applied to towns in lieu of "aids" and gifts. Certainly he had no conception of the people or the nation as beneficiaries of his measures. His aim was the peaceful and profitable functioning of the baronial society under his hand.

Nevertheless, Dr Warren does well to point out that Henry's legal and administrative innovations did in fact give a share in the day-to-day governance of England to classes of society hitherto out of the picture—the local knights and small landholders, who were so soon to be caught up into Parliament and as members of juries; later, as taxpayers and justices of the peace, they became part of the network of self-government at the grass-roots. "It did represent", he writes, "a major shift in emphasis from feudal to non-feudal elements in the community."

He does not answer a further question: why and how was it that England, so long distracted by baronial feuds, should have become so rapidly amenable to a widely thrown net of legal demands and actions, and this during the reign of a monarch often absent on wars or quarrels? The answer may lie at the deep roots of society. By 1160 English and Norman blood was everywhere mingling, while economic prosperity was increasing, with the expansion of arable land and demographic advance, making it possible for small men, even villeins, to buy land and thrive.

The reign of Henry II has been treated too often in the past as little more than the story of the king's quarrel with his archbishop, which in fact occupied only seven of the thirty-five years of his reign, and even during those seven years was merely one of the many matters occupying the king's attention. Even Dr Warren cannot escape from the framework of the quarrel, and his 150 pages devoted to it form a watertight bulkhead in the book.

His account is careful and on the whole impartial. He considers that Thomas in his first year as archbishop was to blame for provoking the king needlessly and almost ostentatiously. He does less than justice, however, to Becket in relation to his treatment of Philip de Brois, a criminous clerk. The archbishop, in imposing exile on the culprit, was in fact outbidding the king's appeal to ancestral customs by applying the royal legislation of the pre-Conquest church. According to this a homicidal priest was to "forfeit both his ecclesiastical orders and his country", that is, to go into exile. As for Clarendon, Dr Warren recognizes the king's mistake in insisting that the bishops should take an open-ended oath to accept the ancestral customs, and he has no defence for Henry's unreasonable, unjust and tyrannical treatment of the archbishop at the council of Northampton. He also acknowledges that in the matter of the Constitutions of Clarendon the bishops were in principle solidly behind their chief. In what happened later he considers that Thomas was the more difficult of the two with his insistence on a global "freedom" for the church which not only was unrealistic but had been abandoned by the papacy itself in dealings with the Emperor. The king was in the wrong again over the coronation of his son, but for the last weeks of his life the archbishop's conduct was once again provocative.

On the main issues Dr Warren's sympathies are with the king. Had Thomas been willing to negotiate, leaving his options open (to use a current phrase), a working arrangement might have been agreed on similar to the understanding which in fact ensued among all parties a few years after the murder. To regard the king's violent tactics in 1169–70 as threatening a break with the papacy and a total "submission of the clergy" was a fatal and anachronistic misjudgment on Becket's part. The freedom he died for was a mirage. It is perhaps unfortunate that two books—David Knowles's *Thomas Becket* and Beryl Smalley's *The Becket Conflict and the Schools*—and an article in the *English Historical Review* (October, 1972) on "Henry II's Supplement to the Constitutions of Clarendon" appeared too late for Dr Warren to consider them; the article in particular emphasized the authenticity and drastic nature of the 1169 extension of the Constitutions of Clarendon, which included an oath against the Pope.

No doubt with hindsight we can say with some assurance that if Thomas had been more of a realist all would have been well, and that no twelfth-century monarch conceived of a church without the papacy, or of himself without an effective control over his own bishops. But, without historical hindsight, was this the only reasonable view? Were those who in 1932 thought of Hitler as no more than a passing nuisance, or those who in 1956 took Nasser for another Hitler, altogether numskulls or hysterical? The decrees of 1169, read out of their context, are almost identical with the measures of Henry VIII and Cromwell in 1532–35. The restraint of appeals, the submission of the clergy, the diversion of Peter's Pence to the royal benefit, the oath against the papacy—all are there. The Tudor statutes were almost certainly remotely inspired by the study of "divers sundry old authentic histories and chronicles", which included the literature of the Becket controversy. It is one of the ironies of history that Becket should have taken seriously measures which when repeated with serious intent in a later century were discounted as harmless by almost all contemporary clerics, and that it should have been left to Archbishop Warham to make out his defence along the lines of Becket's manifestoes.

Dr Warren, as is only natural in such a long book, is not always of the same opinion. Early in the book, the archbishop is "hysterical"; at the end of the day the great quarrel is "a classic tragedy—the story of heroic men with remarkable qualities, undone by equally great flaws of character, flaws of passion and of pride."

And what, at the end of the day, of Henry himself? We can ponder the impressions he made upon four intelligent and highly articulate contemporaries. Walter Map, his servant, tells us that he was "one upon whom men gazed closely a thousand times yet took occasion to return". Gerald of Wales, a critical spirit, judged him "beyond comparison among the princes of this world for his many natural gifts". John of Salisbury, no idolator, agreed that "he had such remarkable gifts of nature and grace that no prince, I would think, is his equal". Peter of Blois ends his long encomium by opining that Cicero and Virgil would have had a hard task to describe Henry's physical and moral excellence. Yet all these, except the last, balance their praise by noting his lack of self-restraint and honest dealing. That Henry had many natural gifts and qualities, and performed many feats of energy and endurance is certain, and we have only to look backwards to Stephen and forward to John to realize that he was a leader of men who could attract and retain in his service, and exploit to their full capacity, a notable group of ministers. Certainly he was faced more than once with serious rebellion, but this was primarily the work of ambition and insubordination, not the result of any incompetence on the king's part.

He had a complex character. He could be not only charming and genial, but genuinely tolerant and good-humoured. He befriended and was respected by the three saints (not including Thomas) who were his subjects: Gilbert of Sempringham, Ailred of Rievaulx and Hugh of Lincoln. Yet he could be ruthless, heartless, and implacable, as with Archbishop Thomas and his relatives and supporters. Dr Warren sees him as a young man, impetuous, drastic and "thorough", who learnt in time and by the hard way to get his will in later years by skilful bargaining and a sense of the possible. He inspired admiration and devotion, but perhaps not personal affection. His family relationships were deplorable, and he was guilty of the death of the only man outside his family for whom he had had deep affection. Those who knew him best acknowledged his mental powers and intellectual interests, but in action he avoided any recourse to a programme of ideas. He was not a good man, as was Alfred the Great, nor one with firm principles such as the Conqueror. Sexually he was morally loose without being dominated or distracted by his desires. Though concerned only with his personal interests and success he was not, so to say, a case-study in egoism, as was Henry VIII. Though extraordinarily able and forceful, he lacked the intuition and the coordinating genius of a statesman. He was, indeed, not a great man; he lacked the self-control, the magnanimity, the breadth of sympathy that can lead a ruler to subordinate many activities to noble ends: the liberty and happiness of his subjects, peace and good order and religion, the guidance of a nation in justice and the service of God.

Yet Henry II, like Henry VIII, though not a great and good man, was certainly a great king in his ability to assert his authority in support of others, who were making wide changes that affected English life long after they had passed away. The old legal system of England that developed into Common Law, the nation-wide administration of social, fiscal and judicial business that was an heirloom from pre-Conquest England, and had lived on under a feudal blanket—all these, as the constituents of much that was to make up the strength and character of the country, might have been submerged in feudal anarchy, to be replaced later by Roman Law and the bureaucracy of an absolute monarch. That they not only survived, but throve, was due mainly to the clarity of vision and perseverance of an unusually gifted band of royal servants; but Henry, for whatever reason, supplied the understanding and the support without which their work could not have come to fruition. It may well be that the personal merit of Henry for achieving the end-product has been exaggerated by Kate Norgate, Lady Stenton and even by Maitland, but it was the king who made the achievement possible.

Looking back over *Henry II* three or four of its merits stand out. A fresh, and to some extent an unfamiliar, impression is given of Henry's courage, energy and decision when in his teens and again in his early twenties. Here he deserves comparison with Augustus and Napoleon. Next, the great legal and administrative innovations are set out fully and clearly. Maitland's great history of medieval law must remain the *locus classicus*, but Dr Warren mediates the master for those pressed for time. Then there is the illuminating survey of Henry's "Angevin empire", which is rightly presented as a family federation rather than a single sphere of dominion. And finally, there is the survey of the long period of *détente* after the murder in the cathedral. Henry's end was lacking in dignity, his "empire" was almost entirely lost by his sons, and for a century the history of England is, on the surface, that of a country unsure of its own identity. Below the surface, however, the changes wrought in the reign of Henry II were working to produce the law and the governance of a later age.

(b) THE ECONOMY EXPANDS

THE MORE OR LESS simultaneous publication of the collected papers of Georges Duby, Maurice Lombard and M. M. Postan, together with another masterly essay in synthesis by the first of these authors, may well indicate that the study of the medieval economy is booming. Whether or not that is so, the fact that Postan's published work spans the period from 1928 to 1970, while that of Duby and Lombard fills the period since the Second World War, invites a stock-taking of the progress that has been made in this branch of historical inquiry.

In order to appreciate the advances of the past generation, some account must be taken of how things stood when Postan was undertaking his first researches. The founding fathers of economic history had cast their studies into a mould which they borrowed from the political historians. The notion of the Middle Ages, of course, derived from the scholars of the Renaissance. These ages were the waste land which intervened between the enlightenment of Rome and the new enlightenment of Bruni's and Leonardo's Italy. Later historians, of course, modified this essentially static view. In the nineteenth century, in particular, painful progress was discerned from what was in every sense a "dark age" down to the "rebirth" which ushered in the beginnings of modern times.

The new science of economic history followed in this tradition. For its practitioners the Middle Ages began in economic, as well as in political and cultural, barbarism: an "economy without markets", almost purely agricultural, and dominated by the motives of subsistence. Recovery was a long and slow process; but at least from around the eleventh century recovery was basically continuous. A money economy arose, trade expanded, towns grew, a middle class developed, even "industrial revolutions" were discerned. In other words, elements of the later industrial economy were being assembled, steadily and cumulatively, over the medieval generations.

This approach to the medieval economy had certain corollaries. Economic institutions were assessed in terms of their contribution to the establishment of the industrial economy of the future, and elements in the economic situation which anticipated that future were sometimes given a disproportionate significance. Further, there were few attempts to comprehend the economic attitudes to their medieval context. Rational economic behaviour was that which was found in the industrial age; medieval men were sometimes assumed to have responded to economic circumstances in the same sort of way; and all other behaviour was deemed "non-economic" and evidently irrational.

A critique of these views of the medieval economy gathered momentum between the world wars. Postan was active in England and Marc Bloch emerged as the pre-eminent figure among French economic and social historians. They were scholars of very different

types. Postan's work is founded upon the methods and the pre-
scriptions of the social scientists, above all of the theoretical economists. His essential achievement has been twofold. First, he has
endeavoured, so far as imperfect evidence permits, to give some sort
of dimensions to a variety of elements in the medieval economy, and
that of England in particular; and to show how these elements were
related to each other. Secondly, he has tried to chart the fluctuations
in the economy as a whole, at least from the twelfth century down to
the fifteenth. In pursuit of these aims his method has been to abstract
from the totality of historical phenomena those components which
are strictly economic.

Marc Bloch was no less responsive to the findings of social scientists, although for him the work of geographers and anthropologists
was probably more influential than the theories of economists. This
influence, however, is to be seen rather in the questions he asked of
his sources than in his method of tackling problems. His instinct
was, moreover, to place economic phenomena in their total setting,
and above all to give full weight to the "mentalities" of past ages
as something which conditioned men's way of getting and spending.

New approaches, therefore, both before and after 1939 have owed
something to new questions formulated in the light of findings by
economic theorists, sociologists and anthropologists; but they have
also involved the exploitation of new sources of evidence. Bloch
was something of a pioneer of topographical study of the landscape,
both from old plans and on the ground; and air photography has
added new dimensions to the story which the land itself will tell us.
Duby's *Guerriers et paysans** shows how widely the economic historian
must now cast his net.

If written sources remain his staple, he must also take account of
the rates of flow of Alpine glaciers and the size of tree rings; and to
an increasing extent he is dependent on the findings of archaeologists
and their associates. These latter, more than anyone else, have
provided a reasonably precise picture of the material culture of
Merovingian Gaul and settlement types in early Germany. They
have provided great collections of early coins for numismatic
analysis. Martin Biddle and his collaborators are, at long last,
adding new evidence to that hitherto available for the history of the
Anglo-Saxon town; skeletons from Hungarian graves of the tenth

---

* An English translation appeared in February 1974 as *The Early Growth of the
European Economy* (292 pp. Weidenfeld & Nicolson.£4).

century are affording new evidence for demographers; and pollen analysis of soil samples is enabling a picture to be constructed of the natural vegetation of long past ages.

These volumes of collected essays, then, take us into the workshops of historians who have played an important part in re-interpreting the economic history of the West during the Middle Ages. Among them Lombard stands in a sense apart. His originality was that he sought to do for the Mediterranean region of the early Middle Ages, when it was dominated by the civilization of Islam, something of what Braudel did for it in the age of Philip II. The main fruits of his researches are only now appearing, six or seven years after his death; and the essays reprinted in *Espaces et réseaux* concern part only of the vast canvas which interested him. They deal with the routes, the markets, the trade and the money of the Islamic Mediterranean; and their subject-matter inevitably involved him in a great controversy. Henri Pirenne had argued that the Western "economy without markets" was a product of the Muslim closing of the Mediterranean to long-range commerce rather than a result of the protracted barbarization of the Western Empire. The closed economy of the Carolingian age he attributed in the last resort to Muhammad.

Lombard all but set this doctrine on its head. He illustrates the new external contacts of the Carolingian West by three small but significant events:

In 801 the first elephant from India trod the soil of Gaul, having got there by the Mediterranean and the land route from Italy. In the middle of the ninth century dromedaries from Africa, sent by the land route from Spain, appeared on the banks of the Rhine. In 986 an Asiatic camel with two humps, after travelling the routes of eastern Europe, appeared within the walls of Quedlinburg in Saxony.

The incidents are indeed evocative and they can be supported by evidence for less exotic traffic. The idea of a closed Europe, utterly cut off from contacts with the Muslim masters of the Mediterranean, can no longer be sustained. On the other hand, the quantitative importance of this or any other branch of long-range trade in the total economic activity of Carolingian Europe was probably very small indeed. For this reason, if no other, it is also difficult to attribute to the Islamic monetary system, as Lombard does, a formative influence upon the monetary development of the early medieval West.

At the same time, Lombard's positive demonstration of ninth-century economic contacts between Western Europe and a wider world, given no more than their proper weight, must now be fitted into any general view of economic development during the early Middle Ages. Duby, as the essays printed in *Hommes et structures* indicate, has studied these centuries from a variety of angles. He investigated in depth the feudal society of Burgundy. He then turned to a general study of medieval agrarian history, the main fruit of which, his *Rural Economy and Country Life in the Medieval West*, is known to every student of the Middle Ages. From the start, however, the history of the medieval nobility has been his special interest, extending beyond the material basis of the noble household to the nobleman's position in society generally, his relations with his peers and other social classes, and his attitudes of mind. A number of his essays on these themes, reprinted in *Hommes et structures*, have already become classic; they represent a fruitful continuation of the tradition initiated by Bloch; and they provide foundations for some of the conclusions about the early development of the Western economy which are worked out in *Guerriers et paysans*.

Duby begins much where his predecessors started: a secular process of economic decline set in during the troubles of the third century and reached its low point in the plague-infested Europe of the sixth century. In the seventh century, however, he discerns not (like Bautier) a temporary revival but a turning-point. Regression gave place to expansion, and expansion even longer-term than the contraction which it followed. Initially, of course, the rate of improvement was painfully slow. Locally it was liable to interruption by epidemics, famines, raids, civil wars. Over time, however, population, the settled area and the volume of exchanges all increased; and regions which had been "barbarian" fell increasingly under the economic influence of the more advanced lands. The pace of expansion increased rapidly after about the year 1000, when a better peace, the end of major raids and a measure of technological progress made enterprise more rewarding and human endeavour more productive. The momentum of advance not only carried Westerners south into Spain and east into the Slav lands. It also generated qualitative changes in the basic structure of society. Genuinely urban communities multiplied everywhere in the West; and foundations were laid which in the future would make the towns the principal agents of economic change.

Duby's economic rehabilitation of the Dark Ages will not altogether surprise English readers, for Reginald Lennard has taught us to see Domesday England as an "old-settled land", with much of the land that ever was arable already under the plough. What is most interesting, however, about Duby's reconstruction is the part he allots to the consumer demand of nobility and higher clergy in initiating economic expansion. To eat and drink amply and well, to decorate their persons and tables and sanctuaries with magnificence, to dispense largesse were social attitudes shared by nobles and prelates: their lands and their dependants were the means of realizing them. The evolution of the nobility and economic expansion were closely related.

The Carolingian and succeeding generations witnessed the development of a society the essential features of which were pithily described by eleventh-century commentators. It was a society in which certain functions had become the province of specialists. Specialists in war (a nobility of dukes and counts and barons and knights) and specialists in prayer (the clergy whose upper ranks followed a way of life in many ways similar to that of the lay nobility) occupied its superior echelons. These classes multiplied, they extended their control over more and more of the land and men of the West, and their lordship was reinforced by the acquisition of political and judicial powers which had once been vested in the Carolingian crown. In order to support their noble way of life the nobility stimulated the activities of merchants and craftsmen; they organized agricultural production on a large scale on lands they kept in hand; they levied charges on the peasantry that sometimes look very like an organized form of pillage; and ultimately, in the twelfth century, they played some part in the work of agricultural development and colonization which was a feature of the time.

True, by then, in many places, profits from an expanded tenantry and from political lordship enabled many lords to withdraw from direct economic enterprise. Except, perhaps, in England, agricultural production became principally a peasant activity. The nobleman continued to spend, even to waste, conspicuously; but he ceased to be an active producer at the moment when the appearance of mercenary soldiers was also robbing him of his military specialism. Here again Duby sees an economic turning-point: the nobility, which had been the main instrument of economic development down to the twelfth century, ceased to play that part by the end of it. In this sense the close of the twelfth century marks the end of a major phase in European history.

Duby leaves the development of the Western economy when the tide of advance was still running at full flood. It is at this point in time that Postan takes up the story. His approach is fundamentally different from Duby's. His grasp of the basic structure of medieval society, and of the economic consequences which flowed from it, is in no way in doubt. To take just one example, his essay on the Peterborough peasant charters is a brilliant exposition of the relationship between the organization of peasant families and the shifting distribution of land in East Midland villages. His basic instinct, however, is to attribute quantitative dimensions to economic phenomena. He seeks to measure the number of people, the extent of the cultivated area, the size of tenements, the volume of production and exchanges. He seems generally to infer that economic behaviour reflected these basic economic circumstances; consequently when, as is all too often the case, the evidence available precludes measurement, trends in population or production or distribution can be inferred from men's economic behaviour.

Along these two lines Postan arrives at a view of the economic chronology of the later Middle Ages which stands in greater contrast to traditional views than Duby's notion of the earlier Middle Ages. The thirteenth and perhaps the early fourteenth centuries were the high point of medieval expansion; but they were followed by "an age of recession, arrested economic development and declining national income". The late medieval recession affected all sectors of the economy; and the onset of endemic plague in the mid-fourteenth century, drastically reducing the number of producers and consumers, was crucial to its inception.

In recent years, however, Postan has added certain new components to this economic model, in which the influence of modern theoretical and empirical studies of under-developed economies is to be discerned and which involve some change of emphasis. He reveals, in particular, some of the flaws in the thirteenth-century movement of expansion: the growing evidence of overpopulation, the putting of marginal land under the plough, certain indications of soil exhaustion, the decline in the average amount of land per head, the mounting charges many peasants paid, the growth of a rural proletariat.

In this regard, it is unfortunate that a decision has been taken not to reprint the latest statement of his views on these matters from the first volume of the *Cambridge Economic History*, despite the fact that his chapter on Northern trade from the second volume has been reprinted. It seems a pity, too, that his essay on the medieval English estate labourer finds no place in these collections, for it contains the best short account there is of labour organization on the medieval manor. In brief, however, Postan's conclusion is that there was something like a Malthusian crisis of subsistence in much of the Western countryside by the end of the thirteenth century, which was already slowing down the rate of economic expansion and raising levels of mortality. The way was prepared for the demographic catastrophe occasioned by bubonic plague.

Postan's general view of economic trends during the last centuries of the Middle Ages now commands a good deal of assent. Even J. D. Chambers, no apologist for Malthus, accepted the likelihood that a Malthusian situation existed in much of pre-plague England. Nor can it easily be denied that production, and probably exchanges, expanded in the thirteenth century and contracted after 1350. Of course, refinements may have to be made to these propositions. Postan himself has subtly modified his initial portrait of the thirteenth-century "boom", and he drops hints here and there of the ways in which his view of the succeeding centuries might also be developed.

More might be made, for example, of Carlo Cipolla's suggestion that an important feature of the generations after 1300 was the extent to which some regions which had been relatively "backward" began to catch up the areas which had been relatively "advanced". England is perhaps numbered among the late developers. Possibly it could also be argued that in this country the reduction of population, by reducing the supply of labourers and the demand for (and therefore the price of) land, left the great peasant majority sole heirs to English farmlands and more prosperous than it had ever been in the great days of manorial lordship. In other words, the peasants now disposed of spending power which stimulated industrial production catering for a mass market, and in this way contributed towards the formation of that more balanced economy which began to expand once again in the closing years of the fifteenth century.

Lombard, Duby and Postan approach the problems of economic history in very different ways; but each of them is a major contributor to the recent rapid extension of our knowledge of the medieval economy. Some of what they have done has become accepted learning; some of it is, in the nature of things, debatable. The material published in these five volumes, however, is proof positive that out of the debate comes discovery.

8

THE THREE LADY Cs

LAWRENCE HIMSELF told us that he wrote *Lady Chatterley's Lover* three times over. Version One, now commonly, if not very sensibly, called *The First Lady Chatterley*, was published in America in 1944; but Version Two has so far been publicly available only in the Italian translation by Carlo Izzo. Both are now published in England for the first time, the second under the title suggested sarcastically by Juliette Huxley. Now that—the censorship battle having been lost and won—it is no longer mandatory on the liberal conscience to claim that *Lady Chatterley's Lover* is a great work of literary art, central to the understanding of Lawrence, the question of the interest and value of these earlier versions can be inquired into with such detachment as one can bring to so deliberately controversial a work. Their importance certainly should not be simply taken for granted: E. W. Tedlock's assertion—quoted in the introductory note to *John Thomas and Lady Jane*—that "the three versions are unique in the opportunity they afford to study the development of an idea by a creative mind" is obviously nonsense. The history of art affords a good many opportunities to study the development of ideas by creative minds, as critics and historians have found: Wordsworth, Beethoven, Rembrandt and Wren offer a few examples against which to measure the importance of the three Lady Chatterleys.

Does this new publication, then, matter very much? Though there are extensive differences between the three versions, and though, as Geoffrey Strickland has argued, there are strong reasons for preferring the first above the other two, probably few of those—admirers of Lawrence or not—who dislike *Lady Chatterley's Lover* will feel that there is enough in *The First Lady Chatterley* to make a major work of literature; and those who admire the final version are likely to go on doing so in preference to the quieter, less brutally

---

D. H. LAWRENCE: *The First Lady Chatterley*. (The first version of *Lady Chatterley's Lover*.) 232 pp. £2.50. *John Thomas and Lady Jane*. (The second version of *Lady Chatterley's Lover*.) 372 pp. £4. Heinemann.

assertive but also less clearly purposeful, first. But if Mr Strickland is right that Lawrence altered the novel disastrously in the rewriting, if F. R. Leavis is right that *Lady Chatterley's Lover* is a bad novel, violating Lawrence's artistic integrity, then the study of the "development of the idea" becomes more than a matter of curiosity. Professor Tedlock's formula will strike many as sadly apt—sadly, for he cannot be presumed to have had this point in mind, and because in the event the outcome really is so unhappy, so un-Lawrentian. In his essay "The Orthodoxy of Enlightenment" Dr Leavis observes that "'will' and 'idea' (terms, in his use of them, intimately related) ... certainly play a part in *Lady Chatterley's Lover* that the normal creative and critical Lawrence would have diagnosed and condemned"; and what we can see in the "development" from the first Lady Chatterley to the third is the hardening of the idea under the determination of the will.

Frieda Lawrence gives us the real clue in the introduction which she wrote for the American publication of Version One and which is here reprinted:

Lawrence said grimly after he had written *The First Lady Chatterley*, 'They'll say as they said of Blake: It's mysticism, but they shan't get away with it, not this time. ... The tenderness and gentleness hadn't enough punch and fight in it, it was a bit wistful.' Anyhow another mood came over him and he had to tackle the novel again. He wanted to make the contrast between the cynicism and sophistication of the modern mind and the gamekeeper's attitude sharper.

Yes: he had to work up the punch and fight, he needed intellectually to sharpen a contrast which his material did not offer of itself. This gives the lie to Lawrence's own statement that his characters "just came pretty much as they are", that "the story came as it did, so I left it alone". As is now open for all to see, he did not leave it alone: under the spell of a certain idea—the determination to make the contrast between cynicism and spontaneity diagrammatically sharp— he falsified such honesty of experience as there is in the first version and wrote a deeply immoral novel: immoral not because the language is indecorous but in its precommitment, which precludes honesty of record. "Morality in a novel", Lawrence wrote in 1925, "is the trembling instability of the balance. When a novelist puts his thumb in the scale, to pull down the balance to his own predilection, that is immorality." Two or three years later he himself demonstrated this with painful piquancy.

This is not to say that either of the earlier versions is free of all sense of *parti pris*. The treatment of Clifford Chatterley, for example, shifts a good deal in emphasis and detail, but from the start it is hard not to feel that he is the preordained symbol of the world of the mechanical will and is denied any possibility of a life on any other terms. His paralysis was always a part of this symbolism:

Clifford was killing her. Killing that part of her soul which was her true body. He would have done just the same if he had never been wounded in the war. Only then she would not have seen so clearly. The terrible catastrophe had made her clairvoyant. (I)

So it was not a catastrophe to him: we are not to waste any sympathy on Clifford for the terrible injury he suffered; he would have been as evil without it—only it makes it easier for Connie to see. Yet Lawrence's intention towards Clifford in *The First Lady Chatterley* is not quite unambiguous. Certainly he is offered as the polar opposite of the gamekeeper (called Parkin in the first two versions) and, in consequence, it seems, is subjected to passages of such vilifying scorn as to call in question the sanity of the mind which they are supposed to express:

Meanwhile the voice of the other man, Sir Clifford, went on and on, clapping and gurgling with strange sound. Not for one second did she really hear what he said. But it sounded to her like the uncouth cries and howls of barbarous disconnected savages dancing round a fire somewhere outside of the wood. Clifford was a smeared and painted savage howling in an utterly unintelligible gibberish somewhere on the outskirts of her consciousness. She, deep within the sacred and sensitive wood, was filled with the pure communication of the other man, a communication delicate as the inspiration of the gods.

When the reading was ended she looked at Clifford, and his peculiar naked face, with the rapacious eyes of the men of our civilisation, made her shudder. It was the face of a most dangerous beast, domestic but utterly crude, inwardly insensitive.

And with the swift instinct of self-preservation, the deepest of all the automatic instincts, she smiled to this cultured gentleman, to her softly throbbing blood a dangerous domesticated savage, and said to him:

"Thank you so much, dear! You do read Racine beautifully." (I)

Nothing is shown, though so much is said—and in whose voice? Why should Racine sound like howling gibberish? Of course it has nothing to do with Racine. The syntax slips easily from how "it sounded to her", through what Clifford "was" (to her) to the seemingly "objective" statements about Clifford's face and her blood. The voice in fact shows a return to the technique of *Sons and Lovers*: it is that of an alliance between Lawrence and Connie, which makes it literally impossible that Clifford should be disinterestedly, that is honestly, observed: as he is a character in a novel this means that he is denied an existence independent of the interpretation of a partial witness. (So, later, "he was no longer really human. She looked on him now as some weird bird or some creature whose soul has suddenly left it, while it lives on a sharp, often dislocated will of its own" (I). The bird image—how Connie "looked on him"—is instantly taken over as the new focus to which the reader's view is directed.) Parkin, interestingly, seems to be rather more sensitive to the possibility that Clifford might suffer and be hurt, until, prompted by Connie, he admits that he does not care if Clifford dies—"maybe better if he did".

But on occasion we have a glimpse of something else. In the first version there is a dialogue, entirely missing or changed out of recognition in the other two, in which Clifford's sense of his human "uselessness" comes out, a little stagily perhaps but with real poignancy, exposing for a moment that there *is* a suffering creature behind the façade of machine-made abstractions. (Connie's silent reaction is—characteristically—that "he was now letting off his agony on her".) More interesting, in tracing the development of Lawrence's idea, is the transformation of a fragment of dialogue during the famous scene in which Clifford's mechanical chair gets stuck and he must, much against his will, be helped by the keeper. In Version One he apologizes frankly after an evident effort of self-control, and is answered with straightforward decency:

> "I'm sorry I lost my temper, Con," said Clifford at length.
> "Oh, I don't mind," said Constance.
> "Parkin, do you mind wheeling me? I beg your pardon for the way I spoke to you."
> "The pesterin' things 'ud make anybody get their rag out," said the keeper. (I)

There is implicit a real considerateness on both sides. In Two, Clifford's tone has become "rather offhand" (so has Parkin's), and he is still plainly out of temper with the world:

> "I'm afraid I rather lost my temper with the infernal thing!" said Clifford at last.
> "It is annoying!" said Constance.

"Do you mind pushing me home, Parkin?" said Clifford. "And excuse anything I said", he added rather offhand.
"It's nothing to me, Sir Clifford!" (II)

Finally all note of true apology vanishes, and the scene becomes merely one more small piece of evidence of Clifford's inhuman callousness and lack of scruple (reinforced by the keeper's being made in this version to be weak from the after-effects of pneumonia):

"I expect she'll have to be pushed", said Clifford at last, with an affection of *sang froid*.
No answer. Mellors's abstracted face looked as if he had heard nothing. Connie glanced anxiously at him. Clifford too glanced round.
"Do you mind pushing her home, Mellors?" he said in a cool, superior tone. "I hope I have said nothing to offend you", he added, in a tone of dislike. (III)

It seems to be a part not only of Lawrence's technique in *Lady Chatterley's Lover* but also of his fundamental intention (viewpoint) that the total human scene should be reduced to a handful—perhaps no more than a pair—of sheep among a world of goats or baboons from whom all traits of decent, ordinary humanity have to be expunged. There is a fairly nasty scene early in the novel in which Connie comes upon the keeper with his child (usually abandoned to her grandmother) crying after he has shot a marauding cat. In the first version, Parkin's voice "was strangely caressive, and yet irritated", "it was obvious that the child was afraid of him", but though she is a little coy, there seems no harm in the girl and Connie simply takes her home, away from the unattractive man. In Two the scene is totally altered. Parkin's voice is now "snarling", and what he says to the girl is first cutting, then derisive. Connie gives her sixpence and is told off for rewarding the child for lying (a point which the final version is careful to correct). But the episode turns viciously on the girl herself, who is now "a sly, false, impudent little thing, already full to the brim with tricks", so that, thinking about the scene on her way home, Connie can easily turn her dislike away from Parkin on to the girl:

The man had been insolent, insolent! Yet she could forgive him most easily. He might be a bit of a brute, but he was no cringer, and she didn't mind his temper. How he disliked that brat of his! She could sympathise with him there! It was an unattractive piece of femininity, that one! She could tell his skin simply crawled at the child's false airs and ways. Crying over a 'pussy', and as hard-hearted a little piece of goods as ever emerged! (II)

So Parkin's conduct and dislike are all right, because his own daughter is sly and false! Lawrence did fortunately remove that passage from Three, but the girl remains "simpering" and "false", and the impression is inescapable that she has been deliberately made so in order that Mellors's lonely virtue should stay essentially intact.

Though there is unfortunately no doubt that Lawrence endorses Connie's reactions, she comes pretty badly out of the intermediate version of this episode. She is "bored" with her self-imposed job of taking the child home; it is in her mind that the unpleasant docketing of the child takes place, and she shows the characteristic reaction of the "gentry" in winning the child over with a present. (Near the end of Two she even tries bribery to secure Parkin a better job.) In Two indeed there is a lot of—somewhat bewildered—hardness remaining in Connie, absent from Three, in which she is near to being treated as a pawn in the symbolic opposition of the two men. Strikingly, in the first version it is she who makes all the running: she has far more of the modern, independent woman (far more, too, of Frieda Lawrence) than the familiar Lady Chatterley, of whom it could hardly be said that she was "quite good at thinking in symbols". Nor on the other hand would *that* Lady Chatterley talk so blithely of hating all the local people "for having no nakedness as they should have". In the final version that sort of jargon is Mellors's property; whereas it is the spiky, scathing, outspoken first Lady Chatterley who, "quite determined against any sort of bullying", nevertheless drives Parkin on. Her fantasy about wanting to be a "common woman" is, as he says, "nawt but foolery"; she keeps plenty of will of her own, as Parkin feels keenly:

"You come when you like, an' you go when you like", he said, "an' you take no count of me. But what about me, when I wait and watch across th' park, an' you never come? An' I say to myself: 'She wants none o' thee tonight, lad! Go whoam an' hang thy gun up!'—Ay, I'll wait! Yi, an' go home, an' wait again th' next day. But I know right enough. You think nothing of me. You look down on me. Only you enjoy a bit of cunt wi' me. But you look down on me, cunt an' all." (I)

It is not a fair retort, but it has more justice than she will allow. The Constance who can say of her life with Clifford, "What had she got? Misery, anger and a horrible blank life ahead" is a woman intensely, even morbidly, self-centred and self-dramatizing, conscious almost alone of her own feelings and reactions: her boredom, her lurid hatred of Clifford ("that ghoulish Clifford", "a pinky grey baboon who ought to die. [He] only lived in order to make everything baboon-horrible") imply an absorption in the self which is as ugly as the mechanical mindlessness of the Clifford on whom she spits:

It was strange, once her soul roused itself, how she hated Clifford: the deadness and fixity that had turned to obscenity in him: the morality that was so ghoulish. Never a breath of fresh life, never, never. Always that soft, putrescent tolerance, a tolerance that consisted in turning a false light on everything, to make everything, everything, even her very technical adultery, an event flattering to himself. Always subtly flattering his own vanity: like some highly bred, cunning ape, like a young gentleman-baboon! No, she hated him, and her pity for him was an evil thing, a cunning sort of selfishness of her own. Let him die! Let the tidal wave sweep him and all his sort away for ever. (I)

Whatever of truth there is in this indictment of Clifford is scarcely visible in the intense glare of hatred which fills the paragraph. By the end of the book her violence has made her, "curiously", a soul-mate for Clifford as she had never been before.

Where Connie in *Lady Chatterley's Lover* is so much a victim caught between two kinds of violence, in *The First Lady Chatterley* it is Parkin who is constantly driven into a corner, trapped in a way which Connie is incapable of understanding, or perhaps much caring about. Though we get an occasional routine blow-off against the gentry, Parkin is an incomparably more sensitive human being than Mellors. His discovery, early on in *John Thomas and Lady Jane*, that the gentry do not have things all their own way, his perception of actual suffering in Connie and even in Clifford, is a touching moment of truth which is also a moment of self-discovery unlike anything, even in the "tender" passages, of *Lady Chatterley's Lover*, in which indeed Mellors's reactions are as calculable as Clifford's.

Parkin is solidly working-class. The change made in converting him into Mellors, who had been an officer, could speak standard English and had decided intellectual pretensions, is the most obvious nail that Lawrence drove into his novel. The reassurance that we get through Hilda that Mellors was "instinctively much more delicate and wellbred than herself" is, with much more, written into Three for the sake, obviously, of making Lady Chatterley's giving herself to one of the people both more palatable to a certain kind of sensitive social conscience and more plausible. But it is obviously a cheat. Mellors can "go anywhere", he has social poise, and Connie gets no

nearer the working-class than his mother with a smudge on her nose
whom she shuns and runs away from.

But Parkin, on leaving Wragby, goes to live and work in Sheffield,
and Connie does some rather clumsy slumming—as his hosts, the
Tewsons, instinctively recognize. The embarrassments of the tea
party in which both sides are on guardedly good behaviour are
nicely caught (Parkin himself plays little part in it, but he is at home
with the Tewsons as she cannot be): the nerve of such exploration
of the class theme as the book contains is here, where class is itself
the main preoccupation. Connie "longed to say to their noses:
'I'm pregnant by this Oliver Parkin here: been pregnant for three
months'", but Parkin has become a Communist, to whom the
owners are "nobbut sort of fishes, an' what they've laid hold on
they'll keep, if you tear 'em to bits to get it from 'em". To Bill
Tewson, Connie is a friendly upper-class socialist, a second Countess
of Warwick: and as she cannot understand why it is insulting to
speak of Parkin in their presence without a "Mr" before his name,
the hunch seems right. When she has left the Tewsons with Parkin,

> "They're nice people," she said.
> "I'm glad they were so simple with me."
> "What else should they be?" he said.

That little exchange is a wonderful piece of honest observation: it
leaves a chasm between them which she is not humble enough to
recognize; and her dream, with which the book ends, of the bliss of
life as "just Mrs Parkin . . . in an ordinary house in some suburb"
is little short of ludicrous.

The rewriting of the novel, therefore, involved an essential exchange of positions between Lady Chatterley and her lover (the
element of possession implied, doubtless unintentionally, in Lawrence's final title is much more appropriate to the first version).
Though it would be odd to speak of Parkin as a victim, there is no
place in his story for the hectoring bullying to which Mellors
subjects Connie and which so disfigures *Lady Chatterley's Lover*
(where it is associated with the deliberate injection of dialect and of
the "obscene words", largely missing from One and Two). Parkin
does on occasion deliberately *use* dialect—"defiantly . . . when he was
suspicious or angry" (I)—but it is at first more in self-defence, "a
kind of ironical refuge" (II), than as an assault on the world he
hates. Moreover, since it differs from his normal speech much less

than from Mellors's (it is not far from the notably sympathetic
Bill Tewson's), we register in it much less of a deliberate challenge:
Lawrence is not himself obviously in league with the impulse behind
its use. Then, as the rewriting goes on, the function of the dialect
changes: in Two it has become a part of the mystique of primitivism
which turns Parkin finally into the violent crusader of Three,
gripped by antagonism:

He seemed to slide through centuries, thousands of years of human
culture, in his hour with her. When she came, he was an ordinary man,
not very different from Tommy Dukes or Clifford. But when his eyes
began to dilate and flash, he began to slide back through the centuries.
His curious hiss of passion, sudden indrawn, when he touched her naked
body, was far back almost as the snake itself. And that crooning voice:
"Th'art nice, th'art nice!"—was something pre-human. And then he
used the dialect as a sort of armour and a weapon, forcing her to
physical compliance. (II)

That is still the voice of the first Lady Chatterley, but her Parkin
never forced his Connie to physical compliance, a forcing which
seems looked on as a sign of a kind of elemental sexuality anterior
even to the creation of man.

This may be moonshine (*The Plumed Serpent* is sometimes too
near for comfort); but in the main Parkin is recognizably human: he
is always strongly aware of class differences (and afraid, in consequence, of being merely used by Connie as an escape from
Clifford), but there is still little, in his opposition to Clifford and
the other "bosses", of the abrasive hatred which is so much the
dominating motive of *Lady Chatterley's Lover*. Though hatred has
been instinct as a motive for action from the start (in the self-
obsessed Connie), it is only in Three that it is consciously elevated
into a principle. Even in Two there is still something random in the
way Connie flings around her condemnations, discovering with
happy relief that the proletariat is "a state of mind, embracing Clifford
and the gambling Lady Eva, and Mrs Bolton and the beastly Bertha
Coutts, but missing Parkin and missing herself". If that seems merely
childishly spiteful in the kind of particularity it offers, what follows
is by implication a good deal nastier:

She felt a great relief, when she was no longer forced to think and feel in
terms of class. The warm-blooded were the warm-blooded, they were the
sons and daughters of god, in all the world. And the cold-blooded and the
cold-willed were the proletariat, the world over, from colliers to kings. . . .
Against the proletariat she could bear to fight. (II)

So much for the elimination of class. The fighting resolves itself into simply wishing all the rest in perdition—"I shouldn't care if the bolshevists blew up one half of the world, and the capitalists blew up the other half, to spite them, so long as they left me and you a rabbit-hole apiece to creep in, and meet underground like the rabbits do." It is not, alas, the carefree abandon of young lovers who will let the world go by on its own ways: there is undoubted relish in the prospect of the world's self-destruction. So, it might be said, is there in some of Birkin's more bitter prophecies in *Women in Love*. But Birkin's spleen never goes unplaced or unchecked; it is never suggested that it is in itself an idea; and it is set against the profound study of the effect of "proletarianization" on one man who had given himself to it thoroughly and deliberately.

There is little evidence in any of the Lady Chatterley novels that Lawrence was much interested in the "industrial" theme, and the suggestion that Connie's sexual tensions are somehow identical with the difficulties of modern industrial civilization always had something fraudulent in it. The attempt to gain a ballast of "significance" for the marriage theme from Mellors's diatribes on the evils of industrialism (as if the theme were not important enough to do without such factitious bolstering) is merely nominal.

And the objection to the identification in *Lady Chatterley's Lover* of physical sterility or impotence with mechanization lies deeper than the feebleness of the picture of Sir Clifford as industrial magnate, which is at best a silly parody of that of Gerald Crich: the positive side of Lawrence's "case" is weaker still, and the merely woodsy setting of the keeper's activities and of his meetings with Connie is made to imply literal potency only by blatantly sentimental associationism. There is a flabby lushness which clogs the descriptions of the natural scene, so designedly contrasted with the strident images of hideous modern Tevershall, so romantically linked with the story-book past of Robin Hood. But there is worse: the diagrammatic contrast is the excuse for an offered escape into an equally storybook future—for those who are lucky enough to be able to live the forest life. As for the rest, why, their future is none of our concern: they are simply the world which Connie will jettison for her own personal salvation:

She realised there were two main sorts of energy, the frictional, seething, resistant, explosive, blind sort, like that of steam engines and motor-cars and electricity, and of people such as Clifford and Bill Tewson and

modern insistent women, and these queer vacuous miners: then there was
the other forest energy, that was still and softly powerful, with tender,
frail bud-tips and gentle finger-ends of awareness. She herself was seized
by both kinds of energy. With Clifford and Mrs Bolton, and at Bill
Tewson's house, and with her sister Hilda, even, strange frenzies of the
explosive energy came over her, she felt herself full of force. Sometimes
this seemed to her the utmost desirable. But lately, she felt a great desire
to escape it. That sort of energy, that sense of force and power was
accompanied by a craving restlessness and unsatisfaction, something
seething and grinding deep within, that she longed with all her soul to
escape. She had tasted the other, the fullness of life, which is so different
from the frenzy of energy. "Then shall thy peace be as a river." She
knew what it meant. It meant the wood where she had been in stillness
with Parkin. It meant the fullness of life that trees have, which never want
to wander away to something else.

And Parkin stood to her for this peace. Then lately, in Sheffield, he
too had lost it, and this had thrown her out of her reckoning. She was
almost afraid of meeting him: that pinched, rather insignificant little
working-man of Blagby Street. (II)

There is of course a central truth within this; and fitfully the forest
does come alive as an *emblem* of natural, rooted energy and life—
what Lawrence marvellously evokes in his vision (in "Apropos of
Lady Chatterley's Lover") of the great rhythm of the Christian year.
But the forest is no more than evoked within the novels: it is not
itself the source of energy. (Energy comes to be as much an issue of
the will in Parkin/Mellors and Connie as in Clifford.) Obviously
in the nature of things *now* it cannot be a literal source for any but a
tiny handful who feel able to live in the "chinks" left by "the
children of men" and who can only do so in self-regarding rejection
of the mass of mankind *as* a mass. (The "warm-blooded" are a
new kind of predestined elect.) So the symbolic contrasts which
Lawrence builds into the obtrusive patterning of the novel make
sense only on the assumption of such a rejection. It does not answer
to say that *Lady Chatterley's Lover* is not a "realistic" novel: its
unreality is that of a false ideal.

There is little point in offering an order of preference between the
three versions. Certainly the first, comparatively free from jargon and
overt bullying, is the least offensive: lacking the crudely opposed
contrasts of *John Thomas and Lady Jane* and more especially of
Lady Chatterley's Lover, it is more honest in observation, though
correspondingly more obscure in purpose. But it does not make
enough difference: Lawrence had trapped himself from the start

by the "symbolic" abstractions which he imposed on his vision of the real world. The "idea" was there from the beginning, with always something of the monstrous in it: only its "development" brought fully into the open how mechanical is the view it offers of the possibilities of the life we can live now—and how much hatred lies within its assumption of tenderness.

9

A HEGELIAN JESUS

IN FEBRUARY 1974, it will be 100 years since David Friedrich Strauss died. The centenary will probably attract little attention, even though Strauss was the author of one of the most radical works of modern theology, *The Life of Jesus*—"kritisch bearbeitet". A reprint of this famous "critical treatment" of the Gospels as history is a more fitting reminder of what Strauss achieved than any commemorative books or articles about him could be. For his own story is a disappointing one and his theological thinking scarcely less so. Karl Barth went so far as to declare of him that, though Strauss may have "thought existentially" more than most men, he was "even more certainly not a thinker. . . . What he completely lacked was the thinker's ability to build up consecutively, to construct, to synthesize." And Barth commented on Strauss's biggest attempt at dogmatics, or rather polemical anti-dogmatics, for *Die christliche Glaubenslehre* denies Bible, Church and dogma: "All Strauss was able to do was to steer the ship of dogmatics carefully on to the rocks of a somewhat facile confrontation with Spinoza's and Hegel's philosophy and have it founder there with all hands."

Clobbering Strauss has been itself a somewhat facile way of drawing blood from the anaemic body of modern religious thought, ever since the first rush of forty and more essays that appeared on the subject of *The Life of Jesus* in the years immediately after the unmodified edition of 1835. Even when Strauss began to modify his views considerably for the third edition (1839), and thus made it easier for his champion in Zürich, Ferdinand Hitzig, to get him appointed to the chair of dogmatics and church history at the university there, the citizens of that town voted forty to one against his taking up the appointment. (As a result Strauss received an annual "pension" of 1,000 francs until the end of his increasingly embittered life.) Even his popularized *Life of Jesus adapted for the*

DAVID FRIEDRICH STRAUSS: *The Life of Jesus Critically Examined*. Translated by George Eliot. Edited by Peter C. Hodgson. 812 pp. SCM. £3.75.

German People (1864), which strives, still more than the third edition, to accommodate itself to the liberal intellectualism of the time (the preface acknowledges Renan; the text draws much from the conventional scholarship of Baur's historical school), failed to win by its placatory platitudes the success Strauss believed he had forfeited by his earlier polemics.

His final effort at reconciliation, *The Old Faith and the New* (1872), went to the fashionable modern extremes of acknowledging Jesus as at best a "noble enthusiast" and pointing the way forward to a religion of cosmic evolution; but the only fame this book won for Strauss was that of becoming Nietzsche's first victim. We can now see how much the fervour of Nietzsche's attack owes to the spectacle of spilt blood, which for a moment colours the victor's imagination with a flush of genuine religious awareness.

It is a pity that the fifty pages of introduction that Peter Hodgson has written for this reprint are far less imaginative than they are scholarly and academic. If, as George Eliot feared, there might not be one reader who would ever want to read this book right through (the version she translated was a fourth edition which recanted the recantations of the third), a bolder attempt was surely needed to tell us what is at stake in this nearly 800-page *Life of Jesus*. Certainly, Professor Hodgson does list the "critical passages where the logic of the book and its author's convictions become apparent", but he runs his eye over them in a way that suggests professional competence rather than personal concern. Only once does he express a value judgment, to the effect that Strauss's "'speculative reconstruction' ends with trivial bourgeois secularism in place of Christology" (it is odd that it should be the word "bourgeois" that lends most colour even to this judgment). And in the next paragraph Strauss's "difficulty" is described again quite technically as though it were largely a difficulty in the use of Hegelian terminology.

This is not to suggest that Professor Hodgson does not see in Strauss any "lasting theological significance". On the contrary, he thinks that his significance "can be summarized under at least the following points" (O, that academic passive and open-minded regard for other possible points!):

(1) *The Life of Jesus* represented a watershed in the development of a critical method for the study of the Gospels, in virtue of both its destruction of all previous methods of interpretation and its positive elaboration of the mythical criterion. . . .

This is typical of the tone of voice in which Professor Hodgson conducts his opening discussion. If it is typical of the kind of "critical dialogue with the inherited tradition" that the foreword to the SCM "Lives of Jesus" series hopes to promote, then it sounds as if it will be largely a matter of theologians talking to theologians, with the major contributions made by voices from the past. There is a mass of references, many of them in brief footnotes, to more recent writings on the questions raised by Strauss, but it would be hard for a non-specialist to guess whether these questions still trouble theologians otherwise than academically, i e, in terms of having the record straight about who stands where in the history of theology. (Why is it that "dialogue" is a favourite word among groups who intend, in fact, to talk in a specialized way of their own?)

Albert Schweitzer—whose *Quest of the Historical Jesus* is, of course, alluded to here—managed in half the space to give a livelier feeling of why these questions mattered to Strauss and must continue to matter:

> However far criticism may go in proving the reaction of the idea [of God-manhood] upon the presentation of the historical course of the life of Jesus, the fact that Jesus represented that idea and called it to life among mankind is something real, something that no criticism can ever annul. It is alive thenceforth and unto this day, and for ever more.
>
> It is in this emancipation of spirit, and in the consciousness that Jesus as the creator of the religion of humanity is beyond the reach of criticism, that Strauss goes to work, and batters down the rubble, assured that his pick can make no impression on the stone.

Schweitzer, however, did not shrink from beginning his discussion with the avowal: "In order to understand Strauss one must love him."

The closest Professor Hodgson allows himself to come to any personal appraisal of this book is with regard to its literary quality— and this he does not seem to have distinguished at all clearly until one of his students pointed out to him that "it could be likened to a great tapestry: threads woven through each other, making each incomplete without the other". From a student of literature, this would have been a banally unhelpful remark, since it is true presumably of *all* works having any artistic merit. A student of theology might have turned this observation to some more spiritually profound account had he gone on to reflect on the relationship between the beauty of art and the truth of religion, and more generally between imagination and history (since *that* is surely the first "lastingly significant point" raised by Strauss). But no such thoughts seem to have occurred to either professor or pupil.

If the fabric of Strauss's text is "novel-like"—and this is also "precisely the fabric of the Gospel story itself"—then Professor Hodgson sees a problem only of "theological opacity" and lack of systematic presentation. And that he will sort out with his list of "critical passages", and his careful, scholarly instruction on how to place Strauss so as to provide a better balanced view of the Bible:

Strauss allows for historical development of the stories through tradition, but lacks both the form-critical tools and perspective on the writings necessary to trace it. Baur's overemphasis of "tendency criticism" (or redactive criticism) should be viewed as a reaction to Strauss's one-sided criticism of stories apart from their literary context and traditio-historical development. The best results can be obtained from a combination of the two methods, and indeed Strauss and Baur *together* lay the foundations of modern form criticism and redaction criticism.

To say that "the best results can be obtained" surely begs the question —and this too is Strauss's question—of what "the best results" might be when we read the Bible. To scrutinize and compare every scrap of evidence and so form as accurate an historical judgment as possible on what really happened? Or to try to realize in our own imagination the spiritual meaning of what happened? (Is "the best" that we *believe* it?)

These two ideals may not be mutually exclusive, but they are not immediately the same. It may be possible to criticize Strauss, as Professor Hodgson does, for having broken up the Gospels "to investigate the internal grounds of credibility *in relation to each detail given in the Gospels*". Professor Hodgson has italicized the part of the sentence he objects to, and he concludes that it is "because the stories are abstracted from their literary, historical and theological context, [that] the negative results are inevitably accentuated and the credibility of the Gospel writings as a whole called into question". But it does not follow that by looking at the Gospels "as a whole" their credibility will thereby be established. Strauss did not make a minor mistake in method because he tackled the details of each story separately. His mistake, if that is the right word for his massively sincere attempt to know what he believed with regard to every detail of the life of Jesus, is revealed in the first part of the sentence quoted above, rather than in the second: "*To investigate the internal grounds of credibility*", is the phrase that deserves the italics, because it assumes that there is a scale of credibility, which rests upon grounds which are open to investigation. Strauss's object is not to show how much of the Gospel rests upon these grounds, but how little. And this "accentuation of negative results" was deliberate, of course, not accidental (thus it was not something that scholarship should try to mitigate). For precisely *this* critical method was intended to save the Bible in a "higher" sense.

Behind this method looms the figure of Hegel, as Professor Hodgson points out, though here again the emphasis is placed on a scholarly detail rather than on the larger issue of truth and belief. Hegel allowed that the idea of divine human unity must once have manifested itself fully in the historical person of Jesus; Strauss does not allow this: "This is indeed not the mode in which the Idea realizes itself; it is not wont to lavish all its fulness on one exemplar." There is undoubtedly a potential wealth of significance in Strauss's conclusion that if the Idea cannot be credibly seen as manifest in one individual, it must be fulfilled by humanity as a whole. The lost cause of the individual is redeemed by the "sinless existence" of mankind in the mass. But since this conclusion is reached in the last pages of the book, and not dwelt upon, it should not distract attention from the main burden of the *Life* itself and of the method Strauss uses to investigate it.

The method is dialectical: that is to say, the Gospel record is analysed into opposing details (Jesus is the son of Joseph; Jesus is the son of God), and opposite interpretations of each incident are then surveyed—supernaturalistic, on the one hand, and rationalistic, on the other. This procedure, Strauss recognized, "would for the most part annul the life history of Jesus as history". But it is well known that when Hegelians "annul" something they are not simply destroying it, but simultaneously "raising it up"; the dialectical process passes beyond mere contradiction to contemplate the synthetic wholeness of a higher idea. Like many another exponent of the dialectical method, Strauss found it easier to analyse the contradictions than to contemplate the whole, which receded at the very end into a brief glimpse of mankind's glorious self-realization as one with the divine. The meaning of the process does not entirely depend, however, upon reaching this goal; it becomes an end in itself, in which a new kind of meaning is constantly being raised up out of the discordant facts. That meaning is what Strauss called the *mythus*.

The aim of Strauss's long analysis is to show that a mythological imagination has been at work at every point in the Gospels. This creative spirit operated, he contends, in various ways, sometimes inventing scenes and happenings outright, sometimes embellishing fact with an aura of supernatural significance and occasionally reporting (but in many variant forms and contexts) some of the things Jesus of Nazareth may actually have said. Now, the manner in which Strauss's *Life of Jesus* demonstrates this truth about the Gospels—which it exceeds in length, incredibly indeed, by almost sevenfold—is by making us *see* this constant ferment of intellectual activity. We see it, however, in Strauss's text, rather than in the Scriptures. Where the Gospels narrate with an equally astonishing degree of simple statement (even John's theology is quite unlike philosophic discourse), Strauss's pages are a tissue of speculation and argument. Not one fact, not even one idea, is allowed to exist there for us to accept at its face value; everything is caught up into the higher realm of thought—and thus annulled.

We come to recognize, however, that Strauss neither adds nor takes away anything from our understanding of the Gospels other than this one insight into their universal character as works of the mythological imagination. He is careful to stress that he does not wish to distinguish any particular passages of fraud or deception, but merely different types or gradations of myth; what is at work in the production of the Gospel *mythi* is no private or personal fancy— against which some publicly acknowledged reality could conceivably be set in contrast—but an all-embracing "spirit of the people". The reality behind the myth is by definition inaccessible; so Strauss is achieving his effect by pointing to something that we cannot see. This has the double result of making what we do see more wonderful (as imaginative vision) and at the same time more doubtful (as history). He is like a conjuror who makes familiar things appear and disappear. Since that is all he can do with them, he fails to interest us after a while in the significance of his trick.

The Life of Jesus is in the end nothing but a *tour de force*, which reduces all the varied happenings, practical teachings and unimaginable wisdom of the Gospels to a mental routine, the repetition of essentially the same thought, the application of the same question and thus the discovery of the same answer, to everything. Inevitably, our sense of the importance of that mythological answer fades; as with the conjuror's tricks, we do not really believe the magic, and assume there must be some very ordinary explanation for these feats of the mind. For here lies the crux of Strauss's dubious achievement: he has changed the character of the Gospel stories from an actual marvel into an abstract problem. What those marvels mean, and indeed whether or not they are true, has been from the beginning, from the first apostles, the challenge and call to live and think in that way which is called "the faith". Also from the beginning it has been evident that the ability to live in faith and the ability to see the marvels as true have been inseparable. The truth of the marvels cannot ever have totally excluded the knowledge that they happened to quite ordinary people; otherwise the marvel of seeing their lives to have been so extraordinarily transformed could not have been such good news.

Was it, then, a marvel only of *seeing*? That is precisely what cannot be known. *Of course*, the quality of vision in those who believed has been changed; but since no one else bothered to report on what they were looking at—presumably because to other eyes it was not worth reporting—we cannot know anything about this change. If the mind tries to "speculate" on its experience of transfiguration so as to bring its own visionary powers into focus, its mirror image of itself will seem unreal and deceptive. The light, if there is any, can only be used to lighten the world; the spirit will only be believed if seen incarnate—it cannot be known in the abstract as an idea.

Strauss's intellectual feat, achieved before he was thirty, not only produced the opposite from what he wanted in his career, but also the opposite of his avowed intellectual purpose. Far from saving the truth of Christianity from the disputing claims of supernaturalist apologists and rationalist debunkers, Strauss succeeded in making the issue itself not only self-cancelling, but a matter of indifference, and hence *boring*. George Eliot appears to have felt something of this boredom, though her sense of oppression may have been due to the immense burden involved in translating this work. It is difficult to find any sentences, even to the very end, where either her accuracy or her prose flags. What is perhaps most remarkable in a future writer of such great latent power is that she should have been able to imitate so steadily the scholarly monotone in which Strauss expressed himself.

IO

LORDS AND LADIES

(a) SPONTANEOUSLY BYRONIC

WHEN A CLERGYMAN challenges an officer of Dragoons to a duel about a woman whom other men know to be a whore, the comic spirit will certainly be in attendance. Should death and injury be averted, the comic spirit will easily prevail. Byron, the friend who carried the Revd Robert Bland's challenge in 1811, managed to adjust things peaceably. Ten years later he was to recall how difficult this had been, mainly owing to the unhelpful obstinacy of Susan C., "the d——st b——h that I ever saw, and I have seen a great many" ("Detached Thoughts", 36). Another friend, the "Sentimental & Sensibilitous" Francis Hodgson (June 29, 1811), due to be ordained in the following year, had also patronized Susan C. for a while. In an immediate report of the matter by letter to his old travelling-companion, John Cam Hobhouse, Byron emerges as the spokesman of the comic spirit. He is hard-headed, positive, pugnacious, exuberant, and scornful:

Bland (the *Revd*) has been *challenging* an officer of Dragoons, about a *whore*, & my assistance being required, I interfered in time to prevent him from losing his *life* or his *Living*.—The man is mad, Sir, mad, frightful as a Mandrake, & lean as a rutting Stag, & all about a bitch not worth a Bank token.—She is a common Strumpet as his Antagonist assured me, yet he means to marry her, Hodgson meant to marry her, the officer meant to marry her, her first Seducer (seventeen years ago) meant to marry her, and all this is owing to the *Comet*!—During Bland's absence, H[odgso]n was her Dragon, & left his own Oyster wench to offer her his hand, which she *refused*.—Bland comes home in Hysterics, finds her in keeping (not by H[odgso]n however) & loses his wits.—Hodgson gets drunk & cries. & he & Bland (who have been berhyming each other as

---

(a) *Byron's Letters and Journals.* Edited by LESLIE A. MARCHAND. Volume I: *In My Hot Youth.* 288 pp. Volume II: *Famous in My Time.* 298 pp. John Murray. £4.75 each.

(b) A. L. ROWSE: *Shakespeare The Man.* 284 pp. Macmillan. £4.95.

you know these six past Olympiads) are now the Antipodes of each other.—
I saw this *wonder*, & set her down at seven shilling's worth. (November
16, 1811)

The rough, candid, steady affection that linked Byron and Hobhouse
encouraged such humorous plain-spokenness in their communica-
tions. But Byron grows equally forthright both in his assertions and
in his suppositions when he continues the story a month later in a
letter to William Harness, a younger man whose protector he had
been at Harrow:

Bland is ill of a Gonorrhea, a clerical & creditable distemper, particularly
to a despairing Corydon.—Hodgson I should conjecture to have a
Syphilis at least, if I may judge by his querulous letter.—So much for
these Sentimentalites who console themselves in the stews for the loss,
the never to be recovered loss, the despair, of the refined attachment of
a brace of Drabs!—When I compare myself with these men my Elders
& my Betters, I really begin to conceive myself a monument of prudence,
a walking statue without feeling or failing.—And yet the World in general
hath given me a proud pre-eminence over them in profligacy.—Yet I
like the men, & God knows, ought not to condemn their aberrations, but
I own I feel provoked when they dignify all this with ye. name of love, &
deify their common Strumpets.—Romantic attachments for things market-
able at a dollar! (December 15, 1811)

His more customary tone with Harness is that of an elder brother.
Playfully he parodies the kind of advice that most men think age
authorizes them to dispense to their juniors:

Now, Child, what are thou doing? *reading I trust*. I want to see you
take a degree, remember this is the most important period of your life,
& don't disappoint your Papa & your Aunts & all your kin, besides
myself, don't you know that all male children were begotten for the
express purpose of being Graduates? (December 8, 1811)

A similar playfulness will flourish later in his letters to his half-sister
Augusta, but he hardly knew her well enough for this to develop
fully before the end of 1812. During his earlier years, he wrote
affectionately and earnestly to her and relied greatly on her sympathy
when his mother's irascibility made home life unendurable.

Though he disliked his mother personally, their relationship
obliged him to show respect for her. Throughout his Mediterranean
grand tour of 1809–11, he wrote to her regularly. But his letters to her
have a greater sobriety than have those to Hodgson and—following
Hobhouse's return home half-way through Byron's pilgrimage—to

"Hobby". They are reserved, even guarded. To Hodgson, he could say, "damn description, it is always disgusting" (August 6, 1809), but description is precisely what Mrs Byron gets. His letters to her constitute an interesting travelogue with carefully limited glimpses of the traveller.

He reveals himself more fully to Lady Melbourne, the intelligent and worldly sexagenarian who became his honorary "aunt" during his years of fame in England. He writes to her about Lady Caroline Lamb, the lover who long continued to pester him, and about Annabella Milbanke, who eventually became his wife. Lady Melbourne communicated to Annabella, her niece, his first proposal of marriage. Annabella rejected this in a letter which she wished her aunt to show to him. Byron's shrewd analysis of her behaviour is characteristic of this correspondence between two alert and curious observers of, and participants in, the human comedy. He acknowledges Annabella's "abilities & her excellent qualities" and goes on:

Still there is something of the *woman* about her; her *preferring* that the letter to you should be sent forward to *me per esempio* appears as if though she would not encourage, she was not disgusted with being admired.—I also may hazard a conjecture that an *answer* addressed to *herself* might not have been displeasing, but of this you are the best judge from actual observation.—I cannot however see the necessity of it's being forwarded unless I was either to admire the composition or reply to ye. contents. (October 18, 1812)

A year later, his letters will be carrying to Lady Melbourne a witty running commentary on his inconclusive intrigue with Lady Frances Wedderburn Webster, whose husband—absurd, uxorious, jealous, and yet promiscuous—almost asked to be cuckolded.

But, while the comic spirit generally prevails in Byron's more intimate correspondence, graver and gloomier passages certainly occur. Becalmed on his return voyage from the Mediterranean, he ends a letter to Hobhouse by breaking off from a humorous performance and confessing to the dejection which underlies it:

We have had a tedious passage, all except the Straits where we had an Easterly Gale, and glided through the Gut like an oil Glyster.—Dear Hobby, you must excuse all this facetiousness which I should not have let loose, if I knew what the Devil to do, but I am so out of Spirits, & hopes, & humour, & pocket, & health, that you must bear with my merriment, my only resource against a Calenture.—Write to me, I am now going to patrole the melancholy deck. God be w'ye! (June 19, 1811)

Nearly a fortnight later, he describes himself to the same friend as "in bitter bad spirits, skies foggy, head muzzy, Capt. sulky, ship lazy" (July 2, 1811). The neatness and compactness of the eight words in which he accounts for his condition invite us to smile at it. Nevertheless, his gloom is genuine.

The bereavements which followed closely on his arrival in England had an effect upon him which he notes with surprise:

I am very lonely, & should think myself miserable, were it not for a kind of hysterical merriment, which I can neither account for, or conquer ... I have tried reading & boxing, & swimming, & writing, & rising early & sitting late, & water, & wine, with a number of ineffectual remedies. ... (August 10, 1811)

He is serious, too, when he writes to Lord Holland, the leader of the moderate Whigs in the House of Lords, about the Nottinghamshire weavers whose desperate recourse to Luddite violence the Tory government planned to check by making frame-breaking a capital offence. "I have seen the state of these miserable men", he declares, "& it is a disgrace to a civilized country.—Their excesses may be condemned, but cannot be subject of wonder.—The effect of ye. present bill would be to drive them into actual rebellion" (February 25, 1812). This was to be the theme of his maiden speech in the House of Lords two days later.

Byron's vivid sense of the distinctive individualities of his various correspondents, and his readiness to allow frank expression sentence by sentence to his own shifting moods, give his letters a fascinating variety and a deep human interest. We know from Thomas Moore, whose acquaintance with him was ripening into warm friendship by the end of 1812, that Byron made a habit of answering letters as soon as he received them. He scribbled swiftly and fluently in what he himself judged "a sad scrawl" (September 26, 1811). So little normally intervened between the occasion and the words that sprang from it that his correspondence generally has an unrivalled spontaneity and aptness.

His delighted observation of the life around him never flags. "There is nothing like inspection, and trusting to our own senses" (November 2, 1808), he assured his mother in justification of his projected grand tour. In due course, he portrayed Ali Pacha for her and recorded his impressions of Portugal, Spain, Albania, Greece, and Turkey. When he sent home his servant Fletcher, he gave her his reasons:

... the perpetual lamentations after beef & beer, the stupid bigotted contempt for every thing foreign, and insurmountable incapacity of acquiring even a few words of any language, rendered him like all other English servants, an incumbrance.—I do assure you the plague of speaking for him, the comforts he required (more than myself by far) the pilaws (a Turkish dish of rice & meat) which he could not eat, the wines which he could not drink, the beds where he could not sleep, & the long list of calamities such as stumbling horses, want to tea ! ! ! &c which assailed him, would have made a lasting source of laughter to a spectator, and of inconvenience to a Master.—After all the man is honest and in Christendom capable enough, but in Turkey. . . . (January 14, 1811)

Such a catalogue had already helped him to tell Hodgson about his life in Portugal:

I am very happy here, because I loves oranges, and talk bad Latin to the monks, who understand it, as it is like their own,—and I goes into society (with my pocket-pistols), and I swims in the Tagus all across at once, and I rides on an ass or a mule, and swears Portuguese, and have got a diarrhoea and bites from the mosquitoes. But what of that? Comfort must not be expected by folks that go a pleasuring. (July 16, 1809)

Back in England, he observes his pretty Puritanical cousin,

... the religious Julie, poor Soul! why does not the pretty (& she is pretty) Muggletonian get a spouse?—Failing in that I observe the Ladies transfer to God what Man has neglected, & become as lovingly religious as they would have been religiously loving. (August 27, 1811)

An old school friend was his guest at Newstead Abbey:

Claridge is gone after a lethargic visit of three perennial weeks.—How dull he is! I wish the dog had any *bad* qualities that one might not be ashamed of disliking him. (October 14, 1811)

"Sotheby the scribbler" turned out to be "a disagreeable dog, with rhyme written in every feature of his wrinkled Physiognomy" (November 9, 1811). These last two miniatures went to Hobhouse. In April 1812, a portrait of Lady Caroline Lamb went to the subject herself:

I have always thought you the cleverest most agreeable, absurd, amiable, perplexing, dangerous fascinating little being that lives now or ought to have lived 2000 years ago.—I won't talk to you of beauty, I am no judge, but our *beauties* cease to be so when near you.

A further five months' experience of Lady Caroline made him discuss her in very different terms to Lady Melbourne:

"*Manage her*"!—it is impossible—& as to friendship—no—it must be broken off at once, & all I have left is to take some step which will make her hate me effectually, for she must be in extremes.—What you state however is to be dreaded, besides—she presumes upon the weakness & affection of all about her, and the very confidence & kindness which would break or reclaim a good heart, merely lead her own farther from deserving them. (September 15, 1812)

Though Lady Melbourne was to receive the account of his flirtation with Lady Frances Wedderburn Webster, Byron's earlier impressions of the Websters' married life went to Hobhouse. "Bold Webster", as he ironically termed him, doted ridiculously on Lady Frances:

His wife is very pretty, & I am much mistaken if five years hence, she don't give him reason to think so.—Knowing the man, one is apt to fancy these things, but I really thought, she treated him even already with a due portion of conjugal contempt, but I dare say this was only the megrim of a Misogynist.—At present he is the happiest of men, & has asked me to go with them to a tragedy to see his *wife cry*! (November 3, 1811)

A fortnight later, he reduced "five" to "three":

W[ebste]r will be a noble subject for Cuckoldom in three years, though he has managed to impregnate her Ladyship, which consequently can be no very difficult task. She is certainly very pretty, & if not a dunce, must despise her "Bud" heartily.—She is not exactly to my taste, but I dare say Dragoons would like her. (November 17, 1811)

Byron is astutely aware of each person he addresses; he allows his natural mobility of temperament to express itself in rapid and sometimes subversive alternations of mood; vigorously and racily, he describes what he has observed; and he comments wittily, sympathetically, humorously or mockingly upon whatever has excited his interest. He is one of the most versatile and provocative of our letter-writers. More perhaps than any other, he has left us a collection of writings that constitute a brilliant and incisive portrait of their author.

He had written all the letters that have been quoted here before he was twenty-five. By this time, *Childe Harold's Pilgrimage*, I and II, had made him famous. But the Turkish tales—*The Giaour*, *The Bride of Abydos*, *The Corsair*, *Lara*, and *The Siege of Corinth*—were still to come. T. S. Eliot wrote appreciatively of the first of these; admittedly, it leaves enough to the reader's imagination to make it more tolerable than the others. In all five, however, the extravagant postures assumed by the characters, the stilted declamation which does duty as talk, and the theatrical lighting which illuminates every scene drive the reader to ask whether this writer had ever encountered a human being. Yet this writer had already written with insight about Bland, Fletcher, Annabella, Lady Caroline Lamb, the Websters and others, and had voiced his own feelings to a variety of correspondents in the frank, flexible, mainly serio-comic, manner we have been admiring. Six years were to elapse before Byron discovered how to import this clear-sighted realism and lively sense of comedy into what were to be his major poems: *Don Juan* and *The Vision of Judgment*.

The appearance of the first two volumes of Leslie A. Marchand's new edition of Byron's correspondence is welcome, timely and important. R. E. Prothero's edition of 1898–1901 has served well. It contains 1,198 letters; its texts, when based on manuscript originals, are reasonably reliable; and Prothero's copious and richly informative notes will long continue to enlighten scholars. But as many letters again have been printed in whole or in part in books and periodicals since 1901; and Professor Marchand will be adding a further 500 or so in the edition now initiated. When finished, this will contain about 3,000 letters, four-fifths of them printed from the original manuscripts or from facsimiles or photocopies.

The remaining fifth will include many letters to Thomas Moore and others, which Moore himself cut for publication and which are no longer available in manuscript. But extant originals will enable Professor Marchand to undo the less extensive bowdlerizing of Prothero. A few examples will show where Prothero drew the line. Concluding a letter to Harness, Byron speaks of ending "my chapter or rather homily in an orthodox manner, 'as it was in the beginning, is now & ever shall be'" (March 18, 1809); Prothero cautiously omits everything after "homily", presumably as profane. Sometimes Prothero softens and weakens the original language. He allows Byron to suspect that Leander's "conjugal affection" was "a little chilled" by swimming the Hellespont; but what Byron suspected was that the swimmer's "conjugal powers" were "exhausted" (May 3, 1810). Later in the same letter, Byron compares the Turks and the English. Prothero preserves decency while permitting comprehension, by substituting asterisks for the word "foreskins" in the sentence, "I see not much difference between ourselves & the Turks, save that we have foreskins and they none, that they have long dresses and we short, and that we talk much and they little". But he completely omits the sentence that follows, in which a mischievous play of alliteration points Byron's deliberately outrageous observations: "In England the vices in fashion are whoring & drinking, in Turkey, Sodomy & smoking, we prefer a girl and a bottle, they a pipe and pathic." With Professor Marchand's reinstatement of this sentence, the assertion that follows, "They are sensible people", regains its cheerful impudence.

There are also minor errors of transcription in Prothero's text. Professor Marchand can clear things up wonderfully, as when he transfers a puzzling mention of the Miss Pigots to "the Miss Parkyns's" (June 22, 1809).

Clearly, this edition will give us more of Byron's correspondence than ever before, edited more scrupulously than ever before. To each volume Professor Marchand appends a list of the letters contained in it, with an indication of the source of his text of each. There follows a list of detected forgeries of Byron's letters bearing dates that fall within the range of the volume. Finally, a series of compact biographical sketches of the chief correspondents and of other persons frequently mentioned presents material that would be less conveniently housed in the concise explanatory footnotes.

A few literal errors have escaped the notice of the proof-reader. Perhaps "deprecation" for "depreciation" in Professor Marchand's introductory essay is one of these (I, page 12). But "temerity" for "timidity" one page earlier can only be a malapropism (I, page 11). "Alternative" for "Alterative", occurring as it does three times on two successive pages, seems also to be something more than a misprint (II, pages 86–7). Another blunder occurs when Byron, recovering from a fever in Greece, describes his situation "in a parody on Pope's lines on the Duke of Buckingham". He is evidently thinking of "Epistle III. To Allen Lord Bathurst", often described as the third of the *Moral Essays*, lines 299–314. The passage, which begins, "In the worst inn's worst room, with mat half-hung", is well-known and much anthologized. Byron's parody is amusing enough as an impromptu but suffers by clinging too closely to the original. Professor Marchand misses the resemblance and tries to relate the "parody" to a totally dissimilar short poem which Pope addressed to a different Duke of Buckingham in gratitude for a set of commendatory verses (II, page 15). When a scholar of high distinction in the early nineteenth-century field fails to recognize a conspicuous landmark in an adjacent area, many readers will experience renewed doubts about the increasing specialization of academic life.

But there can be no doubt about Professor Marchand's erudition as a student of Byron or about the skill with which he places this erudition at the service of his readers. Acquaintance with the first two volumes will cause them to look forward with some impatience to his presentation of the later sequences of letters, and of Byron's incomparable journals, in the many volumes that are still to come.

(b) DARKLY SHAKESPEAREAN

OF THE WELCOME for A. L. Rowse's first biography of Shakespeare the memory is yet green. The advance articles in *The Times* announcing answers to perennial questions posed by the Sonnets, the spirited exchanges that followed in the correspondence columns (had he really come up with the final solution?), the publication of the book on the eve of the quatercentennial celebrations, the blasts from reviewers and counter-blasts from the author—can all this have taken place a full decade ago? To be sure Dr Rowse has himself occasionally raked the embers of debate by forays into *The Times*; for a while he even contemplated writing a book about the reception of his book. Now he has chosen instead to favour the world with another life of the Bard. Like Sam in *Casablanca*, Dr Rowse is playing it again, and if his tune is not quite so beguiling as Bogey's it has, thanks to its haunting Dark Lady theme, already set the Shakespearean world humming.

This biography is like the previous one, and also different. Inevitably the author follows in his own footsteps. Once again we perambulate Stratford. The story of the Sonnets, taken as fourteen-line rhymed instalments in an intimate autobiography, becomes a twice-told tale. Phrases are repeated, paragraphs lightly recast. Surely the procedure is perfectly understandable and appropriate; previous biographers of Shakespeare have followed the same course, and anyway most readers will not have the 1963 *Shakespeare* under their belt. Tone and substance suggest that Dr Rowse is this time round casting his net to capture an even more popular kind of readership than that for which his earlier best-selling biography catered. Fair enough—he has the touch, and the popularizing tradition is an honourable one—but it is at least debatable whether a work addressed to an essentially uncritical readership is the most suitable vehicle for a new and controversial thesis. That thesis concerns Emilia Lanier, *née* Bassano.

Dr Rowse found her in the Bodleian Library, in Simon Forman's case books, where for centuries her indiscretions had lain covered by the kindly dust of oblivion. A contemporary of Shakespeare, Forman was an astrologer, physician, and lecher, at all of which occupations he enjoyed considerable success. If he failed in his quest for the philosopher's stone, he did correctly predict the date of his own demise—although sceptics have unworthily suspected that he cheated by committing suicide. Scholars have long known of this curious individual by reason of his *Book of Plays*, in which he gives eye-witness accounts of performances of *Macbeth*, *The Winter's Tale*, and *Cymbeline*. In 1844 J. O. Halliwell (later Halliwell-Phillipps) published, in a limited edition for private circulation, *The Autobiography and Personal Diary of Dr Simon Forman*. This volume, which Dr Rowse does not mention, is slight and hard to come by, and suffers from Victorian inhibitions respecting "halek", which is Forman's code word for sexual intercourse. For being apparently the first to tackle the mass of Forman papers Dr Rowse has earned our admiration; it is one of those scholarly inspirations that appear perfectly obvious after the fact. In Forman, for Dr Rowse, the dark mistress of the Sonnets becomes visible.

For the benefit of readers—there must be some—who missed the hoopla in the media, the facts about Emilia Lanier are quickly summarized. She was the daughter of a court musician, Baptist Bassano. Orphaned by the time she was seventeen, she became (according to Forman) the mistress of the elderly Henry Carey, 1st Lord Hunsdon. As Lord Chamberlain he supported the players in their running battle with the municipal authorities, and was himself the patron of an acting troupe; in 1594 he became briefly the patron of the new Chamberlain's company. Finding herself pregnant, Emilia made a marriage of convenience with William Lanier, a minstrel. They did not get on well together. When Emilia in 1593 visited Forman to have her horoscope cast, she told him that noblemen had made much of her; Forman, expert in such matters, concluded that this dark beauty (for he describes her as "very brown in youth") would "for lucre's sake . . . be a good fellow". Later he enjoyed halek with her, and after one or two mentions more "this deleterious woman" (in Dr Rowse's phrase) disappears from the case books. Was she the seductress who led the poet his last—or was it his last?—tango in London?

Dr Rowse notes that her husband's christian name lends itself admirably to word-play, and that Sonnet 135 begins:

> Whoever hath her wish, thou hast thy Will,
> And Will to boot, and Will in overplus.

But of course Shakespeare's name too was Will, *will* means desire, and also (as Dr Rowse helpfully points out) the sexual organs. So the word in context has three significances without a contribution from Will Lanier. A quadruple pun would be neat, but a treble serves for the nonce. Emilia's dates fit in snugly with Dr Rowse's assignment for the Sonnets, but that assignment, notwithstanding his protestations to the contrary, remains conjectural; in such matters, as the Variorum editor ruefully conceded three decades ago, the quest for certainty is an idle dream. Emilia was musical, and so was the Dark Lady. Dr Rowse observes that a character in *Othello* who takes a light view of adultery is called Emilia. That is about it. It has been hinted in the press that Dr Rowse holds in reserve additional evidence sufficient to club his critics into submission, but, if so, he is still keeping it to himself.

So we are left with a musical woman, dark-complexioned, married, promiscuous, and in the 1590s still young. There may have been other such, even in Forman's limited circle, for he had no trouble finding partners for halek; on January 15, 1601, the athletic astrologer enjoyed one mistress at 9 a m, and another at noon. Neither was Emilia. Most crucial, no record of any sort links her name with Shakespeare. It is not clear to what extent the mistress of the Sonnets represents a real individual. The imperatives of art, no less than the circumstances of nature, dictate her complexion. Her darkness is emblematic of character, and furnishes the antithesis, moral as well as pigmental, to the Fair Youth. The polarities are summed up in Sonnet 144:

> Two loves I have, of comfort and despair,
> Which like two spirits do suggest me still;
> The better angel is a man right fair,
> The worser spirit a woman colour'd ill. . . .

The aesthetic design of the cycle must give pause to the biographer, searching for clues to personal identity.

Dr Rowse professes scorn for "absurd conjectures and guesses *in vacuo*", and extols certainty, rigour, and method. These are no doubt virtues, but they here assume a talismanic potency, as though their invocation by itself constituted rigorous method. This is mystical scholarship. In effect we are being invited to accept on faith the authority of, in Dr Rowse's words, "the foremost historian of the society of Shakespeare's Age". But no authority, however eminent, holds the laws of evidence at his commandment. Dr Rowse has said that, for this period, we cannot expect to find corroborative letters and the like; we must content ourselves with a chain of plausible circumstance. It is no doubt true that documentary records are often scant, but this frustrating state of affairs does not entitle us to settle for less than adequate proof. It means, rather, that fewer things can get proved. In his preface Dr Rowse claims that his critics will find it "quite impossible to impugn" his findings. The burden, however, rests not with the critics, but with the historian. It is a pity that Dr Rowse should regard speculation in much the same way as nature esteems the vacuum, for there is a place in scholarship for conjecture, and he has come up with rather an intriguing one. Other investigators—or perhaps even Dr Rowse himself—may one day prove it right or wrong. If he is right, the world will applaud his intuition and tenacity, while not necessarily attaching to the discovery the immense significance claimed for it. Meanwhile one suspects one hasn't heard the last of Emilia.

She is only one ingredient in a book which makes for a better read than its predecessor. For one thing it is only a little more than half as long. To achieve his drastic economies Dr Rowse has had to suppress ruthlessly his urge to expatiate on topics that interest him, and evidence of the struggle surface in such poignant formulas as, "We must resist the temptation to go into this appealing play . . .". Mainly he has sacrificed critical commentary; a wise decision, for his genius does not lie that way. As he confessed himself in *The English Spirit*, "Heaven forfend that I should be a critic". What remains of literary interpretation even novices may find excessively elementary: "The subject of *Othello*, innocent love injured and destroyed, inspired Shakespeare to one of his highest flights of imagination and poetry"; or: "His (Shakespeare's) knowledge of human beings, of the human condition, has never been surpassed." True. So uninformed are readers presumed to be that they must be told that the *Henry IV* plays come after *Richard II* and before *Henry*

V, and that the whole lot make up a sequence. Dr Rowse does better when he sticks to dates and sources.

Style, robust without elegance, befits content. The author does not disdain cliché or such colloquialisms as "family-wise" or "fell for". He keeps footnotes to a minimum out of regard for the reader's comfort, but why such frugality should make for greater rather than less convenience is not clear: even the non-scholarly enthusiast may occasionally wish to follow up a point. The practical result is that authorities quoted and documented in the 1963 life—Eccles or Fripp or Spurgeon—here go paraphrased without acknowledgement. If this be an improvement, it is one that the fastidious will disrelish.

Dr Rowse is now keen to see Shakespeare as a writer whose primary allegiance was to the theatre. Thus we have such chapter headings as "The Player Becomes Playwright" or "At the Globe" or "The King's Men". The strategy is unexceptionable, but Dr Rowse is no stage historian, and what he has to say comes at second hand and tends to be superficial. A couple of sentences do to sum up the characteristics of the Elizabethan playhouse, with the vexed question of the existence or non-existence of an inner stage by-passed in a phrase. Mostly, Dr Rowse depends on G. E. Bentley— a good choice, surely, but it is a pity that the latter's *Profession of Dramatist in Shakespeare's Time* appeared too late for the biographer to draw upon it. Still the new bias is salutary.

Here and there the author has changed his mind or taken advantage of later work. In 1963 Dr Rowse thought Shakespeare no intellectual; now he is prepared to concede that the creator of *Hamlet* and *Troilus and Cressida* had egghead proclivities. We are also told that he was equipped with a "sexy nose", no doubt an appropriate appendage for the "sexiest writer in the language". Dr Rowse has written more extensively on this stimulating topic in *The Times*, but it remains unclear how the sexiness of writers may be quantitatively ascertained. He takes into account K. B. McFarlane on the riotous youth of Henry V. He has however unaccountably missed Hugh Hanley's important article in the *TLS* (May 21, 1964) with its revelations, from the Sackville manuscripts, about Susanna Shakespeare and Thomas Quiney. These records show that Shakespeare's elder daughter was in May 1606 cited for failing to receive the sacrament the preceding Easter, and that the poet's son-in-law in March 1616, shortly after his marriage to Judith Shakespeare, confessed having had carnal intercourse with one Margaret Wheeler, who died that month in childbirth. These facts, which are not without interesting implications for the biographer, have provided matter for E. R. C. Brinkworth's recent book, *Shakespeare and the Bawdy Court of Stratford*. In another quarter, Warren Austin has lately sought to demonstrate, through computer-assembled data, that Robert Greene's notorious death-bed slander of Shakespeare was in fact composed by the same Chettle who afterwards apologized for it. This challenge to biographical orthodoxy may not convert the sceptical, but Professor Austin presents his thesis responsibly enough for the biographer to have to reckon with it. Dr Rowse does not reckon with it.

A distinguished historian becomes a public figure in his own right, so the present book has a Rowsean as well as Shakespearean interest. The author's mood, exuberant as regards his subject, otherwise waxes melancholy. "Shakespeare scholarship has reached a dead end", he proclaims. (Is he so readily dismissing the new direction given to imagistic criticism by R. A. Foakes and Maurice Charney? Or the contributions to knowledge of Shakespeare's text we owe to Charlton Hinman and Fredson Bowers? Probably not—he is thinking of biography, which has indeed grown moribund of late. But surely it is careless to equate the part with the whole.) The golden age, represented by the England of Elizabeth, is past, and worse and worse days have succeeded the former. Our speech is "etiolated", "half-baked intellectuals" control the mass media, dons suck up to press-lords and television, honey comes home diluted in a jar. It is a democratic illusion—specifically the illusion of "superficial liberal intellectuals"—that they may be trusted to govern themselves well. Dr Rowse's outburst against the common man has its unintended irony, coming as it does in a book which will exercise its greatest appeal to unsophisticated readers.

At the end what chiefly impresses us is the powerful force of the author's personality. We can only admire the unflagging energy which during the past two years has given us two sweeping volumes of social and cultural history, an illustrated account of the Tower of London, a book of poems, and the present biography, and which promises us a life of Forman next year. No wonder Dr Rowse detects symptoms of exhaustion in the Shakespeare Establishment. With his energy, and also his flair, he has certainly enlivened the scholarly scene. Who else could have made a conjecture about the Dark Lady matter for feature articles in newspapers throughout the world? In this respect Dr Rowse may remind us of the brilliant and controversial young American chess expert who turned a sedentary competition, the preserve of a staid élite, on its heels, and attracted reporters from the four corners of the globe to an obscure hall in Reykjavik. But of course Bobby Fischer defeated the Russian grandmaster, whereas Dr Rowse has declared a victory without checkmate.

II

THE CLASSICAL HOUSMAN

WHEN A. E. HOUSMAN in his will expressed the wish that none of his contributions to periodicals should be reprinted, he was showing an attitude to his own writings that is not uncommon among learned men. A scholar often prefers that his writings, particularly his early writings, should not be reprinted, at least without his being given an opportunity to correct them. But potential readers of such collections on the whole prefer them to appear uncorrected, unless the corrections are clearly marked as such. The editors of *The Classical Papers of A. E. Housman* have rightly confined themselves to the correction of misprints, and they have added references to the editions of works cited which are now in general use.

One must sympathize with Housman in that his request has been disregarded, and one may wish that this had not happened in the lifetime of his literary executor; but one can hardly blame the publishers. The demand for the book undoubtedly exists; if an author's wishes had always to be respected, the *Aeneid* itself would have been lost and, as the editors remind us, Housman himself prefaced to his London inaugural lecture the words of Horace, "nescit vox missa reverti". The three volumes are handsomely produced, and have been edited by two well-qualified scholars, who have added a list of contents and valuable indexes of passages and of subjects discussed. The publication has atoned to scholars, if not to Housman's ghost, for the undeniably useful but in some respects unsatisfactory selection of Housman's prose which came from the same publishers twelve years ago.

The best account of Housman's career in scholarship is given by A. S. F. Gow in the memoir which he published in the year of Housman's death; a brilliant short appreciation may be found in

---

The Classical Papers of A. E. Housman. Edited by J. DIGGLE and F. R. D. GOODYEAR. Volume 1: 1882–1897. 421 pp. £12.60. Volume 2: 1897–1914. pp. 422–902. £12.60 Volume 3: 1915–1936. pp. 903–1,318. £13.90. Cambridge University Press.

a talk broadcast by the least unlike Housman of modern Latinists, D. R. Shackleton Bailey (published in *The Listener* on March 26, 1959). Now we can read the articles and notes in their order of publication and so follow the author's development.

Housman did not attain immediately to his full power. From the start he writes clearly, elegantly and wittily; from the start his knowledge is impressive and his ingenuity remarkable. But though they contain some brilliant suggestions, the pieces in the first volume, first published between 1882 and 1897, seldom show the quality singled out by Professor Shackleton Bailey as most singular in Housman: "the unremitting passionate zeal to see each one of the innumerable problems in his text not as others had presented it or as he might have preferred it to appear but exactly as it was".

The earliest article specially praised by Gow is a series on Ovid's *Heroides* published in 1897, when Housman was thirty-eight. Before that time Housman published a number of articles on Greek authors, particularly the tragedians; all this work is learned and clever, but very little of it is right. The rhetorical manner which makes it look as if only one approach to a problem—the author's— is worthy of a rational man, is not well suited to the treatment of Aeschylus and Sophocles, whose corrupt texts are made still more difficult by the lack of material for comparison.

After the late 1890s, Housman wrote little about Greek, except when tempted by a new papyrus, though he contributed effectively to the emendation of the new fragments of Bacchylides, Menander, Callimachus and, most particularly, of Pindar. When asked why he had ceased to write on Greek, he said it was because he had come to despair of attaining excellence in both languages. In Greek the law of diminishing returns has set in, and problems are not easily solved with finality. But Housman's younger contemporary, John Jackson, produced a remarkable series of emendations of the tragedians; and, if Housman had chosen to go on with Greek, he would doubtless have improved greatly on his early attempts. All the same, he was wise to prefer Latin, which offered a field better suited to the peculiar nature of his gifts.

The second and third volumes contain an extraordinarily large quantity of detailed work of the highest quality. Few people now living are qualified to praise it, but we may record the impression that hardly any scholar has left a collection of textual notes of similar size whose average quality, over a long period, may be compared to what we find here. The early pieces were learned and ingenious. In the later ones the erudition is enormous, covering every topic which might illuminate the matter in hand, and extending over the difficult and rarely mastered fields of ancient astronomy and astrology. The ingenuity is as great as earlier, or greater; but now it comes to be controlled by a sure and steady judgment not often developed by the notably ingenious.

The second volume contains notable articles on Lucilius, on Statius's *Silvae*, on Martial and on Persius; the third has superb pieces about Ovid (particularly the *Ibis*), Martial again, and Statius's *Thebaid*, besides the famous papers on "The Application of Thought to Textual Criticism" and on "Prosody and Method". Yet articles and notes, because they deal not with a complete text but with a selected problem, give less opportunity to appreciate the quality singled out by Professor Shackleton Bailey than do the commentaries. No one can form a proper notion of the greatness of Housman without working through the *Manilius*, and then comparing with the text of the commentary the text printed in the *editio minor* of 1932. Here even brilliant suggestions are relegated to the foot of the page or dropped altogether if they do not satisfy the editor's standards with regard to probability.

Why did Housman, whose verse belongs so entirely to the nineteenth century, choose in his scholarship to continue an eighteenth-century tradition and concentrate almost exclusively on textual criticism? In nineteenth-century Germany the tradition in question, represented there until his death in 1848 by Gottfried Hermann, a very much greater scholar than his English contemporary Porson, was replaced by the new concept of *Altertumswissenschaft*, the study of the ancient world as a whole. Textual studies took their place together with history, archaeology, and the new discipline of comparative philology and with other ancillary disciplines; and the study of ancient literature no longer stopped at the constitution of the text. Wilamowitz, born in the year of Hermann's death and so eleven years older than Housman, wrote commentaries on works of literature in which every branch of the study of antiquity was used to illuminate the text in hand. He made important contributions to textual criticism, but he did not shrink from attempting literary interpretation, and nothing that he wrote is dull. Leo, three years younger than Wilamowitz, brought out the first volume of a history of Latin literature not only learned but admirably written and exceedingly intelligent, in which the central problems, including purely literary ones, are discussed in a way that even now, more than fifty years after the author's death, commands the attention of any person seriously interested in the subject. Housman was intimately acquainted with the new German scholarship of the nineteenth century; he more than once expressed admiration for Wilamowitz. Why did he stay outside the movement that revolutionized his subject?

That he did so is greatly to be regretted, for English scholars after 1830 failed entirely to profit from the momentous developments in Germany. The triumph of the new scholarship in that country coincided with the moment when the ancient universities of England became absorbed in teaching to the virtual exclusion of research. The opinion of enlightened persons like the great German educational reformer, Wilhelm von Humboldt, that the two activities were necessary to each other was not comprehended in the world of Jowett. Mark Pattison wrote that in the Oxford of his day young MAs of talent abounded, but that each was rapidly set to turning some wheel in the vast machinery of cram. British scholars did indeed attempt the general interpretation of the ancient world, but with few exceptions—most of them, like Grote, outside the universities—they did so in a way that did not increase understanding. In the inaugural lecture which Housman gave at Cambridge in 1911 (first printed in the *TLS* on May 9, 1968), he ridiculed their efforts. They took it for granted, he observed, that the taste of the ancients was identical with their own Victorian romantic taste; they believed, in his words, that "the secret of the classical spirit is open to anyone who has a fervent admiration for the second-best parts of Tennyson". Many of their German contemporaries suffered, as Nietzsche pointed out, from a similar delusion; but most of these were at least active in adding to our factual knowledge of antiquity.

Gilbert Murray, himself a minor poet in the late Victorian manner, assumed that the poetical intentions of such a writer as Euripides were not very different from his own. Housman also was a romantic poet; but he never for a moment suffered from such delusions. He saw that the so-called literary criticism of classical authors in terms of romantic canons was altogether worthless. But why, instead of trying to overthrow it by introducing a kind of criticism that took account of the poetical intentions of the authors criticized, did he take refuge in asserting that literary criticism was no exercise for a scholar?

Housman throughout his life upheld the narrow restriction of the term "poetry" to verse productive, in his experience, of particular emotional effects. That definition excluded most of the poets on whom he worked, poets like Ovid, Lucan, Juvenal and Manilius, whose stock-in-trade was wit, elegance, all kinds of rhetoric. Housman's textual criticism of these poets shows that he was supremely capable of appreciating these qualities, which he justly complains were better perceived by the critics of the seventeenth and eighteenth centuries than by their supposedly more learned successors of his own age. Since by Housman's romantic definition of poetry these poets were not "true poets", one can see why he should not have thought it his duty to explain their literary technique. But it would not be hard to show that these same qualities also formed part of the attributes of poets whom Housman would have agreed to be worthy of the name. Yet Housman equates literary criticism, except as practised by a few rare spirits like Lessing and Arnold, with the wearying repetition of sentimental adulation.

Scholarship, he tells us in his Cambridge inaugural, not to mention the London lecture of 1892 which he later called "rhetorical and not wholly sincere", is a department not of literature but of science. Yet later in the same lecture, when he is warning against the tendency to practise scholarship mechanically—which he rightly saw as one of the greatest dangers that may threaten scholars— he says that "the criticism and interpretation of the classical texts is not an exact science". "Its subject-matter", he continues, "is a series of phenomena which are the result of the play of the human mind. . . . To deal with the mutable and evasive you want no cut and dried method." Exactly; even textual criticism requires not merely exact knowledge of language and technique, but a measure of tact and intuition—a measure, in fact, of literary understanding. Housman cannot have it both ways; the hard and fast barrier which his romantic dogmatism seeks to erect between textual criticism and literary analysis cannot be maintained between two territories which shade so imperceptibly into one another.

Housman, like Nietzsche, deserves our admiration for having ridiculed the false assumption that Victorian taste was like that of the Greeks and Romans; and he was right to remind scholars that the possession of a powerful technical equipment does not by itself convey a gift for literary discrimination. But does that exempt professional teachers of the classics, whose duty is to explain a difficult literature, from any duty but that of constituting the text? Their task requires not only factual and linguistic knowledge, but sympathetic understanding of beliefs and attitudes unfamiliar to the modern man; and if they are to perform it adequately they must have the courage to try to achieve both. Their task is not easy. Many people who have taste and understanding are hampered by inadequate knowledge of the facts; many learned people suffer from an insufficiency of taste and understanding. But a knowledge of the difficulties of the enterprise ought not to discourage a true scholar from attempting both halves of what his choice of a career requires.

People often say that Housman's romantic poetry was a kind of protest against the austerity of his life of scholarship. From a different point of view, Housman's life of scholarship can be seen as a kind of protest against that tyranny of "sub-Tennysonian taste" which he from his earliest years found all around him. Talking about scholars and their personal literary tastes, he wrote in his Cambridge inaugural:

Our first task is to get rid of them, and to acquire, if we can, by humility and self-repression, the tastes of the classic; not to come stamping into the library of Apollo Palatine without so much as wiping our shoes on the doormat, and cover the floor with the print of feet which have waded through the miry clay of the nineteenth century into the horrible pit of the twentieth.

Housman read widely in several literatures and keenly appreciated the quality of many different kinds of verse, even though his romantic dogmatism, tenacious as a Calvinist's belief in hell-fire, always prevented him from according any but a little of it the title of true poetry. As the reader of these three amazing volumes admires the writer's powerful intellect and revels in his wit, he cannot help asking himself what would have happened had Housman by some lucky accident ever thrown off the chains of the rigid romantic prejudice which restricted his attitude to literature. If he had been able to employ his strong and supple intelligence in unison with his imaginative powers, might he not have become a major instead of a minor poet? Might he not, instead of dogmatically upholding the critical attitudes of Arnold, have come some way towards those later voiced by Eliot? If Housman had rightly appreciated Leopardi, an author not to be understood if he is considered simply as a romantic, or if he had come upon Nietzsche at an early age, the thing might have happened. Could he not, as he does in one of his most startling poems, have shot the devil? But perhaps events in his own private life so checked his emotional development as to rule out such possibilities.

Nowadays Housman is from time to time abused by people who wish to insist upon the importance of the literary study of the classics. When such people find it necessary to abuse Housman we usually find that they are ignorant or slipshod scholars. Housman is an object of cult among a few young lions, who with a jacobite-like gallantry which one cannot help admiring a little—unless, perhaps, one happens to be a pupil of one of them—claim that a scholar's chief or only duty is to purify his authors' texts. Some of his tirades against other scholars share with the witticisms of F. E. Smith the annoying quality, not their author's fault, of being specially appreciated by people not especially sensitive to forms of humour less promptly to be apprehended. We should guard against allowing any of these things to prevent us from appreciating and admiring Housman.

12

THE SF STORY

A NEW HISTORY OF SCIENCE fiction might ordinarily be the occasion for a calm and considered setpiece on the subject. On the other hand Brian Aldiss's new book is so continuously stimulating or irritating that it calls for a more point-by-point approach: and this is probably for the best, since the issues raised, partly aesthetic, partly socio-psychological, are not really susceptible of a tidy—perhaps of any —formal solution.

Needless to say, difficulties start with the very definition of what we mean by science fiction. Mr Aldiss's is: "Science fiction is the search for a definition of man and his status in the universe which will stand in our advanced but confused state of knowledge (science), and is characteristically cast in the Gothic or post-Gothic mould." He concedes that this may sound "slightly pretentious" for a genre that has its strong "fun side", and that he is prepared to modify it as he goes along. But it is not simply a matter of "fun": it is the old question of the serious game involved in all art. Moreover, there is much SF—for example much of Arthur Clarke, Isaac Asimov and Robert Heinlein (new selections from whom by Angus Wells have lately been published by Sidgwick and Jackson at £2.50 each)— which isn't in any conceivable sense Gothic or post-Gothic, but is cool, cerebral, classical to a degree.

One must look rather at that which distinguishes SF from other fiction: and here, surely, we must accept Edmund Crispin's view that SF is basically "what would happen if?", and is distinguished from other fiction which could come under the same head by its "if" being, in principle, in accord with natural laws. That is, it is a fiction in which the context (physical, social or otherwise) is the crucial point. Indeed, Mr Aldiss himself elsewhere remarks that "the greatest successes of science fiction are those which deal with man in

---

Brian W. Aldiss: *Billion Year Spree*. The History of Science Fiction. 339 pp. Weidenfeld and Nicolson. £3.75.

relation to his changing surroundings and abilities: what might loosely be called *environmental fiction*".

Nevertheless, Mr Aldiss's "Gothic" approach leads him on to interesting ground. He argues, quite plausibly, that the first true work of SF was *Frankenstein*. But this does lead to his rating Mary Shelley a trifle high, as when he quotes one of her pieces with the comment "it is all three Brontë sisters in one!" We are even given the mawkishly uncritical suggestion that a dream of drowning in one of her stories shows that "she seems to have had some genuine prophetic talent".

The claim that there was no science fiction before her involves his rejecting the claims, usually made in histories of SF, that a variety of work from Lucian of Samosata on should be so regarded. Still, all this is largely a matter of definition. Nor is Mr Aldiss so churlish as to deny us a chapter on these pre-Shelleyan (and in his view pre-SF) progenitors of the genre—though he unaccountably omits the *Timaeus*, and surely the Atlantis story is far more truly fictional than the *Republic*, for a utopia sketched out schematically as an admitted intellectual exercise is one thing, the pretence of its actual existence quite another.

Argument on these matters is fun, though little more. (And this reviewer might be prepared to argue, for example, that the *Divine Comedy* overlaps into SF more than Mr Aldiss would grant. The theological description of the universe was then—or so it might be held—the "scientific" one. Hell and Purgatory, unlike those of Milton's vague and distant drama, are given a strict localization—Purgatory at a point just south of the Austral Islands in French Polynesia.)

Mr Aldiss is—and the fact certainly more than compensates for any faults—a genuine devotee of science fiction. Indeed, he gives the impression of having come to other literature through the genre. He often seems the enthusiastic autodidact, discovering everything for himself for the first time. As a result, some of his comments are fresh and exciting; others (though equally presented in terms of discovery) are well-worn truisms; and others yet are fresh but absurd.

He strikingly argues that Swift did not share Gulliver's admiration for Houyhnhnm culture. His net sweeps wide (if sometimes a little oddly—Gérard de Nerval, Villiers de l'Isle-Adam, Hardy), and often in a most stimulating fashion. It is new (in England at least) to find an excellent case for Restif de la Bretonne as an SF writer—pre-Mary Shelley apparently. Nor is Mr Aldiss impressed by big names: it is good to see E. M. Forster's *The Machine Stops* noted as "overpraised". When not arguing to some peculiar preconception, or indulging some (often admitted) prejudice, his natural taste serves him well. For example, he splendidly gives us a whole page of that great scene in *Hector Servadac* where Nina throws a pebble into the supercooled Gallian Sea. He is admirably fair to the great creative editor of modern SF, John W. Campbell Jr, with whom he cannot be in very great sympathy. He is fair, too, even to the king of space-opera at its high-grade schoolboy level, E. E. "Doc" Smith.

On the other hand, his awe at the intelligence and prevision of Erasmus Darwin leads him to dismiss the *Anti-Jacobin* as reactionary propaganda. So it was. But it is still read and Darwin (except in the *Stuffed Owl*) is not. For his undoubted cleverness was, especially in its expression, a silly-cleverness of a type by no means extinct; and Canning and Frere carve him as a dish fit for the gods. To give a few further negative examples: Mr Aldiss asks of Sir Oran Haut-Ton in *Melincourt*, "Is he a literary precursor of Frankenstein's monster?" (There is an easy answer to that one: no.) He tells us that "suspense entered literature for the first time" with the Gothic novel. He announces that "Swift belongs to the mandarin tradition of his friend Pope, the great Augustan poet; Defoe is much more of the people". We get untruisms too, like "to the Establishment the idea of change has always been anathema".

Then again, he asserts that on the strength of *Dr Strangelove*, *2001*, and *A Clockwork Orange*, Stanley Kubrick "should perhaps be acknowledged the great SF writer of the age". This is a footnote, and perhaps a joke; but (having once admitted that *2001* has in its early passages some superb spaceshots in the style of *Destination Moon*) one can only say that in general Kubrick provides no more than a slick shine on childishly knowing silliness or nastiness.

But in general, it is Mr Aldiss's psychological and similar dicta which jar the most. He is especially free with his attributions of "power fantasy", speaking of "the old pulps-through-*Astounding* tradition of indulgence in power fantasy". Telepathy, too, is a "power fantasy" theme. Again, he tells us, "Robots can embody depersonalization fears. This is perhaps their most obvious psychological function." On that sort of line, one can of course go on perhapsing away for ever. To follow this by reading one of Asimov's robot stories (only one not very typical example is included in *The Best of Isaac Asimov*) is instructive.

What we find, in fact, is a basic common sense continually concealed by a variety of superficial but highly obtrusive blemishes. It is greatly to our purpose that most of these are central to current discussion of the genre.

Eight or ten years ago John Campbell Jr was able to rejoice editorially in *Analog* because Susan Sonntag had ruled that science fiction did not deserve the attention—i e, the interference—of trendy theorists. That is, or so he thought, it could continue uninfected by the blight which has come across so many art forms in the recent past. Mr Aldiss himself, as we have said, derives from the heart of the old science fiction, and he writes of it *con amore*. He remarks truly enough that the abbreviation "sci-fi" is used only by "would-be trendies". But he inclines to go too far along with the trends himself. He appears as an SF pro but one who seems to have been suddenly faced with the (for him) new world of underground culture, disrupted significance, and so forth; and to have bowed to a considerable degree to the voices which told him that, unlike mere story-telling, this was "Art".

He admires J. G. Ballard, for example, well past the point of that writer's decadence (though not so far as his latest and worst convulsions). And, in general, he accepts the now receding "New Wave" as legitimate, or at least fertilizing, and does not realize that it amounted to little more than a dreary rechauffé of surrealist work of the 1920s and 1930s, which had largely petered out in the mainstream. He himself has sponsored as a masterpiece a truly terrible piece by Pamela Zoline which might have appeared in *Transition* on one of its off days, and—above all—has nothing to do with SF. (Just as Michael Moorcock, sponsor of the "new" SF, includes in his anthology of it a story of Mr Aldiss's own which is in no conceivable sense SF and does not even pretend to be—a straight tale of present-day Delhi.)

In fact, SF (like other types of fantasy writing) is a particularly unsuitable area for techniques which confuse or disrupt the sense. When something strange is afoot, in a strange time or on a strange planet, only a measure of clarity will let us know what is supposed to be going on. Something similar applies (as has often been pointed out) to excessive characterization, or excessive concentration on streams of thought or semi-conscious imaginings. The cant phrase "inner space" is little more than an attempt by mere verbalization to incorporate the psychological novel into SF. Similarly with Ballard's thesis that the Phallus will replace the spaceship in SF (or, as Mr Aldiss puts it of the New Wave characters, "they were generally anti-heroes, their destination more often bed than Mars"). Those who want the psychological novel can read it separately, while phalluses are a penny a dozen in modern literature, as we all know. Mr Aldiss inclines to the notion that it is a deficiency in most SF that it is sexless; these days it might be thought a welcome change. But for those who think otherwise, there are many works in the traditionalist style in which sex preponderates. For, after all, the phallus and the spaceship are not mutually exclusive.

Characterization, too, needs to be handled on different principles than those of the psychological novel. Above all, complex idio-syncrasy is seldom appropriate. Nor is too much introspection, or a total obsession with one's own personality and motives, very helpful. If we can find Candide or Figaro adequate to their purpose in holding our interest, we need not insist on their replacement by Vronsky. In SF, *a fortiori*. Mr Aldiss, once again switching to sanity at the last moment, quotes C. S. Lewis, always so sensible in these matters: "Gulliver is a commonplace little man and Alice a commonplace little girl. To tell how odd things struck odd people is to have an oddity too much."

Needless to say, Mr Aldiss does not spare us crotchets of the sociological type either. When it comes to fiction which is no more than barefaced preachifying, he agrees with Kingsley Amis's comment on *Men Like Gods*, that it has "a soporific whiff of left-wing crankiness". All the same, his own views are, generally speaking, those of the decent old Wellsian World State liberal. Why not?— except that it leads him to mark writers down to the degree that they do not serve these principles. He is quite straightforward about this, even admitting that he dislikes Heinlein's *Starship Troopers* on "ideological" grounds.

This attitude also leads, more excusably, to such things as a rather inflated view of Olaf Stapledon. *The Last And First Men* is certainly a remarkable and compelling book, and it is fair to say that it has been underestimated. Still, it can hardly be said to escape from a sort of Bloomsbury smugness. Its causes of the (then unrealized) wars of our time are of a triviality and silliness designed to show that governments and masses are simply not up to subtle and sensitive intellectuals. And though to some degree saved by imagination and inventiveness, the whole work suffers from a cult of sensitivity, a pale pantheist glow.

Again, it is a reductionism rather than anything of any helpful significance to point out (for example) that the Eloi and the Morlocks represent the rich and the poor of Victorian times. It is precisely because Wells has transformed that original piece of grit with the nacre of his imagination that there is any interest in the story. It lives, not as a reflection of any then contemporary society, but as a projection from it of some strange and distant development only barely reflecting it. (Nor does it contain any socially partisan preference for either of the two differently despicable races which have emerged.) And the terrible climax on the sluggish sea at the end of time removes us yet further from the dreary pack-drill of social significance. More basically, Wells might have said with Yeats:

> Players and painted stage took all my love
> And not those things that they were emblems of.

The autonomy of the story is everywhere apparent, the careful recreation of the credible: and *this* is the central and essential thing in all successful SF.

The call for "a song with a social significance" much predates current trendinesses. In hard SF, one already finds a notable tendency to scientism. In particular, as is to be found in certain parts of the scientific community proper, there is the inclination to accept allegedly scientific theories of society—the old notion of the rigorously "planned" economy, the superficial rationalism of premature World Staters. That is to say, it is wrongly felt that the rigours which proved successful in quantifiable areas of study can be transferred to areas where experience has by now shown that they do not readily apply. This has led, on occasion, to shallowly schematic presentations of futures and of other planets. And one notes, too, that the present editor of *Analog*—which remains the hardest of the SF magazines—is inclined to clutter his editorial pages with unsubstantiated and often provably false claims about the situation in the Soviet Union, seen (almost as in the days of Sidney Webb and Co here) as admirably planned and devoted to pure science as other countries are not. One also sometimes finds in hard SF—and it is perhaps connected with this sort of thing—writers like Mack Reynolds showing in fable after fable that Communist politics are just the same as ours really, with the opposite impression blamed on interested, or even war-mongering, propaganda.

On the other hand, many hard SF writers have a surprisingly clear grasp of the nature of politics and of power—A. E. van Vogt, for instance, in his accounts of struggles for power in strange futures; Heinlein, too, in spite of Mr Aldiss's claim that his grasp of politics is "frail"; and Asimov. But above all, the better and more imaginative writers are able to project wholly strange societies, with the motivations of alien species and of future humanity being taken, even in their physical basis, as different from our own. It might be argued, indeed, that the ability to conceive a totally alien society is a useful intellectual exercise when it comes to enabling us to distinguish between, rather than lazily seeing as identical, the great range of political and social orders already in existence on earth.

Moreover, excessive political commitment in the here and now leads to extravagant misunderstandings even at the political level itself. It would be hard to justify Mr Aldiss's extraordinary statement that, as compared with Jules Verne, Heinlein favours "conquest", and is possessed of "strong power drives half-rationalized into a right-wing political philosophy". Heinlein's story "The Long Watch" (printed in *The Best of Robert Heinlein*) is only one example of a thoroughly explicit libertarian stand against military dictatorship. And he is, in fact, an anti-totalitarian "hard" liberal.

Heinlein, whom Mr Aldiss nevertheless grants high status, is unfortunately not very well represented in *The Best of Robert Heinlein*—partly because he on the whole appears at his best at novel length. It would perhaps have been asking too much for the editor to use both of his fine stories on the time paradoxes. In fact, we get "All You Zombies", fast, obsessive, difficult, in which the hero is his own father and mother (owing to a sex change half way through), with its splendid ending: "I miss you dreadfully". One's preference, nevertheless, would have been for "By His Bootstraps", that careful, polished, intricate jewel of a story—which Mr Aldiss incomprehensibly represents as "a good humoured demonstration of the trouble that can come when the father figure is removed". This is so wide of the mark that one can only feel it is due to a misprint of the story title.

One of the various intrusions into true SF was the "committed" notion that it should merely reflect immediate present-day attitudes. Not, that is, the legitimate though not exclusive idea that some of it may dramatize present problems by making logical projections of these into the future, as Harry Harrison has done with over-population for instance. No, it is rather the insistence on narrowly contemporary tones, opinions and feelings. For it is surely a false notion that during a period of pacifist moods, SF should automatically and always celebrate the pacifist virtues. One might argue that it is just this sort of parochialism which SF has the power to release us from. Heinlein, though in his *A Stranger in a Strange Land* (much welcomed as a cult book on the campuses) he has written of a peaceful, highly-sexed Utopia-monger, has also in Mr Aldiss's bugbear, *Starship Troopers*, found it suitable to celebrate the military virtues. As at any period when people have forgotten that these were what saved them a generation ago, such an outlook is unpopular with some. But SF should have the scope to cover occasions unlike the present (or unlike the present as it exists in the minds of many readers).

Mr Aldiss rightly draws attention to the great variety to be found in the genre. It is true that he rather implies this to be a fairly new phenomenon, a product of the current intrusion of surrealism, inner space, the literature of extremity and all that. What is much more remarkable is that an immense variety of idiosyncrasy already existed. Kuttner and van Vogt, Asimov and Heinlein, Clarke and Sprague de Camp were all thoroughly differentiated in tone and theme. Mr Aldiss does these men justice, generally speaking (and it is particularly good to see justice, even if inadequate justice, done to the doyen of British SF, Eric Frank Russell). Yet, diverted by the New Wave irrelevancies, he is less than fair to more recent writers in the genuine tradition. Not so much that he does not to some degree appreciate Larry Niven, Jack Vance, James H. Schmitz. But he gives them the odd half-sentence, in a large catalogue of greatly inferior or justifiably unknown names, while the erratic Philip Dick (at his best a splendid imaginative talent, certainly) gets pages. It simply won't do to say of Schmitz no more than that he "wrote one of the best exoecology stories, *Grandpa*", when one considers vividly realized books like *A Tale of Two Clocks* and *The Demon Breed*.

When it comes to Poul Anderson, Mr Aldiss is not so much inadequate as positively unfair. Lumping him (another liberal) with Heinlein as a conquest-fan, he characterizes this versatile Hugo winner simply as a "sword among the stars man" with an "immense following". In fact, such a typical book as *Let The Spacemen Beware* is simply ecological, while even a comparatively swashbuckling work like *Star Fox* is concerned with liberation rather than conquest—while giving us a most sophisticated United Nations debate, and one of the most subtly depicted of all aliens in Cynbe ru Taren, Alerion's Intellect Master of the Garden of War.

Yet, though erratic, Mr Aldiss's appetite is in principle catholic. Except in his occasional fits he admits that a taste for Tolstoy does not exclude a taste for Tarzan, too. And he can qualify the austere "Wells is teaching us to think. Burroughs and his lesser imitators are teaching us not to think" with the saving concomitant "of course, Burroughs is teaching us to wonder."

Science fiction has become respectable. Much is now being written about it by the "effing Ph.D.s" in America intent either merely to get some sort of publication out with a view to promotion in the English departments, or at best to assemble material which they do not particularly care for with a view to illustrating one or other of the fashionable psychological or anthropological notions currently circulating on the campuses.

Mr Aldiss retains his amateur status, and this is greatly to his advantage. How disarming is his note on Frank Herbert's *Dune* novels: "your critic regrets that he is such a recent convert to them that he is unable to offer proper elucidation: that must wait for strength and a second volume". In such circumstances what Leavisite would hesitate to give us a limiting judgment?

Just as the bulk of Mr Aldiss's own SF, though undoubtedly tending to a certain baroqueness of style and theme, never descends into the disruption and unreason which he is prepared to admire in theory, so his natural good sense time and time again saves him in the present book. He provokes to assault, but on the whole evades the counter-stroke by cunning footwork. Though tempted by flashy substitutes, he usually prefers the interesting to the boring and the comprehensible to the meaningless, so that neither his dubious general conceptions nor his occasional particular lapses prevent this from being a good book and an interesting book. For it is pervaded not by them so much as by the more positive, if less easily illustrated, characteristics of excitement and devotion to his theme. If we have largely concentrated on his faults, it is because there was perhaps some danger that, as one of the few readable works on the subject, *Billion Year Spree* might have been taken by the general reader as gospel, rather than a highly idiosyncratic gallop of hobby-horses in all directions. In the end one is impressed and sympathetic. For above all Mr Aldiss is not respectable: he does not, in spite of occasional genuflections, really stand for the taming of science fiction and its submission to an ignorant academicism, of whatever type. If this is true even of Mr Aldiss, what a good augury for the genre as a whole.

13

RACE AND IQ

INHERITANCE AND THE WORKING OF THE MIND have no doubt fascinated and intrigued mankind since time immemorial. Allegiance to one's own group, whether family, village, country, race or even species, seems to be almost instinctive, and with this instinct comes its complement, racialism. Put these three ingredients, genetics, intelligence and race together, and we have one of the most emotionally charged topics of the day, linking science and social affairs.

The scientific background needed for a proper discussion of the extent to which genetic factors can contribute to racial differences in intelligence is complex and highly technical. Folklore on inheritance of behaviour and preconceived notions on racial differences are, however, so widespread as to make difficult technical discussions a poor answer to politically motivated arguments. The borderline between science and politics may be hard to define, but the scientist's responsibility to the public is most important and the need to explain the scientific issues as simply and as objectively as possible is paramount.

The possibility that racial differences in ability are inherited has been discussed sporadically for many years. Although writers before Galton and Mendel, such as Gobineau, could hardly have been on a firm scientific footing, some of the early human geneticists of this century were hardly less ardent in their claims. The most recent eruption of this issue has been due to Arthur Jensen, a Professor of Educational Psychology at the University of California, in Berkeley, closely followed by William Shockley, the Nobel-prize-winning physicist and co-inventor of the transistor in the United States, and the psychologist, Hans Eysenck, in this country. The hub of recent controversy is an article by Professor Jensen called "How much can we boost IQ and scholastic achievement?" published in 1969 in

---

ARTHUR R. JENSEN: *Genetics and Education*. 379 pp. £3.50. *Educability and Group Differences*. 407 pp. £3.90. Eyre Methuen.

the *Harvard Educational Review*. This article is the centrepiece of Jensen's book *Genetics and Education*, published in 1972, while his more recent book *Educability and Group Differences* is essentially a very much expanded version of the same article.

The essence of Professor Jensen's argument is as follows. He starts from the assumption that IQ, as determined from a variety of more or less standard tests, is a quantitative measure of some aspect of human intellectual behaviour. Genetic studies within the White population of the United States and of Europe, and in a few cases also within the Black population of the United States suggest that a major part of the variation in IQ, perhaps as much as 80 per cent, may be genetically determined. Some racial groups, notably American Whites and Blacks, differ very substantially in their distribution of IQ. The mean IQ of American Whites, for example, is in many studies 10 to 15 points higher than that of American Blacks. This is comparable to the standard deviation of the IQ distribution, 15 points, which means that about 95 per cent of the typical American White population, whose mean IQ is 100, have IQs between 70 and 130.

Professor Jensen's argument then continues with an assessment of possible environmental factors which can influence IQ, the conclusion being that none are known which could explain such a large racial difference. Thus, he would say, since IQ is largely genetically determined within Whites and Blacks, there is most likely to be a substantial genetic component for the race difference. The socio-political overtones to the argument derive from the idea that IQ, which does vary appreciably with socio-economic status as usually defined by sociologists and economists, is a major determinant of success in our society. So it is important to know how much of the race-IQ differences really are genetic.

Stated baldly in this way, Professor Jensen's not-so-novel thesis may sound simple and logical, but is it really so? Embedded in the argument are many scientific concepts and questions whose analysis does not flow so easily. What is IQ, and what does it really measure? How can one sort out the inherited and environmental components of a complex, quantitative character such as IQ? What is a race, and how can it be objectively defined? Can one extrapolate from knowledge of genetic components within a race to genetic contributions to the mean difference between two races? Is it really true that IQ is a major determinant of success in our society? And last, but by no means least, even if a genetic component of the race-IQ difference were established, what practical use could be made of this information?

Many scientific papers and books have been written on these questions, to which the interested reader must turn to judge Professor Jensen's arguments properly. Each of his two books concludes with a bibliography that covers much of the subject, including his own writings. Although the bibliographies are not annotated, Professor Jensen's comments on them throughout his books leave one in no doubt about which he would recommend, so it is possible to choose among them according to taste.

Intelligence must not be confused with IQ as measured by an IQ test. Over the years psychologists have devised many types of tests, various combinations of which are used in any given situation to assign an IQ to an individual. This single number can hardly be considered the complete definition of intelligence, though it presumably measures some component of intellectual ability. Psychologists seem to be divided into two schools, namely those, like Professor Jensen and Professor Eysenck, who believe that there is some basic property of the intellect called "g" (for general intelligence) that is measured by an IQ test, and those who believe that intelligence is multi-dimensional and cannot properly be measured by a single number. The geneticist can stand aside from these arguments and simply use the number given him by the IQ tester for his genetic analysis as he would for less contentious measurements such as height or weight. Thus, even though the real significance of the IQ measurement may be in doubt, the geneticist can still try to answer questions about the extent to which whatever it is that is measured by an IQ test has a genetic component.

A major key to Mendel's original success in uncovering the basic laws of inheritance was to work with simple, easily defined characteristics. The subsequent development of genetics and molecular biology, leading to the chemical definition of the gene in terms of the DNA molecule and of its mode of action through the specification of proteins, has similarly depended on working with precise, well-defined biochemical differences. Given a simple characteristic that is determined by one, or at most a small number, of identified genes, its patterns of inheritance can be unequivocally defined.

Many genes are known which cause severe mental retardation and so, of course, have a catastrophic effect on IQ. These genes, however, are quite rare and so have no substantial impact on the overall distribution of IQ in a population. IQ, as measured by an IQ test, must be a composite and complex character. Its expression is dependent on a combination of the effects of environmental factors and the products of many different genes, each of which has on average a very small effect on IQ and so cannot be individually recognized. As a result, one has to resort to complex statistical analyses to sort out the relative contributions of heredity and environment to IQ. The aim of these analyses is to assess the extent to which relatives tend to be more like each other than they are to unrelated or to more distantly related people.

The results are usually expressed in terms of a quantity called the *heritability* which, loosely speaking, measures the proportion of the variation in IQ that can be ascribed to genetic factors. If the heritability were 0 then all variation would be environmentally determined, while if it were 1 all variation would be genetic. The true answer nearly always lies somewhere between these two extremes. Heritability is not like a physical constant; it is a very rough and ready statistical measure of a property of a quantitative character, such as IQ, in a given population. As the population and its environment changes, so does the heritability.

Methods for measuring heritability were originally devised for plant and animal breeders, who can do controlled crosses at will and can, to a fair extent, control the environment in which their crosses are made. The human geneticist is in a much more difficult position since he can do neither of these things. Even worse, the most convenient types of relatives to study—namely parents, children, and siblings—are, for the most part, found in the same home environment. This means that one can never really be sure whether similarities between parents and children or between siblings are due to the genes or to the environment which they share. The only partly satisfactory answer to this problem is to study adopted children (especially identical twins separated at or near birth) who do not share a common environment with their immediate relatives.

Most studies on IQ, the majority in White American and European populations, suggest a substantial heritability for IQ, with estimates ranging from 40 to 80 per cent, according to the sources of the data and the types of analysis performed. This certainly suggests that there are substantial genetic differences in whatever it is that is measured by an IQ test.

Apart from identical twins all people look and behave differently. The outward physical features by which we distinguish people are paralleled by simple inherited differences such as blood types, which can be defined at a chemical level. One of the most striking results of population genetic studies over the past ten years is the demonstration of just how much genetic variation there is in human (and other) populations. Even the genetic differences one can test for now, which can be only a minute fraction of all those that exist, are enough to make the chances of finding two unrelated identical people much less than one in a million. It will not be long before it should be possible to give everyone a unique genetic typing in terms of well-defined, simply-inherited chemical characteristics.

The potential for genetic differences between individuals is staggering, even within a single family. The numbers of genetically different types of sperm or egg which any one individual could in principle produce is many million times more than the numbers of human beings who have ever lived. This extraordinary genetic uniqueness of the individual must apply to all his attributes, including intelligence, and is presumably the basis for the genetic component to IQ.

The existence of genetic variability in a character does not in any way imply the absence of environmental effects. Some of the most severe, simply determined genetic diseases, such as phenylketonuria, can be almost completely reversed by an appropriate, though complex, diet. There is, as might be expected, plenty of evidence for environmental factors affecting IQ. Among the most striking are the consistent, approximately five-point difference between the IQs of twins and single births, and the extraordinary IQ differences between adopted children and their biological parents which have been reported in some adoption studies.

Most IQ studies on different racial groups have used a sociological definition of race. In the United States, for example, children of mixed Black-White marriages would be classified as Black, though even the Black parent could be from a mixed marriage. Genetic studies, in fact, show that all American Blacks have, on average, between 10 and 30 per cent White ancestry. To a biologist a race is just a group of individuals or populations which form a recognizable subdivision of the species. The group is identified by the fact that individuals within it share characteristics which distinguish them, at least to some extent, from other groups. These characteristic differences are maintained because individuals belonging to a group are most likely to find their mates within the same group.

Traditionally, human races were defined using outwardly obvious features, such as skin colour, hair colour and texture, facial and other physical characteristics, whose inheritance is still poorly understood because of their relative complexity. Nowadays, geneticists agree that the only genuinely objective and biologically valid approach defining races is in terms of simply-inherited, well-defined differences, such as the blood types. The frequencies of the various genetic types often vary from one population to another, and it is these frequencies which are used to characterize population groups. The group is thus a statistical concept and the borderline between races may therefore be blurred and hard to define. Any particular genetic combination may be found in almost any race, but the frequency with which it is found will vary from one race to another. Some features, of course, such as skin colour, which show very marked differences between races, are most probably adaptations to different climatic conditions and resulting life-styles. But these are the exceptions rather than the rule. Studies of genetic differences within and between races show that at least 60 to 70 per cent of the overall genetic variation in man occurs *within* races.

Since race is a statistical concept, the question of a genetic component to a race difference is logically quite different from that of genetic differences between individuals. The difference between two races is a difference between *averages*, and reflects differences in the frequencies of genetic types in the two races. Individual genes vary in frequency between races for many reasons, some of them just due to chance, and some due to the action of natural selection in one form or another. Professor Jensen and others have argued that, since such differences in the frequencies of individual genes exist between races, why not also genetic differences in IQ? But IQ, as we have seen, must be determined by many genes. If there is to be an average genetic difference in IQ between two races, then there must be a tendency for those genes which on average increase IQ to accumulate in one of the races, and/or a similar tendency for those genes which decrease IQ to accumulate in the other race. This is only likely to happen simultaneously for a large number of genes if IQ is in some way itself subject to the action of natural selection. Nobody, however, has yet offered a convincing model for the way in which IQ test measurements, as we obtain them nowadays, could have been connected with increased ability to survive or to reproduce during the evolutionary divergence of the present-day races of man.

A number of geneticists have emphasized the fact that there is no logical connexion between genetic components determined within a race and the extent to which a difference between races has a genetic component. The environmental factors which distinguish two racial groups, such as the American Blacks and Whites, may be quite different from the environmental variations found within either race. Cultural differences between races may simply have no parallel within races. While Professor Jensen freely acknowledges that within-population heritability may have nothing to do with genetic differences between populations, having once acknowledged this point he seems to feel that he is entitled to ignore it. Nowhere in either of these two books does he discuss this absolutely crucial point with any conviction.

The two books are, apart from the prefaces, not easy reading even for the relatively initiated. There is much statistical methodology, which is not helped by a rather heavy style in which sentences such as the following are not uncommon:

Because variance in achievement test scores reflects a larger gain component at any given time than do intelligence tests, which are designed to reflect the consolidation factor, one should expect populations that differ on the average on intelligence measures to differ significantly less on achievement measures at any cross section in time, and this has been found to be the case.

Professor Jensen says in his preface to *Educability and Group Differences* that "it was written with mainly behavioural scientists and educational researchers in mind". Let us hope he is right in assuming that they have the appropriate background to deal with the material. Certainly, these are not books for the layman.

In *Genetics and Education* only the preface is new. In addition to the *Harvard Educational Review* article there is a long paper on "A Theory of Primary and Secondary Familial Mental Retardation"; three more or less technical papers on estimation of heritability, one of which even Professor Jensen would admit was clearly written before he had become fully conversant with the techniques of quantitative genetics; and a short ethical note on the right to do research on whatever one wants.

Professor Jensen's theory of mental retardation is that there are two hierarchical components to mental retardation, one connected with "associative ability" and the other with "cognitive ability". They are hierarchical in the sense that the first is required for the second, which latter is most closely related to IQ test performance. The two levels of ability are assumed to be under independent genetic control. While the theory may well have some heuristic value it seems a rather simple-minded dichotomy of a complex problem.

The preface to *Genetics and Education* recounts the history of the *Harvard Educational Review* article and the ensuing problems, criticisms and castigations which Professor Jensen has faced. Having related how he gave a copy of his article to a staff writer from the *US News and World Report*, Professor Jensen protests that he was surprised that his conclusions raised such a public furore. He should not have been surprised. After all, few scientists give advance copies of their articles to journalists! Communication of science to the public is an important and difficult task. The non-scientist is generally not trained to deal with scientific arguments based on hypothesis and counter-hypothesis. A reasoned and well-qualified scientific statement does not make good copy for newspaper headlines.

Professor Jensen rightly complains of the treatment which he and others, such as Professor Eysenck in this country, have received at the hands of those who, while protesting they champion freedom, do not seem to support freedom of speech. It is surely one of the great strengths of our society that it can tolerate open discussion of all shades of opinion, scientific, political or otherwise. Those who seek to silence Jensen, Eysenck or Shockley do not help the fight against racial prejudice which they claim to be supporting. Having said this, however, one is not tempted to compare Professor Jensen with Galileo or any other of the more famous scientific martyrs. His scientific contributions hardly seem to match those of these more illustrious scientific forebears. Nor have his writings been suppressed. The *New York Times Magazine* devoted virtually a whole issue to his ideas and the whole of his *Harvard Education Review* article was read into the *Congressional Record*.

Educability and Group Differences is entirely devoted to the problem of the inheritance of IQ and the genetic component to the race IQ difference. It is an extensive and well-documented review of the field. In addition to its complexity, however, the style has a fighting, defensive flavour to it, almost every chapter opening with a salvo against the environmentalists. To give a sample, the second chapter is entitled "Current Technical Misconceptions and Obfuscations", while in the preface we are admonished to "*think genetically*", as if to imply that all right-minded geneticists are bound to come to the same conclusions as Professor Jensen: "The problem on both sides is fundamentally a matter of ignorance, the cure for which is a proper education about genetics."

The book takes us painstakingly through definitions of heritability, statistical approaches to the analysis of data and all the various factors which might influence IQ. There is a touching faith in complex statistical procedures which Professor Jensen seems to believe give to IQ almost the same precision as a measurement made with a ruler or balance. Much emphasis is, of course, placed on the estimation of the heritability of IQ and on its high value, and also on the apparent inadequacy of environmental explanations for the race-IQ difference. Professor Jensen somehow appears to be obsessed with the need to find single factors in the environment which account for a substantial fraction of the 15 point IQ difference. Repeatedly we are told that some given effect—whether schooling, nutrition, socio-economic status or any one of at least a dozen different factors—can explain at most a very small fraction of the difference, perhaps only one or two IQ points. The precision of the data, in any case, hardly excludes effects of this order of magnitude. Surely he must appreciate that such effects are cumulative and may combine to explain the whole of the difference, even though individually any one of them has only a very small effect. Professor Jensen would no doubt argue that the effects he mentions are not independent, but he does not properly document the evidence for this. Others at least as well versed in these questions, such as Christopher Jencks, simply do not agree with Professor Jensen on these issues.

A few years ago W. F. Bodmer and L. L. Cavalli-Sforza, in assessing the evidence of genetic and environmental influences on race-IQ differences, came to the not very startling conclusion that current techniques and data could not resolve the question. While not excluding the possibility of a genetic component, it seemed that the IQ differences could be explained by environmental factors, many of which we still knew nothing about. There is no reason to believe that the situation has changed since then. Professor Jensen, however, seems to have changed his attitude. In his *Harvard Educational Review* article he wrote:

So all we are left with are various lines of evidence, no one of which is definitive alone, but which, viewed all together, make it a not unreasonable hypothesis that genetic factors are strongly implicated in the average Negro-White intelligence difference. The preponderance of the evidence is, in my opinion, less consistent with a strictly environmental hypothesis than with a genetic hypothesis, which of course does not exclude the influence of environment or its interaction with genetic factors.

The first paragraph of his summary of the final chapter of *Educability and Group Differences* ends with the following statement:

All the major facts would seem to be comprehended quite well by the hypothesis that something between one half and three fourths of the average IQ difference between American Negroes and Whites is attributable to genetic factors, and the remainder to environmental factors and their interaction with genetic differences.

Professor Jensen now seems sufficiently convinced of his hypothesis to quote a definite figure for how much of the race-IQ difference is genetic.

Is IQ really so significant as a determinant of success in our society? What action flows from the knowledge of the existence of a genetic component to the race-IQ difference? Nowhere in these two books are these two important questions properly answered.

The answer to the first question given by Professor Jencks in his very readable book *Inequality* (published in the United States in 1972 and by Allen Lane in this country late in 1973) is a resounding "no". (This book, incidentally, is a welcome complement, for some no doubt an antidote, to Professor Jensen's writings.) Many factors are involved in the determination of economic and social success in our society, and measured IQ is only a small part of the story. This does not deny the existence of very significant IQ differences between different socio-economic groups but only emphasizes that the genetic component to these differences must not be exaggerated.

As for the importance of the race-IQ difference, apart from policies of selective breeding, which Professor Jensen would not support, there are such questions as the relatively high number of Black as compared to White children in schools for the educationally subnormal. Quotas based on the racial distribution in the population might prevent Black children from receiving special educational programmes when they were really needed, and this is to be deplored. But the remedy has nothing to do with *genetic* differences between the races. The problem is the same whatever the cause of the differences. In a society which professes to be free of racial prejudice, people are to be treated as individuals and not as members of groups, however defined, whether by race, religion, sex, or otherwise. The only practical case for studying the genetic component of the race-IQ difference is to answer the question that has been raised, and this is a weak case indeed.

There is much to be learnt about human behaviour and the workings of the mind and we may be confident that much benefit may come from such further knowledge. This does not mean, however, that there are absolutely no limits to basic research, though on the whole it must be allowed a free rein. We do, after all, subscribe to ethical codes for medical and behavioural research on human subjects, and this clearly sets some limits to what is allowable. Planned support of major applied research endeavours is quite another matter, and here it is hard to accept the case put by Professor Shockley and to a lesser extent by Professor Jensen for crash programmes to answer such questions as the extent of the genetic component to the race-IQ difference. Professor Jensen is an able scientist and an effective research worker. It is a pity that he does not concentrate his talents in a more profitable area of research. Many interesting and important questions are raised by the existence of genetic variability for all aspects of human behaviour. For example, Professor Jensen himself makes the interesting point that, if individuals in a class learn at different speeds but all are taught at the same pace, then some will be bored, having finished a task early, while others may never have time to finish with one topic before moving on to the next. In this way, perhaps, the most basic skills will never be learnt by some, however much schooling they have had.

We do not at present know the answer to the question of how much is the genetic component to the race-IQ difference, we do not have the techniques at hand to find the answer and the answer does not seem to matter anyway. Let us then forget this question and move on to more important matters for our present-day society.

14

AGAINST CONFORMITY

(a) THE GAPING VOID

TO EMPHASIZE THE PRESENCE of pattern and purpose in Montherlant's life and writings (as he himself did) is to hold a sometimes difficult balance between impressions of external "fate" and of conscious contrivance on his own part. He committed suicide on September 21 1972 and we know that the *Equinoxe de septembre*—the title of a collection of essays published in 1938—had a special place in his private mythology. The act of suicide, too, was in itself a "Roman" gesture about which he had frequently written with admiration and approval (most recently and at most length in *Le treizième César* of 1970).

On the other hand, it was obviously not his choice, yet also a significant fact, that he was born on April 21 (in 1896), the traditional

---

(a) HENRY DE MONTHERLANT: *La Tragédie sans masque: Notes de théâtre.* 300 pp. 25 fr. *La Marée du soir: Carnets 1968–1971.* 174 pp. 19 fr. *Mais aimons-nous ceux que nous aimons?* 234 pp. 25 fr. *La Nouvelle Revue Française.* Février, 1973: *Henry de Montherlant.* 126 pp. 8 fr. Paris: Gallimard.

(b) HERMANN HESSE: *Die Kunst des Müssiggangs.* Kurze Prosa aus dem Nachlass. Edited by Volker Michels. 371 pp. Frankfurt: Suhrkamp. DM 7. *Strange News from Another Star and other tales.* Translated by Denver Lindley. 145 pp. Cape. £1.95 (paperback, 95p). *Gesammelte Briefe.* Volume 1: 1895–1921. Edited by Ursula and Volker Michels with Heiner Hesse. 626 pp. Frankfurt: Suhrkamp. DM 40. *Wandering.* Translated by James Wright. 109 pp. Cape. £1.60. *If the War Goes On. Reflections on War and Politics.* Translated by Ralph Manheim. 185 pp. Cape. £2.25. *Die Erzählungen.* Volume 1: 509 pp. Volume 2: 506 pp. Frankfurt: Suhrkamp. DM 34 the set. *Knulp. Three Tales from the Life of Knulp* Translated by Ralph Manheim. 113 pp. Cape. £1.40 (paperback, £1.10).

VOLKER MICHELS (Editor): *Materialien zu Hermann Hesses "Der Steppenwolf".* 417 pp. Frankfurt: Suhrkamp. DM 6.

HERMANN HESSE and ROMAIN ROLLAND: *D'une rive à l'autre. Correspondance, fragments du journal, et textes divers.* Edited by Pierre Grappin. 185 pp. Paris: Albin Michel. 18 fr.

Hermann Hesse-Karl Kerényi: Briefwechsel aus der Nähe. Edited by Magda Kerényi. 204 pp. Munich: Langen-Müller. DM 16.80.

BERNHARD ZELLER: *Hermann Hesse. An Illustrated Biography.* Translated by Mark Hollebone. 176 pp. Peter Owen. £2.50.

date of the founding of Rome—as he himself tells us. This date gives additional shape to his life—a "Roman" birth and a "Roman" death. Again, there is an appropriateness which comes close to conscious planning in the titles of the first and last works which he published during his lifetime: *La Relève du matin* (1920) and *La Marée du soir* (1972). But it was patterning beyond his personal control which ordained that he should be wounded, during the Second World War, at a place less than forty miles from where he had also been wounded, and invalided out of the army, during the First World War. These are only a few of many possible examples. They suggest that his life had a significance distinctively and curiously compounded of both spontaneity and volition.

Montherlant was, above all, a man of contrasts and even paradoxes. Not the least important aspect of his life and thought has to do with the contrast between the presence and cultivation of those private patterns just touched on, and his strong sense of lack of meaning or purpose in the general human predicament.

In *La Tragédie sans masque* (1972) he combines purpose and meaninglessness in a tragic pattern when he writes, in what is not simply the striking of a theatrical attitude, of "la destinée tragique que j'ai frôlée tant de fois, pour laquelle je suis fait, qui est digne de moi et dont je suis digne, et que j'aime". The opening essay of *Service inutile* (1935) is significantly entitled "Chevalerie du néant" and Montherlant, having quoted Jeremiah—"I beheld the earth, and, lo, it was without form, and void: and the heavens, and they had no light"—adds a comment which explains the coexistence in his thought of private purpose and public nullity: "Je n'ai que l'idée que je me fais de moi pour me soutenir sur les mers du néant." He used his life and writings as a means of keeping the void at bay. In the end, his defence was to prove fragile and vulnerable.

Inevitably, Montherlant's suicide is touched on by several contributors to the very interesting collection of *hommages* published in the February issue of the *Nouvelle Revue Française*. Jean d'Ormesson takes the direct and relatively simple view that Montherlant ended his life because he could no longer live with himself in terms of old age and the threat of total blindness. There is some evidence to support this view in *La Marée du soir*. The accident of 1968 which blinded Montherlant in one eye also involved a fracture of the ethmoid bone and he feared consequent brain damage. Also, he came close to M d'Ormesson's view a few pages later when he admitted that, had the accident blinded him totally, he would certainly have taken his life.

Nevertheless, he did not become blind, and the negative nature of a suicide committed in view of some possible eventuality is out of keeping with Montherlant's positive personality. In fact, in the same collection of essays, Jacques Borel, Henri Petit and others argue—perhaps more convincingly—that he had become increasingly sickened by the vulgar mediocrity of much contemporary life and that suicide was, in any case, the logical consequence of his lifelong preoccupation with nihilism and death.

On the first of these two points, we know that Montherlant felt contempt for many aspects of the modern world, "un monde chaque jour plus ignoble". In *La Marée du soir* he writes of "une société qui ne mérite même pas la peine qu'on soit insolent avec elle" and attacks many fashionable intellectual postures, including a passion for denigrating what is simply good in order the more easily to glorify what is evil. There is even a very unexpected passage in which he praises the concept of the "good deed", familiar to Boy Scouts, and says: "La 'bonne action' ... ridiculisée de nos jours par les Français, et presque objet de haine pour nombre d'entre eux, est un des éléments essentiels d'une civilisation qui se respecte, où part doit être donnée au cœur comme à l'intelligence, aux instincts, et au besoin de bonheur." Where France in particular is concerned, he quotes (for the fourth or fifth time in his writings) Lyautey's "Je meurs *de* la France" and adds:

Je regrette que ces mots de Lyautey ne soient pas ceux sur lesquels se terminent non seulement ces Carnets, mais toute mon œuvre. Néanmoins, même si le hasard fait que mon œuvre s'arrête pour toujours sur d'autres mots, ce sont ceux-là qui, moralement, en auront été les derniers.

At a more general level, Montherlant's nihilism was obvious and all-pervasive. If a man were to catch a glimpse of the truth about human life, he said, there would be nothing for him to do but to lie down, like a donkey in the desert, and wait for the sand to bury him. A related comment is made about the mad queen Jeanne, in the play *Le Cardinal d'Espagne* (and Montherlant admitted that she contained much of himself): "Elle voit l'évidence, et c'est pourquoi elle est folle." He did not expect such statements to bring him popularity and says, somewhat wryly, that a writer who uncovers the world and reveals it as it really is will rarely be forgiven by his readers.

In a sense, of course, this response to the general question of the human condition only served to intensify Montherlant's private anguish. And his private anguish ensured that his metaphysical suffering was no mere intellectualized posture. To this extent M d'Ormesson is right to emphasize his unease within his own skin. A passage from *Aux Fontaines du désir*, a major collection of essays published as long ago as 1927, clearly expresses the priority of personal anguish over generalized nihilism:

J'ai tout, tout m'échappe, et cette équivalence affreuse n'est pas dans le monde mais dans moi, et il n'y a aucun espoir que je devienne autre, que tout de moi soit métamorphosé jusqu'au tréfonds. . . . Ah! que le temps, que j'ai "tué" me tue à mon tour, mais non pas de ces morts où on revit, où on ressuscite . . . mais de la plus morte mort, dissous dans le néant sans souvenir et sans rêves, où tout de bon enfin j'en aie fini avec moi-même.

It is not surprising that Montherlant finally committed suicide. It is not surprising, given his integrity, that he should have acted in the end in accordance with the central preoccupation of his own writings. If we are surprised, it can only be because we no longer take writers seriously (having found that they do not take themselves seriously) and are startled if they act upon their own words.

The "équivalence affreuse" to which Montherlant refers is probably the ultimate basis of his doctrine of *alternance* and the source of many of his apparently paradoxical positions. His sense of the final nullity of everything encouraged him to explore the contrasting faiths by which men live—hedonism and asceticism, instinct and rationality, Roman pride and Christian humility—with that curiously dispassionate intensity which distinguished him among his contemporaries. In a world of increasing intellectual monism, Montherlant was an aggressive dualist—even a Manichaean ("Quoi que ce soit ne cesse d'être faux que lorsqu'on affirme le contraire"). When his fellow-writers of the interwar period moved closer to a single ideological position—fascism or communism—he exercised an often corrosive intelligence in the service of non-commitment.

After the Second World War ideological polarization increased in a number of ways (from the Cold War to Vietnam) and his exposure of the inadequacies of conflicting doctrines—political, social, ethical—proved an irritant to many. He became one of the most highly praised and widely abused of French writers. He stirred in his readers latent contradictions which many of them had worked hard to suppress. He posed insoluble problems to an age in a desperate hurry for easy answers. Jean Grosjean puts the point neatly in the *Nouvelle Revue Française*: "Montherlant juxtapose deux serrures sans donner de passe-partout."

The result is that Montherlant managed to annoy, and even outrage, a large number of readers of quite contrasting viewpoints and persuasions ("Je ne suis et n'ai jamais été un consolateur"). Some, approving his praise of action, are irritated by the fact that he also praised a life of contemplation. Others have been attracted by his sympathy with gentleness only to be repulsed by his fascination with violence. His celebration of Greek and Roman paganism has disconcerted admirers of his deep understanding of Jansenist austerity and purity.

This sense of the multiplicity of truth, and of its contradictory nature, was succinctly put in *L'Équinoxe de septembre* where he insisted that two opposing doctrines are simply deviations from a common truth. He saw confirmation of this view in the fact that the orthodoxy of one century has so often grown out of the heresy of the century which preceded it. In an age when scepticism itself is fast becoming a rigid dogma for many, Montherlant puts the case for an "open" approach to our experience:

Celui qui dit: "Je ne sais pas", emploie à la fois son intelligence, par laquelle il a connu qu'il ne savait pas (ce qui s'appelle *savoir*), sa conscience, par laquelle il décide que, ne sachant pas, il ne jouera pas le personnage de celui qui sait (ce qui serait charlatanisme, au sens propre du mot), et enfin son courage, en s'exposant, à ce qu'une telle réserve le fasse traiter de lâche par les sectaires, d'ignorant par les doctes, et, par les frivoles, d'idiot. Sûrement, le monde étant ce qu'il est, l'attitude qui fait contre lui cette coalition a chance d'être bonne.

An interesting example of Montherlant's "open scepticism" is to be found in his attitude to religion generally, and Christianity in particular. There is much in his writings (particularly in the essays of *Le Solstice de juin* of 1941) to suggest a Nietzschean contempt for Christianity as a servile and debilitating "slave morality"—the source of what is most reprehensible in bourgeois ethics. On the other hand, he was always deeply interested in the more austere forms of Catholicism, wrote sympathetically on the subject of Christian intransigence ("le christianisme est une affaire rigoureuse"), and countered the pagan vein in his writings (expressed in *Les Olympiques, Aux Fontaines du désir, La Petite Infante de Castille, Le Solstice de juin*) with what he called his "trilogie catholique"

(*Le Maître de Santiago*, *La Ville dont le prince est un enfant* and *Port-Royal*).

In the course of conversation about these contrasting aspects of his work, Montherlant attempted to reduce their contradictoriness by arguing that his response to both paganism and Christianity was essentially poetic. About Christianity in particular he wrote, in the relatively little-known *Pour une vierge noire*, that he took from Catholicism whatever happened to suit his spiritual and poetic life; he described this as making use of Catholicism in a fundamentally human way. Given these views, his last published comments on the "Catholic" plays, in *La Tragédie sans masque*, are of particular interest. They arise from the question put to him on more than one occasion: "Pourquoi écrivez-vous si obstinément des pièces à sujet catholique, puisque vous n'avez pas la foi?"

In replying to this question, Montherlant begins by emphasizing how strong has been his feeling, since early manhood, for the "absurdité" of almost everything. This sense of the vanity of human existence, memorably declared in the book of Ecclesiastes, is an essential element in Christianity and thus a direct link with Christian thought from Montherlant's point of view. Without compromising in any way his fundamental lack of faith, he writes: "Je partage avec le chrétien tout ce qu'il rejette", and adds: "Moi, incroyant, je passe de là à exalter le catholicisme dans des œuvres de fiction littéraires. Le 'mépris du monde' débouche ici dans un surcroît de foi, là dans une expression artistique de la religion qui est fondée sur ce mépris."

Having emphasized his emotional and intellectual sympathy for this world-rejecting aspect of Christianity, Montherlant goes on to argue, in more general terms, in defence of his religious plays and the religious elements in his other writings. He points out that any literary artist both needs and wants to portray, in novels or plays, characters who express very different ideas and beliefs from his own. A writer must often call on his best resources of imagination, intelligence and human sympathy in order to portray a murderer, a shopkeeper, a child, etc, in one of his works. Why should not Montherlant, a writer without faith, create imaginative works in which Christian characters and persons of deep spirituality appear? The question is not whether the author himself is a Christian, but whether his Christian characters are humanly convincing to believers and non-believers alike.

This imaginative sympathy with those whose views he does not necessarily share goes a long way towards explaining Montherlant's capacity for presenting apparently contradictory positions with equal persuasiveness. It explains much of the intellectual—and poetic—power inherent in the great "debating scenes" of some of his best plays. It also means, within Catholicism as such, that he was able to convey contrasting viewpoints with the same conviction. It is significant that, in a comment on *Port-Royal* reported by Philippe de Saint-Robert in 1969, he described himself as sympathizing "all the way" with the recalcitrant Jansenist nuns. But he was also careful to add that, had he been Archbishop of Paris in 1664, he would have considered it his duty to harry them in much the way that Péréfixe did. In her contribution to the Montherlant number of the *Nouvelle Revue Française*, Dominique Descotes pays him a justified tribute when she writes: "Montherlant a su éblouir les chrétiens par une image idéale d'eux-mêmes, qu'ils seraient bien incapables de soutenir."

Few writers have been more active than Montherlant in expounding and defending their own works. The Pléiade edition of his plays contains a substantial amount of authorial comment and *La Tragédie sans masque*, though it includes essays on plays written after the original Pléiade collection, does not add a lot that is new. In a sense we are faced here with a further paradox on the part of a writer who, in another mood, expressed his aim as "écrire dans la conviction profonde que son œuvre n'a pas d'importance". In *La Tragédie sans masque* he points—in self-justification— to the commentaries on their own plays of Corneille, Dumas *fils*, Strindberg, and others, and adds, a trifle coyly, concerning his own dramas: "Je leur ai porté l'amour qu'une mère porte à ses enfants, y compris peut-être la classique surestimation maternelle de leurs mérites." In fact, like a number of other writers, he is one of the most discerning critics of his work and it is difficult to discuss his plays individually without referring to some of his own acute and beautifully phrased judgments.

Perhaps the most interesting part of *La Tragédie sans masque* is that in which Montherlant defends his "costume tragedies" against the charge (made by Valéry among others) that they are dated and that "il y a trop de *Sire*, de *Seigneur* et de révérences". One knows that he was much concerned with historical authenticity and rightly located this authenticity as much in the language of his characters as in appearance. As a result, they speak a language and express ideas sometimes quite alien to a modern audience.

Montherlant quotes two examples of reported remarks, made by Richelieu and Louis XIII respectively. In reply to pleas for mercy on behalf of the Duc de Montmorency who had been condemned to death for insurrection, the former said: "Il est trop grand pour que je puisse le sauver"; and the latter: "Je ne serais pas roi si j'avais les sentiments d'un particulier." Montherlant is no doubt right to insist that these very striking phrases came naturally to the two speakers in question. He is on less sure ground when he adds that if the significance of such remarks, incorporated in a play, goes over the heads of the audience, this is their fault and not the author's.

Nevertheless, it remains true that plays such as *La Reine morte*, *Le Maître de Santiago*, *Port-Royal* and *Le Cardinal d'Espagne* have had an enormous success in the theatre despite the historical distance of their setting. If they have not always been thoroughly understood, they have been widely admired and greatly applauded. Indeed, interestingly enough, it is a play like *L'Exil*, set at a much shorter historical distance (the First World War), which Montherlant found to be most dated from an audience's point of view. In fact, he refused to allow *L'Exil* to be performed in Paris because various "period" aspects, essential to its meaning, would appear ridiculous to present-day theatregoers. These aspects include the young hero's snobbery (both of dress and ideas) and his patriotic sentiments (even though these are undermined in the course of the play).

If Montherlant is right, the case of *L'Exil* raises interesting questions concerning how far back in time historical plays need to be set before they are acceptable to an average audience. His own costume tragedies are set in the sixteenth and seventeenth centuries and have proved immensely popular with a certain type of audience, despite his refusal to adapt their speech and sensibilities to those of twentieth-century "swingers".

It is still true, of course, that a number of other plays (*L'Exil, Fils de personne, Celles qu'on prend dans ses bras, La Ville dont le prince est un enfant*) are not historical. Nevertheless, they are set in the period of Montherlant's early manhood rather than in the present. His attitude to the present was in many ways a consistently negative one. This position—which some will ascribe to the exhausted inflexibility of an elderly sceptic cherishing delusions of Roman grandeur—takes the form of a certain preoccupation with contemporary youth in both *La Tragédie sans masque* and *La Marée du soir*. It is not surprising that a man, writing in his middle seventies, should be puzzled, or at least ironic, in his comments on the rising generation. Montherlant refers more than once to the generation gap ("le divorce des générations") and quotes with what seems like approval a statement to the effect that a man of fifty should not concern himself with youth as the gap between them becomes too great.

This is hardly consistent, however, with his claim in *La Marée du soir* that present-day youth is being exploited by its elders (since this implies that the previous generation bears some responsibility for the attitudes and behaviour of the present one). Referring to the many letters which he received from young people, he wrote in 1971:

Ce sont des lettres de garçons de dix-huit à vingt-deux ou vingt-quatre ans, désespérés. On leur a retiré toutes leurs raisons de vivre; depuis combien d'années? Ni instruits, ni élevés, toujours bornés, toujours exploités, toujours dirigés en tout vers le pire, et le meilleur à leurs yeux discrédité. Et eux-mêmes sans défense, bien sûr, fors quelques-uns.

This is certainly not unsympathetic, but neither is it "progressive". *La Marée du soir* is not progressive in the fashionable sense of the term, and indeed Montherlant refers, more than once, to the stupidity of an allegedly progressive "moving with the times". He quotes from Péguy: "On ne saura jamais ce que la peur de ne pas paraître assez avancé aura fait commettre de lâchetés à nous Français." There exist, of course, a cowardice and hypocrisy in certain inflexible and illiberal attitudes and they must be deplored. But not the least valuable aspect of *La Marée du soir* is its several reminders, echoing the closing pages of *Le treizième César*, that cowardice and hypocrisy can also be uncomfortably prominent elements in certain forms of fashionably liberal thinking.

Montherlant's first posthumous publication, *Mais aimons-nous ceux que nous aimons?*, has now appeared. (He had listed, in a note of May 25, 1971, the six completed manuscripts which he then regarded as constituting his only authentic extant work.) This book covers the crucial period of Montherlant's early manhood during the years 1920–25. Inevitably, this means that it deals, among other things, with the revelation of sport after the First World War and with the resumption of his bull-fighting activities.

It also discusses youth, the youth of the *après-guerre*, and a number of comments (e g, "Peyrony, très en avance sur son temps, détestait les adultes") suggest fundamental similarities between the young people of the 1920s and those of the 1970s.

The essays in the book are grouped, in fact, around three of his young companions of the time. Jacques Peyrony is a boy whom Montherlant met when he joined an athletic club in Paris. He figures importantly in *Les Olympiques*. Douce is a girl whom he met in the street when she was eighteen, with whom he had a nine-year-long affair, and whom he describes as "charmante, mais sans piquant". Finally, there is Dominique S . . ., the young woman athlete who was the model for Dominique in *Le Songe* and with whom he had the most complicated and interesting relationship of the three. All three broke off their friendship with him—the two women in a positive way and Peyrony more or less by default. This prompts Montherlant to meditate, in retrospect, on the nature of friendship and love, and to ask the question (a quotation from Maurice Clavel) which provides the title of the book.

In *Mais aimons-nous ceux que nous aimons?* we are back in the unmistakable atmosphere of Montherlant's early works. The themes of war, death, love, friendship, sport, bull-fighting—and the Roman virtues of courage, magnanimity and severity—are woven together with a distinctive blend of irony and idealism. As so often, Montherlant's irony leads to considerable human insight: "J'étais familier avec ces mouvements tendres, très sincères, qu'on a pour une femme qu'on n'aime pas." And his idealism extends to sport so that he writes: "Le sport jouait pour moi le rôle d'une foi, dont je ne devais pas transgresser les préceptes."

This mixture of idealism and ironical insight presides over Montherlant's relationship with Dominique. As he watches her prowess as sprinter, hurdler and high-jumper, he is deeply moved both by the aesthetic perfection of her style and by what he assumes to be the virginal purity of her body. He accepts that there is a sense in which "culture physique égale culture morale" since integrity, self-discipline, club solidarity and respect for opponents are all virtues which link sport with what he regards as the highest moral values. But he also encourages in Dominique, through his fictional transposition of her character in passages from *Le Songe* and *Les Olympiques* which he gives her to read, a sexual self-awareness which seems to undermine her single-minded dedication to sport. This new awareness coincides with a sudden loss of form on her part and Montherlant's ideal image is further flawed by the fact that he sees her "bump" a fellow-competitor in a sprint. When they do eventually make love, it also appears that she is not the virgin he thought.

While this, in itself, is a matter of indifference to him, it brings the Proustian awareness that he had fallen in love more with a creation of his own mind than with an actual human being.

Much of the book is taken up with a detailed and fascinating analytical account of the relationships that develop between Montherlant and his friends. (There is also a reference to his friendship with the Spanish matador Belmonte who, incidentally, shot himself a few days before his seventieth birthday because he could not accept old age.) Montherlant concludes that our affection or love for others—and theirs for us—is something essentially fitful and capricious. We are aware of this in our hearts, he says, but we conceal our awareness under illusions of permanence. As a result, he sees intimate human relations as compounded of clear-sightedness and illusions, and he holds that both these attitudes—and particularly their co-existence—do honour to human beings. He refers again to his three *camarades* and ends on a characteristic note of tolerant disillusion:

De ces trois êtres aucun ne m'aimait; mais les aimais-je? "Aimons-nous ceux que nous aimons?" (Nous, du moins, les hommes). Nous demandons aux autres de nous donner un amour que nous ne leur donnons pas. Les miens s'évanouissaient quand ils avaient donné ce qu'ils avaient à donner, et c'était peut-être le mieux ainsi. Rien à dire si on sait bien d'avance que tout est perdu, soi compris.

(b) THE HESSE CULT

AT FIRST GLANCE *Die Kunst des Müssiggangs*—"The Art of Indolence"—taken from the title of an early essay by Hermann Hesse, looks like a singularly inappropriate heading for a volume by a writer who, during a literary career of sixty years, turned out several hundred essays, more than 3,000 book reviews, well over 35,000 letters, and whose collected works, in the 1970 German edition, fill twelve substantial volumes. One is inclined to agree with Hesse's later pronouncement: "Indolence is a virtue that I have always regarded with awe, but that I have never mastered." As new volumes of previously unpublished or uncollected letters, essays, reviews, and other material appear—thanks mainly to the efforts of Hesse's son, Heiner Hesse, his publisher, Siegfried Unseld, and his editor, Volker Michels—the quantity and variety must astonish even specialists who had some inkling of its extent.

Yet in a larger sense "indolence" helps to explain the appeal of this author, who has now been translated into thirty-five languages, who is acclaimed as a cult-hero in Latin America and as the most popular European writer in Japan, and whose works have sold more than 6 million copies in the United States. For the eighty-three short pieces of *Die Kunst des Müssiggangs*—a sampling of non-political essays that have not previously appeared in book form—expose the principal themes that have promoted Hesse, in the ten years since his death, from an underground cult figure to a celebrity whose name is exploited to advertise products ranging from records and greeting cards to educational tours.

To a surprising extent Hesse's themes are anticipated in the title-essay of 1904. Arguing that industry and technology have produced a culturally bankrupt age which exerts ruthless pressure for conformity, Hesse proclaims individual freedom and cultivation of the personality as man's highest goals, and points to the leisure of the East (as exemplified in *The Arabian Nights*) as a counter-example to the hectic pace of Western society. In subsequent pieces Hesse uses the most varied occasions—travels in Italy and India, early flights in zeppelins and aeroplanes, observations of trees and clouds, reflections on books and carpets—to elaborate this underlying theme. "Indolence" means rejection of a society which has produced water and air pollution, traffic congestion, dehumanization of the individual, blind nationalism, and war. It implies leisure to devote oneself to culture and nature, time to listen to music and one's fellow men, and patience to cultivate the mellifluous lucidity that characterizes Hesse's prose. These occasional pieces, half of which were written more than fifty years ago, resemble a checklist of the problems and goals which concern the disaffected young of the 1970s.

Most readers who have discovered in Hesse's works an expression of their anxieties and ideal became acquainted with him through his novels, not through his essays, which are little known in Germany and less abroad. With his *Materialien zu Hermann Hesses "Der Steppenwolf"*—the first in a series that is to include *Demian*, *Siddhartha*, and *Das Glasperlenspiel*—Volker Michels has provided an excellent introduction to the genesis and impact of one of Hesse's best-known novels. The volume begins with a well-conceived mosaic of letters, essays, poems, photographs, and other material documenting the composition of *Steppenwolf*. The second part presents twenty-two reviews and essays reflecting its reception from 1927 to the present.

From the beginning, Hesse's novel evoked admiration and understanding among thoughtful German critics. The public reception,
however, has been mixed. Not counting his early vogue as a somewhat anodyne *littérateur*, Hesse enjoyed two waves of popularity
among young Germans disenchanted with the wages of a military-
industrial society—immediately after each of the World Wars.
But those successes, paradoxically, account in large measure for the
lack of interest in Germany today. Many young Germans refuse
to believe that an author revered by their parents and grandparents
can possibly have anything to say to them. And most of them refuse
to undermine this conviction by actually reading his works, despite
the seal of approval by the Marxist critic Hans Mayer and the *enfant
terrible* of contemporary German letters, Peter Handke.

In the United States, despite notable scholarly-critical activity
beginning with Hesse's Nobel Prize in 1946, there was no public
response for decades. In 1952 an American publisher notified Hesse
that his works had to be remaindered because of insufficient demand.
But by 1962, just as postwar German interest had reached its low
point and as *The New York Times* obituary asserted that his works
were "largely unapproachable" for American readers, Hesse had
begun to attract a wider following. In a contribution written
especially for *Materialien*, Fred Haines (the script-writer for a version
of *Steppenwolf* currently being filmed) recalls that Hesse was discovered in the United States by the Beat Generation, an early wave
of the counter-culture, who coopted him as a hitherto unknown
forerunner of their obsession with Oriental mysticism and psychedelic experience and who detected in him a proponent of their
own lifestyle.

Of the various authors represented in *Materialien*, probably none
had a greater public impact, for better or worse, than Colin Wilson
and Timothy Leary. Mr Wilson's *The Outsider* (1956) introduced
Hesse's name to a potentially receptive audience of disaffected youth
and proclaimed that, as an example of romantic alienation, "Hesse's
achievement can hardly be matched in modern literature". To back
up his statement Mr Wilson provided lengthy summaries of Hesse's
principal novels, which at that time were not easily available. Dr
Leary, in *The Psychedelic Review* (1963), agreed that Hesse is "one
of the great writers of our time"; but he touted him above all as
"the master guide to the psychedelic experience and its applications".
Mr Wilson's view of Hesse was oversimplified—and perhaps for

that very reason effective publicity. Dr Leary was simply wrong. But their impassioned pieces were heady stuff to a generation just beginning to turn on to pot and the *I Ching* and to embark on the quest for transcendental illumination in their disenchantment with a consumer society and the Vietnam war.

The essays in *Materialien* fail to suggest the extent of the Hesse craze in the United States today. By the late 1960s Hesse was no longer simply Saint Hesse among the Hippies, but an American pop hero. A rock group known as "Steppenwolf", and clad in costumes suggesting the figures of that novel, spread Hesse's name (if not his works) across the continent. Many university communities saw student hangouts spring up with such names as Steppenwolf (Berkeley), Siddhartha's Pad (Bloomington, Indiana), or Demian's Rathskeller (Princeton). Magazines like *Mademoiselle* and *Seventeen* printed articles by and about Hesse. The Hallmark Company brought out greeting cards bearing "Words of Love" from *Siddhartha* and that novel was brilliantly parodied—parody, of course, pre- supposes familiarity—in *The New Yorker* (Roger Angell's "Sad Arthur"). *National Lampoon* featured a "classy comics" version of *Siddhartha*, while Snoopy the Dog—in Charles Schulz's "Peanuts", the leading comic strip of the 1960s—was reading Hesse. The cult was noted and appraised by *Time, Life, Look, The Saturday Review,* and other witnesses of popular culture.

Far from fading, the Hesse fad has reached new heights since 1972. One young American producer has just completed (in India) a film version of *Siddhartha*; another is filming *Steppenwolf* in Europe; and an American composer is completing an opera based on the same novel. A summer seminar in Switzerland offers instruction in Hesse and Jung along with lessons in yoga and sidetrips to Florence. Books are being produced in response to popular demand: John D. Simon's "critical commentary" on *Steppenwolf* in "Monarch Notes"; Robert H. Farquharson's *Outline of the Works of Hermann Hesse*; Edwin F. Casebeer's monograph on Hesse in a series called "Writers for the Seventies"; and a collection of critical essays on Hesse in the "Twentieth-Century Views" series.

The essays reprinted in *Materialien* are misleading in one respect: from early reviews by Oskar Loerke and Stefan Zweig down to recent evaluations by Hans Mayer and Peter Weiss, they are wholly favour- able. Yet the novel came in for its share of censure from the start. Hesse reacted to this mixed reception in one of his most sardonic stories, "Vom Steppenwolf" (1928), also included in *Materialien*. Public opinion, we learn, is sharply divided over the *cause célèbre* of Harry, the Steppenwolf. One party, charging that he ridicules accepted values and corrupts the young, insists that the beast ought to be destroyed. A more liberal group, while acknowledging the threat, pleads that even a Steppenwolf has a right to existence, since he embodies feelings that reside in all men. It is even proposed that an Association of Steppenwolves should be established. Taking advantage of public interest, the owner of a menagerie engages Harry for a guest appearance. On opening day three people step up to Harry's cage. The twelve-year-old boy asserts dogmatically that a cage is the only place for such a beast: perhaps he might eventually be trained for some useful task; but in the meantime he should not be permitted to run around free. His sister, fascinated by the glittering teeth but repelled by the unkempt pelt, regards Harry with more ambivalent emotions. Yet, sensing that the beast has taken a fancy to her, she responds to his blandishments. Their governess interprets the meaning of Harry's behaviour for her young wards. Convinced that she nurtures the heart of a Steppenwolf in her own breast, she is tempted to invite Harry to tea, if only he would become a bit more civilized. Seeing that Harry permits the girl to rub his nose, the governess unwraps a tiny chocolate heart to give him as a token of her sisterly esteem. The wolf bites her hand. The wrathful governess sues the menagerie, but the owner, pointing out that there were adequate warnings against feeding the animals, is confident that he will win the case. The publicity attracts even larger crowds.

"Vom Steppenwolf" was written to allegorize the reception of Hesse's works in Germany forty-five years ago. But it provides a remarkably accurate paradigm of the situation in the United States today. Opinion is of course still divided. To a notable degree Hesse's detractors are still united by their apprehensions regarding his pernicious influence on the young, which Jeffrey L. Sammons in *The Yale Review* has labelled "the Germanization of American youth". George Steiner, in *The New Yorker*, is dismayed because "Hesse seems to offer ecstasy and transcendence on the easy-payment plan" to a generation of youth who have "read little and compared less". Frank Trippett, a senior editor of the (now defunct) mass-circulation magazine *Look*, was speaking for Hesse's American fans when he rejected these elitist critics, "the condescending ones who found Hesse too slight for their brand of maturity". Mr Trippett went on to claim that even without a European cultural background he found himself admirably prepared to cope with the spiritual climate of Hesse's fictional world, for he grew up in an equally mysterious realm—"in the remote and mystical and obscure and impenetrable American South", where one can encounter "Steppenwolf in the sorghum patch".

If Hesse's story anticipated the continuing polarization of critical voices, surely not even in his wildest fantasies did that professional non-joiner ever dream that his other prediction would fulfil itself: the organized alienation, the institutionalized individualism of an Association of Steppenwolves. Yet this year an international Hermann Hesse Society is being incorporated in New York, as one can learn from the *News Notes* that it circulates. Life has a way of imitating art—even in the form of parody.

If all the principal figures of Hesse's allegory have their equivalent in the present, then the enterprising menagerie owner, who puts Harry on display and profits from the controversy, can be none other than Hesse's publishers—in Germany and abroad. But there is yet another twist to the analogy, for the story contains a cynical allusion to the vagaries of literary fame. Harry is given the cage which formerly held a panther who had died unexpectedly—an allusion to the panther who took over the cage of Kafka's "Hunger Artist", a work Hesse had enthusiastically reviewed three years earlier. And of course the Kafka vogue, which made "kafkaesque" one of the trendy adjectives of the 1950s and early 1960s, has been superseded, for a time at least, by the current Hessomania.

Naturally not all young Americans appreciate Hesse. A close parallel to the self-assured boy can be found among representatives of the New Left, who have taken Hesse to task for his apolitical stance. (It has long been typical of Hesse's hostile readers that they cannot simply ignore him; they feel almost morally obliged to attack him.) In the eyes of these readers Hesse exemplifies, as Krystyna Devert put it in the anthology *Literature in Revolution* (1972), "an exhaustion of the spirit . . . and the temptation to withdraw from that painful confrontation with reality" which they demand. As long as he remains in his aesthetic cage, he will be tolerated; but he must be shot down mercilessly if he ventures into the real world, where "there are no political thoughts, only political acts". Who else is the little girl but the Hesse freak *par excellence*, responding intuitively to the affection that Hesse always displayed for youth?

These are the people who buy 400,000 copies of *Siddhartha* and confess in their letters, "I feel for Harry Haller because dammit I too cannot sustain myself in the 3rd realm", or, "I feel that I am living a life similar to what one would find in a Hermann Hesse novel". (Note that the verb "to feel" occurs more frequently in their critical vocabulary than "to understand.")

If we pursue our analogy to the end, the governess must represent the hundreds of teachers and professors who have hastily added Hesse's works to their reading lists in an attempt to engage their students and to profit from the aura that surrounds his name. But will they too draw back in alarm when they understand Hesse well enough to realize that Hesse urges their wards to rebel against them, that in fact he mocks their very pretensions to explicate his works? It is too soon to tell. In reality as in the tale, the case is still in the courts. In the meantime, the customers flock to the bookstores as they flocked to Harry's cage.

If *Die Kunst des Müssiggangs* displays the continuity of Hesse's themes, the handsome new edition of his stories makes it clear why he is known outside Germany principally for his later fiction. This edition of *Erzählungen* is valuable not just because, for the first time, it brings together in two volumes Hesse's most important tales (fifty-four, including six previously unavailable ones), but also because it provides the first chronological overview. Hesse's accessibility to readers around the world today is due in no small measure to the parabolic form of his narratives, which enables readers to transpose their meaning to other times and places. This quality, strikingly evident in "Vom Steppenwolf", also characterizes Hesse's novels from *Demian* to *The Glass Bead Game*. But it is a relatively late development. Almost without exception the stories before 1914 belong to what might be called the "Gerbersau"-type, after the South German town that Hesse created—like Faulkner's Yoknapatawpha County—as the fictional world of his prewar stories. Like the three tales of *Knulp*, these works portray the poignant romanticism in the lives of provincial tramps, servant-girls, schoolboys, and shopkeepers. The moist-eyed humour of these idylls won Hesse his first large audience, which was put off by the mocking irony of his later works. Their bitter-sweet melancholy always backs away from tragedy at the last moment, and they end with a sigh of resignation rather than an angry interrogative. Above all, the tales are so totally localized that they cannot easily be read as anything but comments on life and society in Wilhelmine Germany, although a modern drop-out might well understand the "nostalgia for freedom" proclaimed by Knulp, that flowerchild *ante datum*.

During the First World War, as a direct result of psychoanalysis, Hesse began writing fiction of a wholly different kind. The themes remain constant, but the narrative mode shifts from the minor of the particular to the major of the general. The difference is apparent if we compare "Vom Steppenwolf" of 1928 with "Der Wolf", in which the same motif occurs twenty-five years earlier. These three lovely pages recount the pursuit and brutal slaughter of a wolf by a mob of peasants. Hesse's sympathies clearly lie with the animal, which unlike its pursuers is portrayed as being in harmony with the world and nature; but it is clearly a real wolf in a specific situation, and not the sardonic man-beast of the later allegory.

This allegorizing tendency shows up clearly in the fairy tales that Hesse began writing during the war years. Eight of them, originally published under the title *Märchen* (1919), have been felicitously rendered into English by Denver Lindley as *Strange News from Another Star*. The "Märchen" distinguish themselves from Hesse's more realistic "Erzählungen" principally by their conspicuously fanciful motifs—talking birds, wishes that are magically fulfilled, and other appurtenances of the Romantic canon to which Hesse was deeply indebted. But, as such astute readers as Thomas Mann and André Gide noted, Hesse manipulated conventional forms to express contemporary ideas. The title story exploits the mode of the fairy tale to expose the horrors and absurdity of modern war. Other "Märchen"—e g, "The Hard Passage" and "A Dream Sequence"—reflect the unrelentingly honest self-scrutiny to which Hesse was led through the experience of Jungian analysis. Few novelists of manners could match the unsparing dissection of human relationships—notably, the breakdown of his first marriage—that Hesse undertakes in "Iris", one of the finest pieces of the volume. In general, the fairy tales, by enabling Hesse to filter experience of the most personal nature through the objectifying lens of the parable, anticipate the movement toward mythic generalization that characterizes his later works from *Demian* to *The Glass Bead Game*.

If German readers of the 1920s became increasingly interested in Hesse the man, it was in part his own fault. The curiosity aroused by the pseudonymous publication of *Demian* focused attention on the identity of the author. In addition, Hesse devoted himself more and more to autobiographical reflection (as a psychoanalytic exercise in self-discovery) and less to short fiction: of the fifty-four "stories", only fourteen were written after 1920. Yet he tended to conceal the *facts* of his life. Depressed by a book on the late Tolstoy, he once noted that "it's no good to learn about the intimate affairs of great men". As a result, even his autobiographical writings blur the line between fact and fiction, as Hesse emphasized aspects of his life that seemed to display more archetypal validity.

His readers, intrigued by this literary game of hide-and-seek, continued to "feel" an identity with Hesse and addressed thousands of letters to him. It is a mark of his peculiar notion of "indolence" that he took the trouble to answer almost all of them conscientiously. Many of these letters, including entire correspondences, have been lost or destroyed (for example, the correspondence with his first wife and the early letters to Thomas Mann and C. G. Jung). But the letters now beginning to appear constitute a fascinating record of his life, necessitating in some instances a reappraisal of existing views.

There have been earlier volumes of letters—notably the *Briefe* selected by Hesse himself (1951) and later expanded by his third wife (1964). With few exceptions, however, that edition documented only the state of mind of the sixty- and seventy-year-old, not the development and crises of the writer during his productive years. The most remarkable of the special correspondences is no doubt the highly self-conscious Hesse-Mann *Briefwechsel* (1968). Any spontaneity is undermined by the faintly antagonistic irony with which the magus of Montagnola and the name-dropping, globe-trotting Thomas Mann encountered each other, as keenly aware of their representative roles as Goethe and Schiller in their correspondence. Yet their sense of a common generation and mutual worth, for all the differences in temperament and style, binds them together against readers and critics who from the start attempted to play one against the other. The Hesse-Suhrkamp *Briefwechsel 1945–1959* (1969) is a greater tribute to Hesse's publisher—a fine, patient, solicitous man of taste and sensitivity—than to Hesse, who, from the very nature of the business correspondence, comes across as uncharacteristically crabby and obsessed with problems of money, health, and servants—not to mention technicalities of publication and royalties.

Readers acquainted with the impressive correspondence between

Thomas Mann and Karl Kerényi on myth will be disappointed by the meagre Hesse-Kerényi *Briefwechsel aus der Nähe* (1972). In fact, there was no urgent need for its publication since the few important letters were already available in the *Briefe* (1964). The whole relationship, as Kerényi notes in his preface, "entsprach weitgehend meinem angeborenen Bedürfnis, begeistert zu verehren". This inherent need to venerate helps to explain Kerényi's professional obsession with myth, and it may have produced a personal relationship flattering to the novelist; but it did not provide the basis for any sort of serious intellectual exchange. The correspondence—thirty-six items from Hesse and twenty-eight from Kerényi—consists principally of invitations, thank-you notes, and birthday greetings between 1945 and 1956. It is so slight that the second half of the volume must be filled by a variety of often irrelevant appendix material, including descriptions of the letterhead of each note or card as well as the full text of a letter to Kerényi from his daughter, merely because it happened to be passed along to Hesse. If Hesse and Kerényi engaged in any sort of meaningful discourse, it is not evident in these letters.

The new French edition of Hesse's correspondence with Romain Rolland, *D'une rive à l'autre*, is much richer and very sensibly edited. It contains everything included in the German edition of 1954 as well as several new letters, passages from Rolland's journal concerning Hesse, and Hesse's reviews of Rolland's works (all translated into French). The dialogue between the Frenchman and the German was based not so much on any inherent temperamental or aesthetic sympathy—although they shared an interest in the East— as on their mutual opposition to the First World War and the senseless nationalism that produced it—an attitude which set them apart from most intellectuals in France and Germany. The letters are most revealing during the period from 1915 to 1923, when both men were working actively for the reconstruction of European spiritual and intellectual life. But the older writer was unable to follow Hesse in his literary experiments of the 1920s, when Hesse departed from conventional narrative traditions to write such works as *Steppenwolf*. And Rolland began to be suspicious of Hesse's success with a new generation of readers: "Toute cette fin de *Steppenwolf* m'attriste (littérairement aussi ou, mieux, intellectuellement) et me fait hausser les épaules. Ce serait bon, à 20 ans! Mais à 50!" Hesse noted ironically that he could sympathize with Rolland's difficult position in the

France of the 1920s: "Mais alors j'ai eu la chance que ma patrie ait perdu la guerre. C'est pourquoi les mêmes personnes qui dans le cas contraire m'auraient mis au mur et m'auraient fusillé, me lisent et me louent maintenant." Hesse comes across as the more generous spirit as the years pass; but Rolland's sometimes snide journal entries following visits to Montagnola provide a useful outside view of Hesse during the 1920s.

Apart from the Rolland letters, then, the various published correspondences document Hesse's thoughts (and less so his life) from about 1930 until his death. At the other end, the splendid volume by Hesse's wife, *Kindheit und Jugend vor Neunzehnhundert* (1966), presents his childhood and youth from 1877 to 1895 in letters and documents. The Hesse family seems to have felt compelled by some pietist confessional urge to record every event, every thought, every impulse of their lives. As a result there is an enormous wealth of biographical evidence for Hesse's early years, covering his boyhood in Calw and Basel, his school years and subsequent flight from the seminary at Maulbronn, and the parents' uncomprehending attempts to deal with their prodigal son. The volume ends with a letter of September 19, 1895, in which H. Perrot attests that Hesse had been gainfully employed for the past fifteen months in his tower clock works. But for the period between 1895 and 1930— that is, between Hesse's juvenilia and the "classic" period of *The Glass Bead Game*—we have had virtually no firsthand evidence: a dozen letters in the expanded *Briefe*, six letters and postcards between Hesse and Mann, and the smaller edition of the correspondence with Rolland.

The expanded Hesse-Rolland correspondence, the documentary section of *Materialien*, and notably the *Gesammelte Briefe 1895–1921* (the first in a projected three-volume edition of letters) now provide for the first time virtually uninterrupted epistolary evidence for the period from 1895 to 1930. Though they do not offer many radically new insights, they add depth and differentiation to our understanding of Hesse's development during those crucial years. The 392 "collected letters"—representing roughly one-thirtieth of the extant letters from that period—begin with Hesse's arrival in Tübingen in October 1895, to take up his position in a bookstore. They record his tentative beginnings, his frustrations and first successes as a writer. The years of marriage and family life in Gaienhofen, tranquil on the surface, are punctuated by travels across Europe and to South-East Asia.

Hesse's move to Switzerland in 1912 was an unsuccessful evasive action to prevent the disintegration of his marriage, which led to the need for psychoanalysis—first by J. B. Lang (the "Pistorius" of *Demian* and the letters) and later by Jung himself. After the war, works of a strikingly new kind began to appear—*Demian*, various essays on spiritual renewal, and the expressionist novella *Klingsor's Last Summer*. At the same time, Hesse withdrew from public view in Berne and retired to Montagnola, where he spent five years in virtual isolation, learning to paint and writing *Siddhartha*. The mood of these years is reflected not only in the letters, but also in the collection of prose sketches, poems, and watercolours entitled *Wandering*, which Hesse published originally in 1920 and which has been made available in a pleasing rendition by James Wright.

During the 1920s Hesse's insistence on independence brought with it a great burden of loneliness—not to mention financial hardship—and despair at the insufficiency of his previous literary efforts. The threat of suicide becomes a topos, or at least a recurring refrain, in the letters. The documents of *Materialien* supply detailed evidence not only for what was already known or suspected—the influence of Hesse's life on his works, notably *Steppenwolf*—but also for the reverse: when his second wife brought divorce proceedings against Hesse, she drew her evidence extensively from such works as *Der Kurgast*. In these ruthlessly honest letters Hesse brings out into the open many feelings that he had hitherto repressed, while as a writer he finds dramatic images for them. Hesse's strength does not lie in any particular originality of thought. Rather, as we see from the letters, he is unique in his uncompromising refusal to make any distinction between thought and experience; he insists on living in accord with the principles of his own works. Hence his immense appeal, as a person, to several generations of readers. But hence also, the ambivalence of his political views.

Of the areas in which our understanding of Hesse's thought is modified by the letters, the most conspicuous is politics. Hesse published a collection of "political" pieces, which have recently been translated under the title *If the War Goes On. . . .* But the twenty-eight essays and parables, written between 1914 and 1921 and again between 1937 and 1947, represent the limpid distillate of Hesse's thought—not the murky process through which he reached his conclusions. As Hesse remarks in his introduction, his pieces are "political" only in so far as they were written in a political atmosphere (like the letters to Rolland): "In all other respects they are the opposite of political, because in each one of these essays I strive to guide the reader not into the world theatre with its political problems but into his innermost being, before the judgment seat of his very personal conscience." But this serene detachment was purchased only at the cost of the great anguish recorded in the letters.

Hesse always insisted that he was an utterly unpolitical man; in 1903 he boasted to a friend that he was uncontaminated by politics because he had never read a newspaper. But he became the dupe of his own attitude: in 1918 he conceded that, because of his political naivety, he was taken in at the beginning of the war by the official spokesmen of German policy. The curious ambivalence revealed in the letters is comforting in a way because it corresponds to the dialectical attitude characteristic of his thought in general. A convinced opponent of nationalism, he was deeply committed to the German cause and immediately placed himself at the disposal of the German consulate in Berne when he was pronounced unfit (because of his eyesight) for military service. His disenchantment with the war was not an instant moral perception; rather, it became clear only when he realized how the war was corrupting writers and intellectuals (the topic of his first political essay) to betray cultural cosmopolitanism. As he wrote years later to Thomas Mann, it is fitting for the intellectual to involve himself in politics if he feels a deep personal commitment; but he should resist with all his strength whenever he feels that he is being coopted by external forces—like the German and French intellectuals of 1915 who agreed to sign foolish proclamations. This attitude leads to a position that Hesse's detractors have called an ivory-tower elitism. But the letters make it clear that Hesse's disengagement from partisan politics stems from his conviction that one must commit oneself fully or not at all. Despite his pacifism, he had nothing but contempt for many pacifists who spent their time signing manifestoes and attending rallies yet disdained practical service in the cause of peace (such as Hesse's own war-relief work). By the same token, he urged his sons to join no political party unless they were prepared to carry its principles to their logical conclusions—which, in the case of revolutionary parties, often means killing. To belong to a party without that final commitment is political dilettantism. Since Hesse was unwilling to accept the consequences of the leading political platforms of his age, he chose to withdraw from direct political action for the sake of that revolution of the spirit so dramatically documented in his letters.

For two reasons, little of this problematical Hesse comes through in Bernhard Zeller's readable biography, a pastiche of well-chosen quotations from Hesse's autobiographical writings set in a sensible framework of biographical narrative. First, the book is a translation of a Rowohlt *Bildmonographie* originally published in 1963 (and not to be confused with Herr Zeller's more thickly illustrated *Hermann Hesse: Eine Chronik in Bildern* of 1960). It shares little of the critical sophistication that characterizes more recent Hesse studies; and it was written too soon to make use of the splendid materials that Herr Zeller, as director of the Schiller-Nationalmuseum, has subsequently acquired for the Hesse-Archiv in Marbach. Hence it relies mainly on the retrospective autobiographical writings, in which Hesse often sublimated the events of his own past. Second, the book has been poorly translated and edited. It includes fewer than half of the original illustrations. Zeller's bibliographical apparatus has not been updated, but simply reduced to an incomplete list of Hesse's works in English translation. Worst of all, Herr Zeller's careful text has been altered, words, phrases, even sentences being indiscriminately omitted.

It is a pity that Bernhard Zeller, who probably knows as much about Hesse's life as anyone, should be represented by a work that is so much out of date. But the mentality of the menagerie owner still prevails, anxious to get Harry the Steppenwolf before the public while interest is still keen. What is needed is a biographer who, understanding Hesse's praise of indolence, will take the time to assess the wealth of material now appearing so that the next book on Hesse will not be merely another rehash of everything that has already been written, but a substantial and sophisticated new evaluation. Any such study, needless to say, will have to come to grips with the Hesse cult—and not merely because the sociology of literature has sharpened our perception for questions of literary impact and reception. Rather, in accord with some Heisenbergian principle of criticism, the literary object is affected by the very act of observing; each age sees the writer it wants and needs to see; and therefore the objections of the cultural elitists, that young readers today lack the background to appreciate Hesse, are partly invalid. The Hesse we read today is in fact no longer the bittersweet elegist of Wilhelmine Germany, the anguished intellectual *entre deux guerres*, the serene hermit of Montagnola *après* Nobel. The cult has adjusted the kaleidoscope of Hesse's works in such a way as to bring into focus a Hesse for the 1970s: environmentalist, war opponent, enemy of a computerized technocracy, who seeks heightened awareness (through poetry rather than pot!), and who is prepared to sacrifice anything but his integrity for the sake of his freedom.

15

FICTION OF 1973

(g) VLADIMIR NABOKOV

Transparent Things

Transparent Things is the story of a wintry magus casting up accounts, a conjuror selling off his effects. It is Vladimir Nabokov's first new novel since *Ada* in 1969, and it leaves all that passionate encyclopeadic faking behind to emerge with a new lucidity, the bare boards at last. Well, not quite. The imagined voice behind the novels used to be saying, Look at my riches, my plots and contrivances, my looking-glass history and wonderland geography. Now the author comes forward with a different sort of triumph in his eye, and says, Look at my poverty, this mortal mess and these clumsy machines. He's dressed for the part, too, and looks more like a plumber than a fancy fabulator:

> Presently R. came in. He had not shaved for three or four days and wore ridiculous blue overalls which he found convenient for distributing about him the tools of his profession, such as pencils, ball pens, three pairs of glasses, cards, jumbo clips, elastic bands, and—in an invisible state—the dagger which after a few words of welcome he pointed at our Person.

The trick with the dagger rather suggests that he hasn't abjured all the old vulgar flourishes, but on the whole he seems a workmanlike figure, anxious to be honest and direct. And after all, there are precedents—somewhere in the background hovers another weary

---

(*g*) VLADIMIR NABOKOV: *Transparent Things*. 104 pp. Weidenfeld and Nicolson. £1.75.

(*h*) ANTHONY POWELL: *Temporary Kings*. 280 pp. Heinemann. £2.25.

(*i*) DAVID STOREY: *A Temporary Life*. 248 pp. Allen Lane. £2.25.

(*j*) CLAUDE SIMON: *Triptyque*. 225 pp. Paris: Minuit. 25 fr.

(*k*) GRAHAM GREENE: *The Honorary Consul*. 334 pp. Bodley Head. £2.

(*l*) YUKIO MISHIMA: *Runaway Horses*. Translated by Michael Gallagher. 421 pp. Secker and Warburg. £3.10.

190

wizard, Prospero, taking his magic world apart and putting it all ("The cloud-capp'd towers, the gorgeous palaces") back in the box.

And so we get only teasing, parenthetical glimpses (the lurid cover of a paperback edition, a smattering of exotic synonyms) of the novel we expected to be reading. *This* novel is about the life on the margins and between the lines, a tour of some of the fragile engines that work the magic revelations. The narrative set-up is a double-edged affair, with "R." telling "Person's" story, which is partly about R., and not at all flattering. Person is no poet, but a proof-reader, who lives out his life in the hinterland of fiction, and looks at R.'s language and people from behind the scenes. From this sceptical angle, the author's Swiss citadel dissolves into a wilderness of hotels and ugly villas, physically impossible "walks", sugary snow, property pine-trees and bulldozers. R. himself seems to be falling apart, his fake English peppered hopefully ("you know") with the bogus idioms and precarious colloquialisms that somehow manage to come out on paper as mannerist triumphs. And like the words, the characters R. has tied up neatly in his novels are deserting him, falling away, leading—as perhaps they always did—their own lives. The momentary, splendid coherences of fiction have become transparent, so that we can see the stuff it's made of slipping, flowing away in all directions, into other minds, other uses, other futures.

The slender narrative takes place at the vanishing points where, or when, Person's tragic itinerary crosses R.'s, and vice versa. Early on, for example, Hugh (Person) has enjoyed a fumbling conjunction with dark Julia, and enjoyed it mainly because Julia is famous R.'s stepdaughter, reputed mistress, and favourite heroine; but what Hugh does not see, later, is that his own love Armande, Julia's blonde double, is R.'s secret possession, every hollow and curve of her caressed and chronicled in the other's imaginings. This is not, as R. might say, a joke on you, Hugh: R. is no freer than poor Person in the world of transparent things, where even the most monumental artefacts are doomed to dissolution and dismantling, becoming ingredients in someone else's story. Your possession of them is as real, and as impotent and invisible, as your signature on the words you use; every landmark and property bears the ghostly imprint of infinite minds—and therefore of none. It is easy to make patterns in a world that works like this, impossible to make them stick. All those bright things will elude you, and leave you in the end alone—"Human life", says R. with comic calm, "can be compared

192   *T.L.S. 1973*

to a person dancing in a variety of forms around his own self. . . ."

It is not a thought to conjure with, or to cram the stage with characters. He only hints at Hugh's story, colouring in a few bizarre scenes, soot-and-flame, black-and-gold, to give you the general idea. The tempting particulars, the awful rows, the weeping, the trial, happen in the wings. The real focus is on the mental manoeuvres, on the dream-pangs it takes to relinquish your (imagined) hold on (imagined) beauty—which is as hard as giving up your hold on life, and perhaps the same thing. The book's sparse, studied language hints all the time at the tragi-comic truth; it is full of strategic hitches, like Armande's un-English but horribly accurate idiom, "And now one is going to make love". "One" is right, one makes love, two never do, alas, no matter how often they try. Armande, the essential Armande, slips through poor Person's fingers the instant he lays his heavy, humble paws on her. He is left with solitary mental acrobatics, dodging the jovial threats of quacks and theologians ("You'd better tell Uncle your dreams or you might burn"), fumbling his way towards giving up his last possessions, and becoming transparent himself.

Transparent Things is the best book there's been for a long time about making and breaking fictions. R. says, "Men have learned to live with a black burden, a huge aching hump: the supposition that 'reality' may be only a 'dream'"—but it's not really the case that we've "learned to live with" that slippery, unhelpful paradox, only that we're tired of banging our heads against it. And perhaps that is because it has produced a lot of depressing fiction about the so-called limits of imagination, doctrinaire tracts shaped like circular mazes and populated with identical twins. Nabokov's brief, lucid reverie has nothing in common with those copy-book performances: he is a connoisseur, an insatiable student of the taste and feel of mental events, someone who can speak with a unique kind of tact and authority about the dizzy delights and pitiable humiliations of authorship.

(*h*) ANTHONY POWELL

Temporary Kings

THE DANCE of Anthony Powell's characters to the Music of Time has now become grimly autumnal. In this eleventh novel of the planned twelve, his fascination with the inexorable development of these people in the fulfilment of their life-roles has turned, of necessity, into a sad contemplation of the varying degrees of their decay. As always, the novel ultimately pivots on a concept of the profound comedy of all human postures and strivings. But the humour is indisputably darker; the wry, funny glances at everything from the vanity of the highest ambitions to the merest minutiae of individual behaviour are pervaded by a sense that soon, now, careers will be concluded, aspirations wither away, the places at the dinner tables be filled only by ghosts.

Two scenes of marvellous, unnerving melancholy enclose the intricate and enthralling action of *Temporary Kings*. The opening passages describe a very old man singing with his band of musicians to the guests at the hotel where Jenkins is staying in Venice. This is 1958, and *could* he be the same man that sang there in Jenkins's boyhood? If so, his astonishing persistence has apparently defied Time; and yet, in his pitiful antiquity he is, for all his energy, the representative of Death. In the closing pages of the novel, a small parade of old and new characters pass Jenkins near Westminster Bridge, seated in vintage cars engaged in a rally—cars which might have been new models in Jenkins's youth. The scene symbolically and ruefully juxtaposes present and past. Jenkins disengages himself from Widmerpool, who makes his last appearance in the novel at the same moment. "There's a lot to do", Jenkins offers as a perfunctory excuse. "I want to get home before dark." There is an unmistakable sense that the same dark may soon be closing in on everyone.

If *Temporary Kings* is the saddest novel in Mr Powell's sequence— sadder even than the war novels in the series, where death was less an approaching inevitability than a sudden, tragic curtailment—it is also one of the most rich, complex and original volumes, showing consummate narrative skill of a kind different, in various respects, from before. One new feature is the use of a single (fictitious, and brilliantly invented) work of art to symbolize a large part of the action. Mr Powell has, before now, used paintings placed in significant positions to evoke in Jenkins's memory thoughts of people and periods. He has never before done what he has here with a Tiepolo ceiling in a Venetian palazzo, "the very existence of which was unknown" to Jenkins though Tiepolo ranks with Poussin as one of his "most admired masters". The ceiling depicts King Candaules contriving to exhibit his wife's nudity to the voyeuristic Gyges.

In the legend, Candaules is murdered by Gyges, who becomes king in his stead. In *Temporary Kings*, it is a voyeuristic Widmerpool who more than exhibits his wife Pamela to a left-wing French writer, Ferrand-Sénéschal; in fact the latter dies in her embraces, before Widmerpool's eyes. From this symbolic painting and all that it symbolizes in the life—and the death—habits of Jenkins's friends, radiates a new and startling set of revelations about the characters in *The Music of Time*. To accommodate this sudden, alarming knowledge of what was hintingly described as "the underclothes" in *The Military Philosophers*, Mr Powell has admitted an unusual sexual explicitness into his writing—another new feature. Hidden and unpalatable facts, scarcely treated with overt humour, are coming to light as the dance transmutes into a Dance of Death.

The most skilful, and in a sense the most surprising, innovation, however, is to be found in Mr Powell's narrative technique. Outwardly it is the same method: long passages of elaborate, yet meticulously polished and finely reticent, prose advance the story in a gradual unfolding of incident and character, interpolated references bringing readers up to date with the latest fortunes of the whole gallery of Jenkins's acquaintances. The difference here is the way in which the most crucial facts are built up piecemeal over the entire course of the narrative rather than presented as conclusive surprises. *Temporary Kings* requires attentive reading on another level than that needed simply to recall "who is who" from previous books. It is an accumulating jigsaw in which every piece requires to be remembered as it is set carefully, in place, with nothing complete or explicit until the end. In terms of construction, it is a narrative feat of a new and fascinating kind, something unexpected from Mr Powell at this stage of his enterprise. Yet it fits perfectly into his scheme at the same time as it varies the texture. And it has the effect of leaving the final volume unpredictable as regards the way in which all the drawn-out threads will be finally cut, even if one might guess at the mood and atmosphere of the conclusion. The most avid follower of Jenkins's saga could not wish better from Mr Powell than this.

The "temporary kings" of the title are literary representatives of many nations gathered in Venice for a cultural conference. For one reason or another, many of the earlier major characters find themselves there as well as some new ones. Mark Members has persuaded the slightly reluctant Jenkins to come. Pamela Widmerpool is there in the company of Louis Glober, a middle-aged but virile American film director: both first seen lying flat, as if set out in a mortuary, to gaze up at the Tiepolo ceiling—an attitude presaging their later deaths. Ada Leintwardine, novelist from *Books Do Furnish a Room*, is also of the party. Widmerpool arrives, in inevitable frustrated pursuit of his wife. He is now a Life Peer, but his covert connexions with representatives of Eastern European countries seem oddly dubious (the international politics of the "thaw" period, and their repercussions on the literary community, are caught with considerable skill). The star of the conference, Ferrand-Sénéschal, does not arrive: he has just died in London, in the circumstances mentioned above but not clarified until much later in the story. In Venice, too, Jenkins reacquaints himself with the fellow-travelling Daniel Tokenhouse, a new character here, but someone for whom he worked in publishing in the 1920s. Little happens in Venice, though things begin to be partially disclosed about most of these people.

The action moves slowly, with characteristic and significant flashbacks to the past, through the small-talk, the wining and the dining between conference sessions. The curiously futile air of the whole gathering is rendered perfectly. On its edges hovers Russell Gwinnett, another newcomer, who is writing a biography of the late X. Trapnel and is therefore deeply eager to interview the former mistress who destroyed his manuscript: Pamela Widmerpool. The interview turns into some sort of love affair, the affair ends in a death—not, as it turns out, in Venice, but back in London, where the second half of the novel is set.

It is customary, but even now not superfluous, to praise Mr Powell's unobtrusively perceptive and dexterous handling of any kind of character. The scholarly, laconic, sexually mysterious Gwinnett is his finest new creation—pursuing his biographical data with a kind of diffident ruthlessness, an inscrutable catalyst who finally determines the fate of both Pamela and her husband. In a superb climatic scene, amid a large assemblage of the major characters, she is enigmatically warned (or cursed?) by the aged Mrs Erdleigh, denounces Widmerpool and reveals the truth about the dealings which have nearly landed him in court on official secrets charges, then declares her intention of leaving all of them for ever. Mr Powell has never combined high comedy and the sense of impending tragedy so powerfully; and it is a culmination which both explains and darkens a hundred episodes and characters in *The Music of Time*.

Life itself, which interweaves people and their destinies in an ostensibly casual way—its loose ends, its inconsequentialities have been the main stock of Mr Powell's sequence—makes its most alarming final twists in ways no less credible than those depicted in this scene. The fineness of Mr Powell's art, the near-genius in his sense of design, consists in his ability to perceive and render believable in "fiction" the sheer multifariousness of real human experience in his age. Reputations founded on inventions less true and more feigning begin to wane almost irrecoverably in the light of his achievement. Obviousness, so often mistaken for originality and force, has always been the besetting sin of the inferior novelist. Which of the doubters will now still claim that Mr Powell was wrong, in those unexpectedly solemn, measured cadences of *A Question of Upbringing* twenty-two years ago, to turn away from it and follow his own path?

(*i*) DAVID STOREY

A Temporary Life

THE RESEMBLANCES, and the differences, between David Storey's outstanding first novel, *This Sporting Life*, and his latest may provide an index of the curious direction in which his talent has lately turned; something paralleled by his recent work in the theatre. The immensely strong, inarticulate, bewildered rugby player of the first book was living in a brutal world of sporting success which he knew to be temporary. The grimy realism of the settings, both on the rugger field and in the wider area of the northern industrial township outside it, was generally taken for granted, and rightly praised. Yet there remained in Arthur Machin and his responses to people and society a residue of the enigmatic. And something ominous and shadowy—something, in retrospect rather unreal—hung over the ostensibly realistic background. The figure of the tough, yet sensitive and vulnerable, hero struggling in a place of darkness with human motives and powers he could not easily comprehend, suggested a substratum of allegory somewhere if one wanted to dig down. In *A Temporary Life*, with a not dissimilar hero, tough and vaguely puzzling, and a quite similar urban setting (though it's brought observantly and intelligently up to date) allegory and fantasy have come to the fore and uneasily taken over.

It is an effectively disturbing feature of this unquestionably very clever book that this does not become clear for some time: the real world becomes unhinged only very slowly and unobtrusively. At the beginning, Colin Freestone, once a professional boxer and now an art teacher, is living—temporarily, he knows or hopes—in his wife's home town, to which she has returned to be treated for a nervous breakdown. Colin specializes in life classes, in which he is constantly striving to drag his students back from self-indulgent fantasy. His wife, Yvonne, has no fantasies: her disease is depressive, that of caring so widely for the sufferings of strangers all over the world that she cannot make contact with people close to her. The words of the mental home (without gates) and of the town (including its rundown Art School, dominated by an obsessed, zany principal) are—and the point is taken—not remarkably different. What happens in this outside world, in Colin's temporary existence there, becomes increasingly bizarre and alarming, though he takes everything in a very quiet, off-hand way.

In his shoddy bedsitter, Colin is drawn mysteriously into the orbit of the wealthy family of a girl student at the Art School. Almost imperceptibly, the narrative and characters turn weird, and, one begins to suspect, symbolical of something. The girl, Rebecca Newman, fails to seduce Colin, but her mother does. At a party at the family mansion, he is insulted, and punches the offender on the nose. From this point it becomes clear—or relatively clear in a novel where the bare, lucid narrative is a mask for many obscure implications—that Colin is up against a kind of mafia of the newest sort of rich. The Newmans are property developers moving on from one old town to another, demolishing and raising; rich, arrogant and subtle in their tactics. As they go, they destroy, compromise or absorb all kinds of talent: Mr Newman employs an artist, a sociologist, an architect and—an excellent touch—an environmental psychologist on his new industrial estate, with its factories and skyscraper office blocks. Colin he has destined for use as his utterly ordinary man. But Colin, choosing the violence which is his only real means of expression (see *This Sporting Life*), opts out.

A Temporary Life is an odd book, occasionally brilliant, always intelligent and absorbing. Mr Storey's command both of pathos and of comedy is increasingly sure: he switches here from the harrowing to the farcical with unnerving speed, and complete conviction. But the sum total is both cryptic and frustrating. For some reason,

Mr Storey has chosen to channel his impressive understanding of modern society, the nature of change within it, and the effect of that change on the individual, into a sort of mannered parable. A host of characters who at first actually live, vigorously, through the abundant psychological realism, the quirks and eccentricities, which the author gives them, slip one by one into allegorical roles, and peter out in fantasy. The finely economical staccato prose is clipped and pared down to a portentously meaningful minimalist style. Everything works with clockwork efficiency and intricacy—clues and symbolic pointers are dropped in every sequence and ingeniously explained, or taken up, at some later stage. But the final impression is of a writer putting his intense and disquieting perceptions of the way life is going through a nightmarish square-dance which muffles rather than clarifies the effect of what he wants to say. Few novelists now writing see so vividly, think so intelligently, command so much sheer understanding of people and society. It is sad to watch these abilities turned to an exercise in stylish evasion.

(*j*) CLAUDE SIMON

Triptyque

IT MIGHT SEEM PERVERSE for a novelist as supremely good as Claude Simon at turning the visible into the legible to be also given to the cold and methodical disillusionments of the *nouveau roman*. But the one follows from the other: when naturalism is so detailed and seductive there is a doubly pressing need to expose its artificiality, to show that mental representations are mental representations and not windows on the real world. What is missing from them is reality's one vital property: movement. However intense and analytically exact Simon's descriptions of material scenes are, he cannot make them truly kinetic. The best representation can manage, whether in pictures or words, is a succession of *tableaux vivants*, and this is a particularly obnoxious substitute because it makes time seem divisible. Escapism of this sort will not do and by forever showing divisibility up for what it is—a convention, or fiction—Simon is giving us the bad news: that real time is indivisible and leads only to the grave.

Triptyque involves much disturbing traffic between the mobile and the static. What should not by rights move, like the human figures on a film or circus poster, does move, while what we expect to move, like the meshed bodies of two lovers, may equally well be frozen into the immobility of a representation. The most dynamic scene is liable to sudden arrest, to become a spectacle for an audience or, failing that, a voyeur. The novel is in the form of a private film-show, in which the machinery of projection is constantly intruding, as it alternates between illusion and art.

Rival forces are clearly at work here and *Triptyque* is in fact a wonderfully dense and varied dialectic between physical desire, which animates, and the observing eye, which petrifies: or between sex and geometry. As a contest this was bound to be something of a mismatch, and the novel is more erotic than geometric; Eros has it over Euclid. The two of them fight for precedence in the activities of an obviously privileged character, a schoolboy who sits by a window working dutifully at the demonstration of his theorems. Except, that is, when the call of nature grows too insistent and he abandons triangles and tangents for a furtive consultation of his small but effective hoard of erotic images—a magazine nude and a brief clip from a blue film.

With his twin pastimes, this boy looks very much like the representative in the text of the novelist himself. For the rest, *Triptyque* is made up, as the title promises, of three separate episodes or scenes. The text, too, is in three sections, but the divisions of text and subject-matter do not coincide; instead, the three scenes have been scrambled and introduced into the novel bit by bit, so that none of them is complete or fully explicable until towards the end. The order of their occurrence has been dictated by all kinds of resemblance and continuity between fragments seldom easy to assimilate; the one way to make full sense of *Triptyque* is to try to work out these principles of adjacency.

Two of the three scenes of the novel are urban, the other rural. In the first, a woman—Corinne de Reixach most likely, a disruptively sensual presence in other Simon novels—lies naked in a hotel room in some ritzy but nameless Mediterranean resort, negotiating for a favour from her lover, a local fixer: her son has been caught carrying drugs and she wants the prosecution dropped. Scene two is, by contrast, all northern grime and drizzle: a drunken bridegroom slopes off from the wedding party and his bride of a few minutes to couple clumsily but furiously with a café waitress in an alleyway.

In the third scene, two young boys, in between fishing in a stream, spy on a work-shy nursemaid who abandons her charge for some energetic sex on the floor of a nearby barn.

These three scenes may not share a locale (except for the novel itself) but they do share a preoccupation: with the anarchy of lust. Simon's pairs of lovers in *Triptyque* mate blindly and weightily, their minds seemingly extinguished by the obsession of their bodies. And in each episode sexuality extends its anti-social power, effortlessly perverting in turn justice, marriage customs and simple human responsibilities.

To go with the lovers, there is plenty of livestock in the novel: cows, fish, a water-snake, a performing monkey, together with a disagreeably dead rabbit, skinned for the pot. The rabbit belongs in a still-life, but not so the fish or the snake, which are too slippery and quick for capture. Neither quick nor dead is the monkey, parading round a circus ring on a leash and seeming to show that nature can be domesticated after all. But Simon has always ridiculed the systems and institutions men think up in order to deny their vital urges and the monkey is put in the charge of a clown, a stumbling figure both sinister and undignified. He, like the rest of us, has everything to learn from the crude but honest behaviour of the truly bestial.

(k) GRAHAM GREENE

The Honorary Consul

ART MAY BE infinite, but artists repeat themselves—have their tricks and their obsessions, learn what they can do and what they should leave alone, discover what matters in their invented worlds and what does not. Such repetitions need not imply a flagging imagination, but rather a growing understanding; if a serious writer's later works remind us sometimes of his earlier ones, this may simply be because he has cast aside what is unnecessary, and has refined what is essential to him. There are few surprises in the later Henry James, or in the last novels of Conrad and of Dickens, and Hardy's Wessex novels do not change, but only become more Wessex.

And so it is with the later Graham Greene. It seems strange to write of so vigorous a talent as "later", but in fact Greene will be sixty-nine next month; he is more than ten years older than Hardy

was when he published his last novel, and older than the James of
The Golden Bowl. To take note of his age is not to suggest a diminution
of powers—that is obviously not the case, any more than it was with
James and Hardy—but simply to remind oneself that a new Greene
novel is necessarily an addition to an already familiar world of the
imagination, and that we will read it, inevitably, with a sense of
recognition.

In that curious sport, *Travels With My Aunt*, Greene drew upon
that sense of recognition to create a comic pastiche of the novels
that had gone before; that novel is a broad joke that he can share with
his readers because they already know the climates and characters
of the Greene-world. *The Honorary Consul* is a return to Greene's
more customary manner, but one might also be tempted to describe
it as a pastiche—in this case, though, a melodramatic one. For it
contains a married priest, a minor novelist, a band of terrorists, an
American foreign service officer, a British consul, a Latin-American
police chief, a cuckold and a whore, all of them characters with an-
cestors in the earlier novels. They do the things that one has come to
expect of Greene's characters: they drink, they make love (though
they rarely call it love, or confess to any tender emotion), they talk
about God and the Church, they betray each other, they die; and
these customary actions are narrated in a voice that after all these
years has become as familiar as a hangover—a sour, joyless voice that
has changed scarcely at all since the days when it told us that the
purser took the last landing card in his hand, that Mr Tench went
out to look for his ether cylinder, and that Hale knew, before he
had been in Brighton three hours, that they meant to murder him.
It is all familiar, it has worked before, and it works again. But it is
not pastiche, far from it; it is a new melodrama, skilful, professional,
flawless. Greene is back at the old stand, as good as he ever was.

Once more he has chosen an inherently melodramatic situation.
Paraguayan terrorists enter northern Argentina to kidnap the
American ambassador, seize the wrong man, and draw a local
doctor into their plot against his will. Dr Plarr is a familiar Greene
hero, one of those solitary men who is exiled from life and action
by his inability to feel deeply. He is the son of an English liberal
who died in a Paraguayan jail, but his own politics are neither exact
nor active: he feels compassion for the poor, and grief for his father,
and that is all. Plarr's course through the novel is familiar, too;
for in Greene's novels the public world lies in wait for the private

man, and feelings lurk to ambush the unfeeling man. "Caring", Plarr says, "is the only dangerous thing": Scobie might have said that, or Pinkie, or Querry, or Brown, and in Plarr's case, as in theirs, caring comes, and it is dangerous. One might say of this novel, as of Greene's other important ones, that it is about the terrible expense of caring.

The chosen situation is not only melodramatic, it is also topical, and in this, too, it recalls Greene's other books. In the novels of the 1930s there was usually a hook to the immediate world of the news-papers—a public figure like Kreuger or Zaharoff, or an historical event, the Spanish Civil War or the Mexican suppression of the Church. More recently Greene's impulse to place his imagination in the historical world has been even more insistent, in *The Quiet American*, for example, and *The Comedians*. *The Honorary Consul* continues that direction: Greene is careful to set the action in the 1970s, to mention that Nixon is the American president, and that Nelson Rockefeller recently visited Paraguay, and to insert passing references to Elizabeth Taylor and Richard Burton, and to a Ken Russell film, for what seem only historical reasons. Because the novel is so strictly placed in time, it becomes something unusual, an historical novel of the immediate present. (Greene began his novel-writing career, one recalls, as an unsuccessful historical novelist.)

Greene has often chosen exotic, remote scenes for his fiction, and he has been praised for his skill in describing Indo-China and Haiti and Sierra Leone vividly; but perhaps his unique gift is his ability to locate those unfamiliar places in time as well as in space. Certainly the dates of his best novels are as important as the settings, and the excellence of those novels depends on their historical reality. For one role that art may play is to offer a surrogate memory, and thus sustain the life of forgotten events. The Church was persecuted in Mexico during the 1930s, and what does one remember of that fact? Greene's whisky priest, stumbling toward his martyrdom. Papa Doc Duvalier terrorized Haiti, and we know it in *The Comedians* when we have forgotten the newspaper reports. *The Honorary Consul* gives the same fictional-historical existence to the political kid-nappings by South American terrorists that have been the newspaper melodramas of the 1970s.

Greene's use of the melodrama of current history is one of his tricks. But in this novel it is also one of his subjects, and he has invented an Argentinian novelist, Jorge Julio Saavedra, in order to debate with him on this point. Saavedra is an old-fashioned novelist who has turned to writing political novels, but avoids contemporary materials for aesthetic reasons: "If one is to write a political novel of lasting value", he tells his friend the doctor, "it must be free from all the petty details that date it. Assassinations, kidnapping, the torture of prisoners—these things belong to our decade. But I do not want to write merely for the seventies." And he continues: "A novelist today who wants to represent tyranny should not describe the activities of General Stroessner in Paraguay—that is journalism, not literature." Greene's novel is a refutation of that view: all the things that Saavedra proscribes, the things that belong to our decade, are here. The point is an important one, for Greene is here arguing the social and political relevance of his art, at a time when many of his contemporary novelists are content to play formal games.

It is too early to say whether *The Honorary Consul* is what Saavedra wants—"a political novel of lasting value"—but political it certainly is. Men act and die in it for political motives, and the relations between nations determine and deface private lives. Good men do evil for political reasons, and men with power indifferently destroy men without it. But though the novel is political, it is not ideological: the conclusion is simply that in our time political action is not an option that men can choose or decline—that we are all political, whether we mean to be or not, and that we share political destinies.

The novel is also political in another, less direct, way in the attention that it gives to the concept of *machismo*, that sense of masculine pride that is so deep in the Spanish character. The word recurs through the novel, like a chord in music. Saavedra believes in it, and has made it the only subject of his novels (all of them virtually the same novel, we are told, in which a proud, silent hero dies for his honour). The police chief believes in it: "Here *machismo* is only another word for living", he tells the doctor. "A word for the air we breathe. When there is no *machismo* a man is dead." The whore believes in it, she has seen it acted out on her bed. Only Dr Plarr rejects it, as an irrational anachronism that infects men's motives. "To fight for one's honour with knives over a woman", he thinks, "that belonged to another, an absurdly outdated world, which had ceased to exist except in the romantic imagination of writers like Saavedra. Honour meant nothing to the starving. To them belonged the more serious fight for survival." But he is wrong; the political acts in the book are based on men's sense of themselves as men, and

even the doctor has his *machismo*, in the end. A political ideology
that does not allow for this will fail, the book seems to say; and so,
for that matter, will a private cynicism like the doctor's.

In South America, politics cannot be separated from religion,
and in this novel Princes of the Church dine with General Stroessner
while a lapsed priest leads a terrorist plot against him. Religion is
everywhere in the novel; but God is not. One is accustomed by now
to Greene's God-abandoned world, but here the theme is very
insistent: "I do not forget my old claptrap", the terrorist priest says,
"but I have never yet seen any sign that He interferes in our wars or
our politics." Yet men go on believing in the old claptrap, and the
wars and the politics go on. So the question is simply, how should a
religious man behave in a revolutionary situation; and what God
can he believe in as he acts? The Church, Greene makes clear, offers
no help. He has always been impatient with the Church as an insti-
tution, but here he utters his impatience with a new urgency. Among
the terrorists there is more than the usual Greene discussion of
God, Evil, and Action, and a fiercer rejection of the Church as it
now exists. The priest dreams of a "great Church beyond our time
and place", in which the rules will be changed to suit men's needs,
and Greene, one gathers, shares that dream. But that great Church
is not yet, and the one that does exist in the world has failed its
people. It is a serious and moving indictment, at once religious and
political.

Greene's "historical" novels are also about private lives; no doubt
it is the interaction of public and private that interests him. If the
political point of *The Honorary Consul* is that one can't avoid
commitment, the same is true on the private, sexual level. Dr
Plarr's detachment leads him to take sex casually, and to avoid caring; for him love is a comedy that whores play out for their customers.
Comedy is a word that appears in the novel almost as frequently as
machismo, usually in Plarr's thoughts. It means pretence, lies, role-
playing; to see life as comedy is a way of denying its significance.
And so at the end he prays, "For heaven's sake let this comedy end
in comedy. None of us are suited to tragedy." But tragedy, like
politics, cannot be chosen or declined. And the same is true of
love. Plarr betrays a foolish man and seduces his wife out of cold
curiosity. But the cuckold, the foolish "Honorary Consul", is wiser
than his physician: "People do get caught up by love", he says,
"sooner or later." And so Plarr does.

Greene has always been ill at ease on the subject of love, and clumsy about tenderness. Perhaps that is one reason why he has created fewer memorable women than men, and no really convincing reciprocal man-woman relationship. Love in his novels is always polluted with guilt and pity (like Scobie's), or it is unilateral (like Rose's), and the love-object is often someone beyond the possibility of communication. Still, the novels are full of lovers, and Plarr is another, a man who is afraid of caring, and anxious to avoid involvement and guilt, and who comes to his end loving, involved, and guilty.

But the true lover in the novel is not Plarr but Charley Fortnum, the Honorary Consul. He is, on the face of it, an unpromising one: an elderly drunkard who has married a young whore, an inadequate performer in bed, an unsatisfactory representative of his country who is not even worth ransoming. But he loves his wife, he forgives his betrayer, and he even gives absolution to the priest who intends to kill him.

In his relations with these three characters Fortnum is a father (and in the priest's case a Father) figure. One notices, after a while, that fathers of all kinds are prominent in the novel: nobody has a father, but they all talk about their fathers. Midway through the book a poet-revolutionary describes a poem he has written that begins: "I see my father only through the bars". "I was thinking, you see, of the pens in which they put children in bourgeois houses", he says. "In my poem the father went on following the child all through his life—he was the schoolmaster, and then he was the priest, the police officer, the prison warder, and last he was General Stroessner himself." In all these manifestations, the father is the bourgeois judge and punisher, and these fatherless men are engaged in a revolution to destroy him and his authority. But there is also, in Charley Fortnum, the *other* father, the merciful, forgiving one.

Greene's novels often hover on the edge of parable, and one is tempted to give them the reductive, patterned meanings that parables have. In the present instance it would be easy to take Greene's title as an ironic epithet for God, and one could go a good way with that interpretation: certainly the novel is concerned with men's needs for authority and comfort, and their unwillingness to abide the authorities they have. But it will not reduce itself to any such simplification in the end, and Greene's exegetes will have to work hard on the fathers and their roles in the meaning. And that is one more way of saying that this is a very good novel.

The problem, always, with Greene has been the adaptation of a great story-telling skill to metaphysical subjects. When it works, the result is uniquely moving: *The Power and the Glory* is a masterpiece. But when story and metaphysics don't blend, when the instrument is unequal to the weight of its meanings, then the novel droops. *The End of the Affair* becomes flatulent with doctrine, and even *The Heart of the Matter*, a far better novel, is less impressive on re-reading than one remembered, because it is didactic. That is one reason why the entertainments of the 1930s stand up so well; *A Gun for Sale* has its metaphysics, too, but Greene has held that element in check. This is not to say that one regrets Greene's religion: it would be impertinent to do so. But one may regret his failures to make his religion into fiction, into fable.

The Honorary Consul belongs with the successes. It is in the familiar mainstream of Greene's work, a melodramatic novel with more than melodramatic meaning, a mixture of violent action and religious speculation that is simply what Greene does best. It is not new, in the sense of a formal departure from customary methods (as *Travels With My Aunt* was new), but neither is it simply more of the same: it establishes the idea of "the great Church beyond our time and place", it develops the theme of love beyond earlier expressions, and it deals elaborately with the concept of Fatherhood. It is wiser and less angry about politics than *The Quiet American* was. In all these ways the new novel extends and clarifies our understanding of Greene's imagined world, not only the world of this book, but the whole canon. For the later work of a major artist is always a further explanation of the earlier work, a new survey of old territories. So this story of a priest and a policeman will affect the way we read *The Power and the Glory*, and this sexual betrayal will touch *The End of the Affair* and *The Heart of the Matter* and *The Comedians*. Its appearance is an important event in the world of Greene, which is our world, too.

(*l*) YUKIO MISHIMA

Runaway Horses

OXFORD FILMGOERS of 1965 will doubtless recall an extraordinary double bill at the Scala cinema, combining *High Noon* with a

Japanese feature mis-titled *Hara-Kiri*. The climax of the latter was reached after about ninety minutes of hysterical gloom, when an impoverished samurai, lacking the proper sword, attempted to disembowel himself with one made of bamboo. Not unnaturally the business was prolonged, to the accompaniment of the warrior's groans and the grinding noises made by the useless weapon, while blood spurted profusely over white screens obligingly placed round the suicide as though in a hospital ward. This being before the days of *The Wild Bunch* and *Bonnie and Clyde*, the auditorium was a jostle of undergraduates in various stages of lurching nausea being helped along the aisles by motherly usherettes who had seen it all before.

To the Western mind as yet untutored either by a British Council year in Kyoto or a self-imposed exile in Osaka, there is something either grotesquely disgusting or (dare it be said) wildly amusing in this penchant for self-evisceration. Though Zen, pottery, prints, haiku and netsuke may have travelled well, our cultural liaison with Japan has seldom amounted to much more than a giggling flirt with the slit-eyed Orient of *Madam Butterfly* on the one hand and *The Mikado* on the other. Puzzled irritation is fairly easily provoked at the mesh of ritual and at a xenophobia paralleled only in imperial China, which underpin Japanese civilization. Conversely, the spectacle of a Europeanized society has produced a lengthy footage of anxious television documentary, though perhaps it is only our naive tendency to suppose Japan to have been an island Arcady, its kimono-clad inhabitants frantically counting syllables to the strains of koto and samisen under eternally blooming cherry trees, which stops us from seeing that for large sectors of the population one kind of barrenness has replaced another.

Yukio Mishima was a notable casualty in this jarring of cultures. No artist of any distinction had previously dramatized both a personal and a public dilemma with such an act of self-destruction. Inevitably, wisdom after the event has impelled readers to back-track through his work in search of hints and warnings. In novels such as *Forbidden Colours*, we early detect Mishima's mistrust of women's anarchic force, his characteristic hankering after tradition, and his distaste for Western affectations mirrored in the absurdity of Japanese wishing each other a "Meri Kurisumasu tsu yu". And is it not tempting to view the aging and embittered Shinsuke as the novelist's self-portrait? Now comes a posthumous novel which almost sinisterly reverberates with echoes of its author's final years and seems to defy reading in any sort of critical vacuum that resolutely ignores the significance of Mishima's last gesture.

Runaway Horses is the second instalment of the *Sea of Fertility* quartet. Its forerunner, *Spring Snow*, ended with the death of the young aristocrat Kiyoaki, who here appears, a decade or so later, in a fresh incarnation as Isao, the son of his erstwhile tutor. Though never self-consciously, the narrative makes several appeals to the epic tradition. Isao, the pure warrior boy who has never known a woman, collects his companions for the purpose of dealing a series of violent blows at the political establishment, to be followed by an orgy of suicides inspired by the example of a nineteenth-century Kamikaze league whose various disembowelments are painstakingly recorded.

Treachery and corruption lie scattered liberally in Isao's path. He is deceived in the military and in the imperial family, disillusioned in his father and betrayed by his girlfriend. Part of Mishima's success lies in his continual contrasting of 1930s Japan with the hallowed elder world invoked by the patriot youths (for, redolent of Western fascism though they often are, the values Isao and his myrmidons represent are scarcely to be viewed as an ideology). Here are the anglomaniac nobility, drinking five o'clock tea and calming their nerves with Gibbon and classical music, there the high-hearted heroes clinging with desperate rigour to the ancient rites. The sublime paradox is that the two can even exist side by side. In such a world, samurai heroism can hardly find a place.

Only on this drill ground was the hand of the sun working with a mathematical clarity and precision. Only here! The will of the Emperor penetrated the sweat, the blood, the very flesh of these young men, piercing their bodies like X-rays. From high above the entranceway of regimental headquarters, the golden chrysanthemum of the imperial crest, brilliant in the sunshine, looked down upon this beautiful, sweaty, intricate choreography of death.

And elsewhere? Elsewhere throughout Japan the rays of the sun were blocked.

Biographical detective work, however, must not be our first consideration in taking up *Runaway Horses*. Mishima has been sufficiently well served in Michael Gallagher's translation for us to perceive at once how much it is that he counts as a novelist rather than as the bicep-flexing stormtrooper out of whom the press made such hay. In the end it is the author's sheer technical skills which manage so superbly to contain and filter his obsessions. The book's breathtaking sequence of imagery and its flawless shape endure more impressively than the harpings upon death, nationalism or the imperial will. Thus to be dazzled by Mishima's mature artistry leads un- avoidably to selfish regrets that the author should have followed his own Isao so closely. Good writers, even of bad books, are few enough.

16

THE GREAT GRAMMATICUS

DID OVID ERR by stating in *De Arte Amandi* that the Nile was the habitat of the crocodile whose excrement was used as a cosmetic? Was Polla Argentaria, the wife of the poet Lucan, later married to Papinius Statius? Should not the name "Strotocles" be that of "noster Cocles" in the First Book of Cicero's *De Officiis* (an emendation that has proved to be correct)?

Such topics—explanations, interpolations, emendations of the texts of ancient writers—form the subject-matter of the fifty-nine chapters of Politian's *Miscellaneorum Centuria Secunda* recently discovered and now published for the first time. As the title indicates the book was intended to have 100 chapters, but Politian died in 1494, before its completion. Politian's other *Miscellanea*, the *Centuria Prima*, had been published in 1489. The editor of the *Centuria Secunda*, Vittore Branca, points out that the later work manifests Politian's views about the scope and methods of philological investigation more fully, more clearly and in their most mature form. The manuscript is proof that by the end of the fifteenth century a new, more advanced stage had been reached in the study and interpretation of ancient literature. It is of fundamental importance, therefore, for our understanding of the history of philology.

In contrast to those who interpreted and reconstructed classical texts on the basis of rigid grammatical rules or speculations inspired by prejudiced notions about what a text ought to contain, Politian asserted the paramount importance of two rules. The one is that in suggesting interpolations or emendations of a word that is unknown or of sentences that make no sense, the first step ought to be an examination of all the manuscripts still in existence and the most ancient ought to be subjected to the utmost scrutiny. Indeed,

ANGELO POLIZIANO: *Miscellaneorum Centuria Secunda*. Edited by Vittore Branca and Manlio Pastore Stocchi. Vol I. Introduzione, 80 pp. Vol II. Facsimile dell'autografo. 80 plates. Vol III. Trascrizione sussidiaria alla lettura del facsimile. 133 pp. Vol IV. Edizione critica. 130 pp. Florence: Alinari.

Politian based many of his suggestions in the *Centuria Secunda* on readings which he had found in manuscripts of the libraries of Bologna or Milan, in the Vatican, or in the two Florentine libraries that were his favourite hunting grounds, that of San Marco and that of the Medici.

Politian's other basic rule also has been generally accepted although perhaps it is not always followed: a text ought to be placed in its historical context. It should not be viewed primarily or exclusively as a part of or a link in a chain of philosophical writings or epic poetry or rhetorical textbooks or whatever the genre, but it must be seen as a document of the time in which it was written.

This means that the explanation of any document requires consideration of all the writings of contemporary authors in whatever field they were working and also of all the remnants and monuments which might throw light on the life of the period in which the author lived. For this reason and not for reasons of scholarly vanity Politian in the *Centuria Secunda* deals with a startling variety of topics: from crocodiles and elephants to a list of the jurists who contributed to the Digest and to an investigation of ancient literary genres.

A work which marks a stage in the development of the history of philology must be presented with philological concern for exactitude. The manner in which the *Centuria Secunda* has been published represents a model of editorial techniques. It consists of four volumes: the first contains Professor Branca's magisterial introduction; the second a photographic reproduction of the manuscript; the third an exact transcript of the manuscript with all its underlinings, corrections and cuttings; and the fourth volume provides the text in a final, critical edition with notes on sources, indexes, etc. The fact that Mardersteig supervised the printing of the work is enough to explain why the volumes are a pleasure to look at and a delight to hold in one's hands.

Does a contribution to the history of philology—important as it might be—deserve such sumptuous presentation? The answer to the question is that the *Centuria Secunda* is not only significant for the history of philology but also because the humanist who wrote it was one of the greatest poets of the Italian Renaissance and—one might add—a poet in whose person and writings we still find magic and enchantment.

Every visitor to Florence who has looked at the Ghirlandaio frescoes of the Sassetti Chapel in Santa Trinità has seen the face of

Politian, young, ugly, radiating intelligence, glancing with devotion
at Lorenzo Magnifico towards whom he shepherds his pupils,
Lorenzo's three sons. Politian's name is firmly tied to Lorenzo and
his circle, to which he brought a very personal note. Some modern
verses seem to characterize him and his poetry in an astounding
way:

> Vom jungen Ahnen hat es seine Farben
> Und hat den Schmelz der ungelebten Dinge.

One is tempted to find explanation for the outstanding aptness of
this characterization in the remarkable features which, separated
by four centuries, Politian and Hofmannsthal, the writer of these
lines, have in common. Both were prodigies; both were still schoolboys when they began to attract the admiration of the great literary
figures of their time. And the poems of both show that subtle sense
for the sound-value of words which demands their being set to
music. One needs not to know much Latin but only to have a good
ear to grasp that in the epigram in which Politian summarized
Ovid's complaints about his exile, he wants to describe the contrast
between the sensitive nature of the poet and the grim surroundings
in which he had to spend the last years of his life:

> Et jacet euxinis vates romanus in oris
> Romanum vatem barbara terra tegit.
> Terra tegit vatem teneros qui lusit amores
> Barbara quam gelidis alluit Ister aquis.

Politian's *Orfeo*, of course, was accompanied by music in its first
performance in Mantua in 1480 and in the following centuries its
text has formed the basis for many of the operas on this theme.

But Hofmannsthal and Politian are bound together in a more
meaningful way by having an identical theme which gives their
poetry its splendour and its delicacy. Their works are a poetic
idealization of the society in which they lived and which they saw
perish.

Ever since Lorenzo Magnifico took into his household the nine-
teen-year-old Politian, who had attracted the attention of the
Florentine literati through his poetic translation of the *Iliad*, entrusted
to him the education of his sons and made him his secretary, Lorenzo
was the young poet's idol. We have known for many years now that
Botticelli's *Primavera* and *Birth of Venus* were painted for Lorenzo di
Pierfrancesco de' Medici and not for Lorenzo Magnifico, and that the
famous school of artists in Lorenzo's Palazzo never existed. Historical

scholarship asserts that Lorenzo was not the ruler of Florence but acted within a republican political tradition so that at best he was a *primus inter pares*. Nevertheless, this does not replace in our mind Politian's image "E tu, ben nato Laur, sotto il cui velo Fiorenza lieta in pace si riposa". We still see in Lorenzo and in his brother Giuliano young princes hunting in the woods and hills of Florence, and leaders of a circle of graceful youths and beautiful women united in the cult of art, the service of love and the delight in the display of manly courage.

The manner in which Politian—in his poem on Giuliano's tournament, or in his elegies on the beauty and virtue of the reigning ladies of this circle, Albiera Albizzi and Simonetta Vespucci—presented the Florence of his time as a golden age, has a colourful intensity which our knowledge of how it really was cannot pale. Undoubtedly, these colours seem to us particularly strong because of the darkness of the period which followed. There is no reason, however, to assume that when Politian extolled the life in Florence under the Medici he had a presentiment of the imminence of the end of their regime. But—perhaps because of his almost miraculous rise from abject poverty to a companion of Florence's most powerful citizen—Politian had a feeling for the inconstancy of life and for the rapid passing of time which gives his poetry its fragile delicacy. And when Lorenzo Magnifico died—although his son Piero, Politian's pupil, appeared firmly established—Politian was certainly aware that the end of an age had come.

> Nunc muta omnia,
> Nunc surda omnia.
> Quis dabit capiti meo
> Aquam, quis oculis meis
> Fontem lachrymarum dabit,
> Ut nocte fleam?
> Ut luce fleam?

In his rise Politian had been a favourite of Fortuna, but the feeling of dependence on this fickle goddess made him sensitive and vulnerable. He possessed grace and charm; he was a devoted friend and full of enthusiastic admiration for what his friends achieved; he had a brilliant, quick and sharp intelligence; but he was very much aware of this. He had no respect for established reputations and would ruthlessly and arrogantly attack and criticize whomever he considered to be wrong or stupid. But he himself easily took offence. He was not without vanity and most of all he was spoilt. Perhaps because he was conscious of the insecure basis of his position, he was proud and concerned with his dignity.

Thus, he himself created the difficulties which removed him from the paradise of his youth. The autocratic manner in which he handled the education of the Medici sons aroused the anger of Clarice Medici, Lorenzo's wife, and she turned him out of the Medici Villa in Cafaggiolo. Lorenzo continued to stand behind him. He took care that the books which in the rush of leaving the Villa he had been forced to leave behind—his Homer, his Demosthenes—were returned to him and he kept him on as his secretary. But even Lorenzo's patience with this difficult favourite became exhausted. When Politian at first hesitated to accompany Lorenzo to Naples, on what was considered to be a dangerous trip into enemy territory, and when, after having changed his mind, Politian expected to get from Lorenzo a personal message and personal invitation, Lorenzo cut him off.

The intimacy and the close personal contact which had existed between Lorenzo and Politian was never restored. But Politian could not live outside Florence and Lorenzo never changed his mind about Politian's outstanding gifts. After a short absence from Florence Politian was called back and received a chair for Latin and Greek rhetorics at the Florentine Studio. The poet was transformed into a scholar.

This move to a new field of activity did not diminish Politian's veneration for Lorenzo Magnifico. He remained constant to what he had said in a poem: "Sum tuus, O Medices; fateor tuque ipse fateris/Sum tuus usque." But next to Lorenzo other figures become the objects of Politian's loyal admiration: Pico della Mirandola and Ermolao Barbaro. When, during his composition of the *Centuria Secunda*, Politian received the news of the death of Ermolao Barbaro he interrupted his writing with an outcry about the loss which this death meant for the *bonae artes* and he inserted in the chapter on which he was working a moving eulogy. In Politian's devotion to Pico and Barbaro the personal factor was not decisive. They had the same interests in the reconstruction of ancient texts and an identical approach to this task. Politian served no longer a person but a cause.

It has often been said of Politian that in the pursuit of his cause he was acerbic, almost cruel to his antagonists; he was especially reproached for having printed, after Calderini's death, an attack against the "pseudo-scholarship" of this old humanist. But Politian defended himself by stating that he was not inspired by "fondness for controversy" nor by "any eagerness to find faults in learned men," but by a zeal for truth. "My shots are fired against those who in order to defend their own personal, entirely imaginary interpretations obstinately resist the evidence of truth." Politian was no longer concerned with his personal advancement. He felt that his responsibility extended to future generations who ought to read the famous texts of the ancient world in unmutilated form. The community within which he worked were all those who had the same aims— whether living in the present or in the future.

Politian's *Centuria Secunda* not only indicates the emergence of a new philological method but it also shows that this development was simultaneous with another development: from the diffuse efforts of the humanists in whom the wish to attract attention had been an ever-present stimulus, philology developed into a self-contained and self-conscious discipline. A few decades later this development had become obvious. Budé, Erasmus and Scaliger were the princely rulers of a field which had become autonomous and in which only those who were also philologists and had the same criteria could judge the work of others.

In Politian and his friends we can observe the growth of the conviction that they were members of a special discipline which had its own dignity. In his *Lamia* Politian declined the role of philosopher. He could claim only to be a "grammaticus". But behind this show of modesty there was great pride. "With the ancients", Politian wrote, "this profession had such an authority that the Grammatici alone were the censors and judges of all writers so that they were also called critics." This statement ought to be read together with remarks which Politian made in a letter to Cortese, remarks which are famous because they are an early attack against the fashion of Ciceronianism. Politian was defending himself against the accusation that he is not adopting the style of the writers of the Golden Age of Rome; he maintained that he did not want to be an imitator whose writings lack strength and vitality. "I am reproached that I don't express myself like Cicero, but why should I? I am not Cicero, I am I, and I wish to express myself."

These words reveal the inner springs of Politian's interest in philology and show that as philologist he continued on the path which he had pursued as poet. Politian's main concern was language,

language as a means of expression. In order to be put into words human thoughts and emotions in their many nuances and their endless variety need a vocabulary of great richness and great flexibility. This was the motive of Politian's intense efforts to establish accurately what an ancient writer had said. This was the reason why he refused to limit Latin to the vocabulary and the sentence structure of Cicero's times but extended his study to the writers of every period of Roman history. Of his aims as well as of his success in attaining them his epigrams against Marullus, also a poet and a competitor, are indicative; they have an immensely rich and varied vocabulary which consists entirely of words used by ancient writers, but is also so esoteric that few will understand them fully without looking up a dictionary.

Certainly, Politian shared the hope of the Renaissance humanists who through their work intended to revive the ancient world. But in Politian's case these attempts are engulfed in the pedagogical aim of enlarging the conceptual faculties and the means of expression of modern man. Politian did not shy away from the possible consequence: because of the close relationship between Latin and the *volgare* an extension of the Latin dictionary might not only serve the understanding of the past but might also aid in the acquisition of a greater and more varied vocabulary and so contribute to the sophistication of the *volgare*. Even as a philologist Politian remained enough of a poet to believe in the possibilities of the *volgare* as a literary language.

Thus, the *Miscellanea* of the *Centuria Secunda* have aspects which are not clearly visible on the surface. The manuscript is not only a document belonging to the history of philology but a work in which the precision devoted to the establishment of the meaning of names and things sharpens and extends the cognitive capacities of man. The "revival of antiquity" in the Renaissance has features which are easily noticed: the use of classical concepts in philosophy; the application of a classical terminology to the developments in political and social life; or the "imitation" of classical prescripts and patterns in art. But it is more difficult to grasp and to define the role which the ancient world played in the slow and gradual transformation of man's cognitive faculties. We might get glimpses of this process by the study of a specialized, detailed and almost esoteric work like Politian's *Miscellanea* because, as always, also here "le bon Dieu est dans le détail."

17

THE CONFINES OF TRUTH

(a) A SECOND DESCARTES?

To MENTION A PHILOSOPHER by surname alone is sometimes to rank him—with, say, Kant, as opposed to, say, G. E. Moore. Wittgenstein is making some such point when, in the preface to the *Tractatus*, he expresses indebtedness "to Frege's great works and to the writings of my friend Mr Bertrand Russell". It would be tiresome to discuss the implied ordering, but one does not need to concur with it in order to endorse Wittgenstein's judgment of Frege. However, general acknowledgment, among English-speaking philosophers, of Frege's greatness has been belated, and is still incomplete. Even now, with much of his work available in English, one can find philosophers of language who are hardly aware of him, and misconceptions of his views are abundant. Yet, as Michael Dummett's book makes clear, there could scarcely be a better way to arrive at a satisfying philosophy of language of one's own than by confronting—not necessarily accepting—the doctrines of this profound and single-minded thinker.

Frege's logicist programme in foundations of number theory, which was shipwrecked on the rock of Russell's paradox, had grown out of a more general project: to find a way of formulating mathematical proofs without reliance on intuition. This required him, first, to invent a formal language which could express any mathematical reasoning, and, second, to explain it in such a way as to leave no doubt that his permitted inference-procedures would lead from truths only to truths. In meeting the first requirement, he invented the quantifier variable notation, which made possible, at last, an adequate treatment of expressions of multiple generality. (Nowadays

---

(*a*) MICHAEL DUMMETT: *Frege*. Philosophy of Language. 698 pp. Duckworth. £10.

(*b*) MORRIS KLINE: *Mathematical Thought from Ancient to Modern Times.* 1,238 pp. Oxford University Press. £12.

quantifiers and variables come nearly as naturally to many philosophers as their mother tongues, so we are in danger of forgetting
the magnitude of Frege's achievement; but Mr Dummett's second
chapter averts that risk.) The second requirement seemed to Frege
to demand not merely paraphrases and explications, but a deep
account of what, in general, a theory of meaning for a language
should be like.

Frege's own initial interests lay almost exclusively in mathematical
discourse, but the generality and profundity of his views make it
reasonable to hope that they might illuminate everyday discourse as
well. Certainly it is Frege's response to his first requirement that has
made possible much recent work in this field. W. V. Quine, Donald
Davidson, and others have brought us nearer being able to give a
general and systematic description of competence with various
idioms of ordinary English, by showing how vernacular sentences
may be "regimented" into the syntactic forms of Frege's formal
language. Possibly useful enrichments—e g, predicate abstracts—are
enrichments of, precisely, Frege's framework. As Mr Dummett
says, "we have no other general framework available".

Some will protest at this. Why, they will ask, should we seek a
general framework, at the price of forcing the charming variety of
ordinary speech into the straitjacket of an austere syntax? The
answer is that, largely thanks to Frege, we have ideas about how
to construct a theory of meaning for a language with the syntax of
his formal language (and we can extend these ideas to the enrichments). Thus we can regard a theory of meaning for the regimented
language, together with an account of its relation to the unregimented language, as constituting a theory of meaning for the
unregimented language. If we try to work directly with the attractive
complexities of actual speech, there is no telling even how to begin
constructing a systematic theory. And we must have a systematic
theory, or at least a general view about what a systematic theory
would be like. Philosophers may not properly rely on an intuitive,
untheoretical grasp of the notion of meaning; for, as Mr Dummett
remarks, "philosophy has, as its first if not its only task, the analysis
of meanings, and . . . the deeper such analysis goes, the more it is
dependent upon a correct general account of meaning".

A Fregean theory of meaning for a language would have four
components: theories of sense, reference, force, and tone. ("Tone"
is Mr Dummett's substitute for Frege's "colouring" or "illumina-

tion".) The first three would centre, in different ways, on the notion of truth; the fourth is a catch-all for any aspects of significance that cannot be captured in terms of truth (e g, pejorativeness). Frege is perfunctory and unsatisfactory about tone; the interest of his views lies rather in what he contrasts with it.

That significant expressions have both sense and reference is Frege's best-known doctrine, but it is not well understood. Frege himself first introduced the doctrine in connexion with singular terms. Many philosophers get no farther than finding it plausible that, e g, "the author of *Waverley*" and "the author of *Marmion*" differ in sense but not in reference. Even about singular terms, however, there is more to say, since Frege applies the distinction also to proper names strictly so called (singular terms without significant structure): some balk at this. Moreover, he extends it to functional and predicative expressions and to complete sentences: many balk at this.

Mr Dummett suggests that Frege's conception of reference amalgamates two ideas: first, that a prototypical case of the reference of an expression is the bearer of a name, and, second, that the reference of an expression is what gets assigned to it in an interpretation of the sort familiar from model-theoretical semantics for predicate logic. The second idea explains Frege's lack of embarrassment at ascribing references to functional and predicative expressions and to complete sentences; the first idea, in view of some disanalogies, which Mr Dummett brings out, between these latter cases and the prototypical case, explains our embarrassment at this extension. (Mr Dummett would put this differently, using "referent" for the entity for which an expression stands. But, contrary to his "terminological note" on pages 93–94, *Bedeutung*, in Frege's *official* use, unambiguously applies to that entity, and may as well be rendered "reference" throughout. Mr Dummett's policy of not citing chapter and verse is always deplorable: where, as here, his claims about Frege are controversial, it is unforgivable.)

Two *caveats* must be entered. First, there is a gap between this account of Frege's conception of reference and the doctrine which it is meant to explain. In an interpretation of the usual kind, a predicate (say) would be assigned a set, which is a complete entity (an object); whereas Frege insists that the reference of a predicate is an incomplete entity (roughly, a concept, though such talk needs correction on pain of paradox). Second, a model theory defines truth on an arbitrary interpretation conforming to certain restrictions. A formula which is not logically true or false will be true on some interpretations and false on others. But, for Frege, a sentence which expresses a complete thought has, once and for all, one or other of the two truth-values as its reference. So, obviously, not just any interpretation will do as a theory of reference; we need to select, and specify, from the set of interpretations defined in the model theory, a designated interpretation—one which makes the truths true, by making the right assignments.

If we adopt this view of Frege's conception of reference, the pressing question about functional and predicative expressions and sentences becomes, what it already was in the case of names, not "Why credit them with references?", but "Why credit them with senses?" Mr Dummett's answer is that "reference is not an ingredient of meaning". He explains this by saying that "a theory of meaning is a theory of understanding": the sense of an expression is what someone knows in understanding it, whereas the reference is not. Our designated interpretation would determine extensions (sets) for all the predicates of the language, and truth-values for all the sentences; and one need not know these in order to understand the language. Intuitively speaking, extensions and truth values are determined jointly by the meanings of the appropriate expressions and by the facts. The designated interpretation includes, so to speak, both the meanings and the facts, inextricably intermixed. But one can understand a language without knowing all the facts capable of being expressed in it.

Is there, then, any way of systematically distilling out the meanings? Frege's discussions of sense are, as Mr Dummett remarks, sketchy, but perhaps we can make something of them. For he held, first, that the sense of a sentence can be specified by giving its truth-conditions, and, second, that the sense of a subsentential expression is its contribution to the senses of sentences in which it occurs. (Both these doctrines are expressed at *Grundgesetze* I. §32.) This suggests, almost irresistibly, that a Fregean theory of sense might be constituted by something which Professor Davidson has recently argued would constitute a theory of meaning for a language: namely, an inductive "truth-definition" for the language in the style of Tarski.

Such a truth-definition need not be confused with a theory of reference. As we saw, a theory of reference would be an inductive definition of truth on an interpretation, together with a specification of the designated interpretation, given in such a way as to determine truth-*values* for all sentences. A Davidsonian truth-definition, by contrast, is not relativized to an interpretation. It determines truth-*conditions* for all sentences, leaving truth-values, as we intuitively require, to be partly determined by the facts. (It need not assign entities, complete or incomplete, to predicates either.) In his difficult Chapter 13, Mr Dummett concedes that such a truth-definition would in some sense display, at least partially, speakers' knowledge; hence, we might conclude, the senses of expressions.

Since the designated interpretation must be one which makes the truths true, and since the truth of the true sentences is owed jointly to their senses and the facts, and since one can know the senses of expressions without knowing all the facts, it seems that the theory of sense is epistemically prior to the theory of reference; one could arrive at the theory of reference only by way of the theory of sense and the facts. In the case of predicates and sentences, on this view, references are posterior to senses, and play no role in an account of what understanding consists in. This is the conclusion Mr Dummett reaches, but he does so without directly exploiting the idea of a systematic theory of sense for a language.

Singular terms have a different position. Names (and individual variables) can be treated in exactly parallel ways in a definition of truth on the designated interpretation and in a Davidsonian truth-definition: namely, by assigning references to names (and considering all possible assignments of references to variables). Taking the Davidsonian truth-definition as a theory of sense, we can regard this parallelism as a vindication of Mr Dummett's conclusion that, with names as opposed to predicates and sentences, the notion of reference does play a role in an account of understanding and hence of sense. Here, we might say, reference is prior to sense.

A way of handling names, adequate for the purposes of a theory which generates truth-conditions for sentences, would, we suggested, be to specify a reference for each. This is a point at which Mr Dummett would evidently dissent from the identification of a Davidsonian truth-definition with a Fregean theory of sense. For Frege wanted an account of the sense of a name to include, not merely a specification of its bearer, but a representation of a competent speaker's means of recognizing an object as its bearer; and Mr Dummett thinks he was right.

Arguably, though, this is a mistake, on the part of both of them. It is hard to reconcile with Mr Dummett's remarks about why the notion of sense is not, in the way Frege would have disapproved of, psychological: as he says, "A model for the sense of a word of some particular kind does not seek to explain *how* we are able to use the word as we do; it simply forms part of an extended description of what that use consists in." Sense is to be what a competent speaker knows: a competent speaker's "means of recognizing an object as the bearer of a name" may be nothing but neural machinery, not something he knows at all. No doubt a sophisticated description of someone's ability to use a name might include an account of the identity conditions of things of the kind which its bearer belongs to, and a criterion for identifying the bearer; but not everything in *our* description of the ability can plausibly be held to be known by the possessor of the ability described.

Sense and reference need not, as Mr Dummett fears, coalesce on this austere conception of sense. They are kept separate by an application of his own suggestion that sense is correlative with knowledge. The reference of a name is an object, so knowing the reference of a name would be something like acquaintance with that object; but the knowledge required for understanding a name is not acquaintance but propositional knowledge. Thus a grammatical distinction secures the distinctness of sense from reference, even if the sense of a name is fully specified by saying, in an appropriate way, what its reference is. "In an appropriate way" matters here. Knowing the sense of "Hesperus" and "Phosphorus" should be thought of as knowing that "Hesperus" stands for *Hesperus* and "Phosphorus" for *Phosphorus*. One who knows that need not know that "Hesperus" stands for Phosphorus or that "Phosphorus" stands for Hesperus: so the sense-reference distinction can still be put to Frege's purpose of explaining how someone can understand a sentence like "Hesperus is Phosphorus" without thereby already knowing that it is true.

The third of the truth-centred parts of a Fregean theory of meaning would be a theory of force—i e, an account, employing the notion of truth, of what speakers do with their sentences. Frege's own efforts in this area are limited to some sketchy remarks about assertions and questions: by contrast, Mr Dummett's discussion of this component of the theory is one of the most profound and difficult strands in the book.

His fundamental idea is perhaps this: complete understanding of the notion of truth requires a grasp, not only of the application-conditions of the predicate "true", but also of the point of the classification which it effects, and it is this latter which the theory of force is to make explicit. If we are to be reasonable in supposing that it is conditions for their *truth* which determine the senses of sentences, we must see how making linguistic behaviour intelligible depends on *combining* knowledge of the truth-conditions of sentences with knowledge of the conventional forces with which they are uttered; the possibility of the combination hinges on the fact that the notion of truth figures also in the account of each possible conventional force.

So far, perhaps, so good. What seems questionable is Mr Dummett's extracting, from thoughts like these, the idea of a sort of independence of the theory of force from the theory of sense—e g, in his suggestion that the notion of truth-value required in explaining some conventional force (say, that of assertion) may diverge from that required in describing how sentences figure as constituents in complex sentences. One might think, as against this, that the fact on which the necessary combining of theories hinges should be precisely that the *same* notion of truth, and hence of truth-value, figures in both. But Mr Dummett's subtle views require, and deserve, much less cursory treatment.

We have not even touched on several topics which are extensively discussed in this book. It seeks to evaluate Frege's doctrines as well as expounding them, and the evaluation requires profound consideration of a great number of issues in the philosophy of language. To list just a few: the possibility of recognizing singular terms in any language; abstract objects; identity; *oratio obliqua*; substitutional and referential interpretations of quantification; Professor Quine's views about analyticity and meaning. The intention, avowed on the dust-jacket, "to separate what is superficial from what goes deep" is achieved, and Mr Dummett is always forthright and nearly always clear. Nobody will agree with everything he says. But it is possible to find many, perhaps even most, of his own views unconvincing and yet to admire the book profoundly for raising important questions and tackling them in the right sort of way.

Reading Mr Dummett is not easy partly because of the difficulty of his subject-matter, but partly because of his expansive style: paragraph by paragraph this generates (mostly) a marvellous lucidity, but it is hard to keep hold of the drift of some of the extremely long, undivided chapters, and some topics run over several chapters. Still, familiarity makes the bones of the arguments stick out, and this is anyway not a book for just one reading: it will need to be worked through repeatedly by anyone with a serious interest in the philosophy of language.

The last chapter credits Frege with a shift in philosophical perspective comparable to that initiated by Descartes: Descartes put epistemology at the centre, and Frege substitutes the theory of meaning. Mr Dummett seems to be not just recommending, but contending that the shift has already occurred. Presumably this claim is not to be judged by counting heads; presumably the contention is that the most *important* work is being done from the new standpoint. Of course, the assessment of importance is made from the very standpoint it mentions, so there is an appearance of pulling oneself up by one's own hair. But in this case perhaps that Münchhausen feat can be partly brought off. It is difficult to see how anyone, whatever orientation he began with, could understand Mr Dummett's book without coming to regard it as a glowing example of unquestionably important work, done from the standpoint of the assumption that the most fundamental part of philosophy is the philosophy of language.

(b) THE MATHEMATICAL HERITAGE

AN EMINENT MATHEMATICIAN was once lecturing on algebraic geometry. In the middle of a long algebraic calculation he became stuck, wandered off to one side, and drew a few pictures. He then *erased them* and resumed the calculation.

Mathematics is usually presented to the student in its final polished form. The hesitant and faltering steps by which it was discovered have been neatly erased. There are times when mathematics seems to function as an Orwellian Ministry of Truth, obliterating its own past. This is not a conscious act on the part of mathematicians, who are only too well aware of the obstacles and blind alleys which beset the arduous path to new ideas. But in teaching a piece of mathematics it can be confusing to disinter the moulding remains of the red herrings of the past. So the past is often rewritten to suit the needs of the present, or simply ignored.

In a book of mammoth proportions Morris Kline exposes the muddy history of mathematics and traces its complex tale from dim antiquity to the early twentieth century. A work of this scope should encompass many themes: the triumphs and the failures; the ups and downs of logical rigour; the changes of emphasis and subject-matter; the philosophical trends and cultural links; the motives and sources of inspiration; above all the remarkable ability of mathematical formalism to give fundamental insights into the universe in which we live.

Let it be said at once that Professor Kline neglects none of these themes; that his style is clear and lucid, though dry; and that for scope and detail there is no work which could compete with that under review. The only comparable book is E. T. Bell's *The Development of Mathematics* which is perhaps half the size; Mr Bell is more entertaining, but less scholarly. Students or teachers in search of their mathematical heritage will find most of it in *Mathematical Thought from Ancient to Modern Times*.

One of the questions which any survey of mathematical thought must answer is the question of applicability: why is it that the abstract methodology of mathematics has, time after time, found profound applications in the study of physical phenomena?

It is worth mentioning some instances, all of which are discussed by Professor Kline. The ancient Greek studies of conic sections, in about 200 BC, led to Kepler's laws of planetary motion in 1609, which in turn led to Newton's formulation of the law of gravitation. The coordinate geometry of Descartes in the seventeenth century gave rise to the differential and integral calculus, which even today is the major tool of theoretical physics. More recently, Hilbert's theory of integral equations turned out to be just what was needed for quantum mechanics, and Riemann's differential geometry became the basic tool for general relativity.

The Pythagoreans answered the question by affirming a belief in the mathematical design of the universe. God is a geometer. By the operation of pure thought, of which mathematics is the essence, mankind may deduce the workings of the world. As Professor Kline notes, the concomitant belief in the pre-existence of mathematical concepts led to a disastrous self-limitation of Greek mathematics and a loss of mathematical power.

A similar belief was entertained by Descartes. In fact the idea of mathematics as a God-given subject persisted well into the eighteenth century, with arguments about the true value of log $\sqrt{-1}$, without any realization that the symbols might be meaningless, and that the observed properties of logarithms of real numbers might be misleading if applied to complex numbers.

A major blow to God-given mathematics was the discovery of non-Euclidean geometries: logically consistent geometries in which there may be no parallel to a given line through a given point, or infinitely many. Which is the true geometry? All the while there is only one geometry, it is possible to claim it as a logical necessity. Faced with several equally consistent geometries, one must resort to experiment to test the different *theories* of geometry. And perhaps the true geometry (if such a thing exists) corresponds to *none* of the theoretical ones.

It is now much more surprising that mathematics tells us deep physical truths. For mathematics is revealed as a creation of the human mind. If it is Man, and not God, who is the geometer, then why is the universe geometrical?

And thus we come to the central thesis of the book, and Professor Kline's answer to the problem of applicability: the best mathematics is that which is rooted in nature.

This is not to say that all mathematics must have *direct* physical interpretations. Any mathematical theory runs into technical problems quite unrelated to its applications. The whole rigmarole of congruent triangles in Euclid is a technical device to circumvent purely mathematical problems. The extra methods and concepts needed to overcome these technical difficulties are every bit as important as the more physically oriented ones: perhaps more so. The physical concepts motivate the theory, the mathematical ones give it power.

Which brings us to the "heroic" age of mathematics, where theories plunged boldly ahead without any concern for their logical foundations, and often with little in the way of experimental evidence either. Newton began it, with his *Principia*; and yet he was not a part of it. Newton was more a geometer in the Greek tradition. He was suspicious of the calculus and avoided it in much of his published work. But almost everyone *after* Newton used the calculus without a qualm. The results agreed with experiment: how could there be anything wrong with the mathematics?

In the heroic age, as never before or since, mathematics *was* physics. No need to ask why it applied: it was the tool designed for the job. As for rigour, Clairaut's attitude was typical: "All reasoning concerned with what common sense knows in advance serves only to conceal the truth and to weary the reader and is today disregarded."

Preliminary indications of disaster came from Fourier's work on heat. According to Fourier, every function can be expanded as a trigonometric series, whose coefficients may be found by evaluating certain integrals involving the given function. As things turned out, matters were more complicated. For some functions the integrals do not exist. For others they exist, but the series converges to the wrong function. After Fourier came a rash of similar difficulties, all centred on the calculus and related infinite processes. As the calculus was developed further and further, the absence of logical foundations became ever more embarrassing. Freedom is one thing, licence another. For mathematics is not physics. Physics has its own real-world constraints, whereas mathematics without logic has no constraints at all!

And so began the age of logical rigour, and mathematicians began to study the foundations of their subject, worried that the entire grandiose edifice might be built on sand. Through the work of Bolzano, Cauchy, Klein, and Cantor, the logical structure of mathematics was reduced to that of the system of ordinary whole numbers 1, 2, 3 . . . Poincaré, with apparently justifiable pride, remarked that "one may say that absolute rigour has been obtained".

A parallel development to that of logical rigour was an increasing tendency towards abstraction. Galois introduced the concept of a permutation group in order to solve fundamental problems in the theory of polynomial equations. Work in the theory of numbers led unavoidably to questions about general algebraic number fields. Analysis became dependent on set-theoretic concepts. As methods and problems became more general, mathematicians were forced to consider more general concepts. Ideas which seemed to be different revealed themselves as different concrete embodiments of the same abstract entity. It became so cumbersome and confusing to carry the physical interpretations of mathematical concepts around with them all the time that the physical interpretations had to be put to one side. One should first do the mathematics, then apply the results to physics.

The more abstract the subject became, the more important it was that there should be no logical flaws. Poincaré's pride turned out to be premature. In the attempts to provide a truly rigorous foundation for the subject, it finally became clear that mathematics was not

God-given but man-made. Any logical structure is a legitimate target for a mathematical theory. Mathematics, no longer just a means, became an end in itself. As Professor Kline puts it, "mathematics broke away from nature and science to pursue its own course".

There is little doubt about Professor Kline's opinion of the break-away:

The subject has mushroomed into a welter of smaller developments that have little relation to each other or to the original concrete fields. . . .

And at this crucial moment of time—Professor Kline stops. He tells us hardly anything about the mathematics of the twentieth century apart from a few gloomy paragraphs: "Developments of the second and third quarters of this century are too recent to be properly evaluated." "To continue into the twentieth century . . . would call for highly specialized material of interest only to research men."

But if these were the criteria, the book could have been much shorter. For many of the historical trends discussed were subsequently found to have little or no value. Many of the details included are highly technical. It may be unfair to criticize a book of this scope for not setting its sights more broadly; but one must be unfair, because by stopping where he has Professor Kline has left out a very important part of the story. One says this not out of a misguided temporal chauvinism, but only out of a sense of disappointment. Had this been a book on the development of physics, it would have contained no relativity, no quantum theory, and no electronics. The title is misleading: it would have been truer to call it "classical mathematics". Many of the book's readers will want to know how the developments of the past link up with the present day. All they will deduce from Professor Kline's study is that in the 1920s everyone went overboard for meaningless abstractions and began to degenerate, save for those sane men who carried on the work of previous centuries, but whose results are too technical to discuss.

The truth is quite different. Far from being "a welter of smaller developments" the mathematics of today is a rich and complex fusion of interrelated ideas. It is commonplace to start with a problem in analysis, reduce it to topology, formulate it as algebra, and solve it using number theory. Today's mathematics consists of a large number of powerful tools for solving very general problems: the answers to more specialized problems come as simple corollaries. These tools were developed in order to have some chance of dealing with otherwise insuperable problems inherited from the nineteenth century.

There was, in the 1930s and 1940s, a brief vogue for wild abstractions. This corresponds to what is known in psychology as the "play stage", and is a necessary prelude to the formation of significant concepts. A few decades of unbridled freedom eventually led to a deeper understanding of what are the really significant ideas and problems.

Most interesting is the new twist which modern developments have added to the problem of applicability. All the while mathematics was rooted in nature it was easy to explain its presence in physical theories. Today this explanation has been revealed as facile. Mathematics developed purely for its own sake has suddenly found important and unexpected applications in the sciences.

A striking example of this process is the Index Theorem of M. F. Atiyah, R. Bott, and I. Singer. Beginning with a classical theorem of complex function theory due to Riemann and Roch, and applying techniques of algebraic topology and number theory, Atiyah, Bott, and Singer produced a fantastic generalization which wrapped up in a single package topology, differential geometry, algebraic number theory, and elliptic differential operators. These last are of considerable importance in mathematical physics.

Another example is recent work on the stability of dynamical systems, using ideas from topology which were originally developed for purely mathematical purposes, and in particular the technique of handle decomposition invented by S. Smale to solve the Poincaré conjecture.

A third instance is René Thom's theory of catastrophes (see E. C. Zeeman, "The geometry of catastrophe", *TLS*, December 10, 1971) which applies a massive amount of topology, algebra, algebraic geometry, analysis, and singularity theory to the classification of discontinuous processes. This has applications to biology, especially developmental biology; and has already given rise to a new theory of the propagation of nerve impulses. It should be emphasized that the mathematical techniques include several developed specifically for the study of algebraic geometry over an arbitrary field, a subject explicitly criticized by Professor Kline.

Why is it that despite having broken away from science, mathematics is still producing physically relevant results?

If one trims away from mathematics the lunatic fringe, one finds a tightly-knit body of knowledge, whose harmony and unity is impaired only by gaps due to our enormous ignorance. The major course of mathematics is aimed—has always been aimed—at removing these gaps. The development of powerful general techniques and deep insights is a natural consequence of this aim; and far from being a sign of degeneracy it keeps the subject healthy.

We search for pattern in a chaotic universe. We look for patterns of a kind we can recognize and understand. Mathematics *is* the study of those patterns which the human mind can recognize and understand. Any pattern we see in the universe will be one for which a mathematical treatment is possible; conversely, whenever a new mathematical insight occurs, we are able to recognize new kinds of patterns. If any of these occur in nature, we have a totally unexpected application of the theory. And this is how mathematics gets its power; for a pattern which is hard to recognize in one area may be obvious in another. By taking inspiration from the second we discover the existence of the first.

We could restrict our mathematical motivation to the physical world alone. But to do so would be to shut our eyes to those patterns not immediately available to physical intuition. This is to limit ourselves in a manner as potentially disastrous as did the Greeks. The real world is an important source of mathematical ideas, but mathematics itself has now grown to the stage where it, too, can provide inspiration for new ideas.

The patterns of physics are, by themselves, too limited. Physics has become so obsessed with numbers that it has lost sight of qualitative problems. Two oak trees may have different heights, different numbers of leaves, different arrangement of the branches—yet they must have something in common which is accessible to our gross physical senses, otherwise we would not recognise them as oak trees. No amount of delving into the microscopic structure of living matter will tell us what it is. But one is bound to bet that there's a marvellous mathematical theory there, if only we could work it out.

INDEX

This index, in addition to referring to articles and reviews in the present volume, also shows other major reviews of the year which have appeared in the *T.L.S.* Date references and page numbers in *italic* are to articles and reviews in the *T.L.S.* not reprinted in this volume. Page numbers in parentheses are given only where the reference is not immediately obvious from the article.

Adorno, Theodor W.: 'Gesammelte Schriften', *9 March*

Aesop's Fables, *7 Dec.* (*p. 1515*)

Agrarian history, *25 May*

Aguilar, L. E.: 'Cuba 1933', *12 Jan.*

Albaret, Céleste: 'Monsieur Proust', *21 Dec.*

Aldiss, B. W.: 'Billion Year Spree', 144

Alexander of Tunis, Field Marshal Earl: Biography (Nicolson), *30 March*

Alexandria, Ptolemaic, *9 Nov.*

Amery, Julian: 'Approach March', *16 Nov.*

Amis, Kingsley: 'The Riverside Villas Murder', *6 April*

Andersen, Wayne: 'Gauguin's Paradise Lost', *25 May*

Anderson, W. E. K. (ed.): 'The Journal of Sir Walter Scott', *5 Jan.*

Andreas-Salomé, Lou: Sigmund Freud and, *26 Jan.*

Anthropology, Social: Special number, *6 July*

Anzoinó, Tommaso: 'Pasolini', *12 Oct.*

Aragon, Louis: 'Henri Matisse', *16 Feb.*

Archaeology, Industrial, *31 Aug.*

Architecture: Special pages, *23 Feb.*

Aristocratic finance, *13 July* (*p. 805*)

Art:
  and Culture, *14 Sept.*
  Pre-Raphaelite landscape, *10 Aug.*

Artists: Education, *21 Sept.*

Ashe, Geoffrey: 'The Finger and the Moon', *24 Aug.*

Athenian Empire, *18 May*

Athens, Ancient: Property and power in, *23 Feb.*; Agora of, *11 May* (*p. 522*)

Aubrey, John: 'Three Prose Works', 'Aubrey on Education', *16 Feb.*

Auden, W. H.: 'Epistle to a Godson', 19; Tributes to, *5 Oct* (*p. 1172*), *16 Nov.* (*p. 1398*), 'Forewords and Afterwords', *12 Oct.*

Austria: After the Hapsburgs, *24 Aug.*

Avant-Garde, Concept of the, *25 May*

Bainbridge, Beryl: 'The Dressmaker', 72

Balzac, Honoré de: Biography (Pritchett), *14 Sept.*

Banta, Martha: 'Henry James and the Occult', *30 Nov.*

Barker, Dudley: 'G. K. Chesterton', *17 Aug.*

Barker, Elisabeth: 'Austria 1918–1972', *24 Aug.*

Barthelme, Donald: 'Sadness', *7 Dec.*

Barthes, Roland: 'Le Plaisir du texte', *22 June*

Bartley III, W. W.: 'Wittgenstein', *17 Aug.*

Bataille, Georges: 'Oeuvres complètes', *15 June*

Beaton, Cecil: 'The Strenuous Years', *5 Oct.*

Beck, J. H.: 'Jacopo della Quercia. . .', *30 Nov.*

Beckett, Samuel, *12 Oct.*

Beckford, William: 'Recollections of an Excursion. . .', *22 June*

Beckmann, Max: Biography (Fischer), *24 Aug.*

Behaviourism, *2 March*

Bellotto, Bernardo: Biography (Kozakiewicz), *5 Jan.*

Benamou, Michel: 'Wallace Stevens and the Symbolist Imagination', *6 April*

Bénichou, Paul: 'Le Sacre de l'écrivain', *5 Oct.*

Benjamin, Walter, *14 Dec.*

Bense, Max, *12 Oct.*

Bentley, Eric: 'Theatre of War', *25 May*

Bernstein, Basil: 'Class, Codes and Control', *29 June*

Berryman, John: 'Delusions, Etc.', *25*; 'Recovery', *30 Nov.*

Besterman, Theodore (ed.): 'Studies on Voltaire and the Eighteenth Century', *20 April, 4 May, 13 July, 31 Sept.*

Beurdeley, Cecile and Michel: 'Guiseppe Castiglione', *21 Sept.*

Bevan, Aneurin: Biography (Foot), *12 Oct.*

Bibliographica, American, *9 March (p. 276)*

Biedermeier literature, *19 Jan.*

Biochemistry, *9 March*

Biology, Theoretical, *18 May*

Biswas, R. K.: 'Arthur Hugh Clough', *12 Jan.*

Bizet, Georges: Whose 'Carmen'?, *24 Aug.*

Blainey, Geoffrey: 'The Causes of War', *15 June*

Blake, William: Woodcuts, *18 May;* Illustrations of the Book of Job, *30 Nov.*

Bligh, Captain: and Mr. Christian, *26 Jan.*

Bonavia, David: 'Fat Sasha and the Urban Guerrilla', *19 Oct.*

Bonsal, P. W.: 'Cuba, Castro and the United States', *12 Jan.*

Bookbinding today, *7 Dec.*

Book-collecting in the 1930s, *11 May*

Book illustrations, *7 Dec. (p. 1505)*

Book production, *5 Jan.;* Special number, *7 Dec.*

Book Short Title Catalogue 1641–1700, *26 Jan.*

Boss, Valentin: 'Newton and Russia', *24 Aug.*

Boston, L. M.: 'Memory in a House', *9 March, 15 June (p. 676)*

Boswell, James: 'Boswell in Extremes 1776–1778', *23 March*

Boucé, P.-G.: 'Les romans de Smollett', *26 Jan.*

Bounty, Mutiny on the, *26 Jan.*

Bowlby, John: 'Attachment and Loss', *23 Nov.*

Bowra, C. M.: 'Periclean Athens', *23 Feb.*

Bradford, Sarah: 'Portugal', *27 July*

Branca, Vittore (ed.): 'Politian's Miscellaneorum Centuria Secunda', *210*

Brandon, Henry: 'The Retreat of American Power', *19 Oct.*

Brecht, Bertolt, *23 Nov., 28 Dec. (p. 1591)*

Bremond, Claude: 'Logique du récit', *12 Oct.*

Brenan, Gerald: 'St. John of the Cross', *24 Aug.*

Brenner, H. (ed.): 'Ende einer bürgerlichen Kunst-Institution', *22 June*

Briggs, Dennie: 'Dealing with Deviants', *16 Feb.*

Briner, Andres: 'Paul Hindemith', *16 March*

Broadcasting: Politicians and the media, *16 Nov.*

Brontë, Charlotte: Study of (Peters), *3 Aug.*; an unpublished tale of, *23 Nov.*

Brontës, The, *3 Aug.*

Brophy, Brigid: 'Prancing Novelist', *30 March*

Broué, Pierre: 'The Revolution and Civil War in Spain', *16 March*

Brown, G. G.: 'Literary History of Spain: the Twentieth Century', *23 March*

Bruce, Lenny, *26 Oct.*

Buber, Martin, *28 Dec.*

Buckingham, Duke of: Copy of 'The Country Gentleman' found, *28 Sept.*

Burgess, Anthony: 'Joysprick', *15 June*

Burney, Fanny: 'Journals and Letters', *13 July*

Byron's Letters and Journals, *122*

Byzantine Empire, *11 May (p. 523)*

Cain, M. E.: 'Society and the Policeman's Role', *2 March*

Callaghan, James: 'A House Divided', *7 Sept.*

Calvino, Italo: 'Le città invisibili', *9 Feb.*

Campbell-Bannerman, Sir Henry: Biography (Wilson), *2 Feb.*

Camus, Albert, *12 Oct.*

Canada:
Canadian Writing Today: Special number, *26 Oct.*
Economic problems, *26 Oct. (p. 1311)*
French Canadian, *26 Oct. (p. 1317)*
Poetry, *26 Oct. (p. 1305)*

Canaletto of the North: *see* Bellotto, Bernardo

Carlyle, Thomas: Meredith's meeting with, *9 Nov.*

Carroll, Lewis: as Logician, *15 June*

Carswell, John: 'From Revolution to Revolution: England 1688–1776', *19 Oct.*

Casement, Roger: Biography (Inglis), 12

Casini, Paolo: 'L'universo-macchina', *1 June*

Castiglione, Guiseppe: Biography (Beurdeley), *21 Sept.*

Castles, Stephen and Kosack, Godula: 'Immigrant Workers and Class Structure in Western Europe', 46

Caute, David: 'The Fellow-Travellers', *6 July*

Cecil, Lord David: 'The Cecils of Hatfield House', *12 Oct.*

Celtic art, *21 Dec.*

Chapman, R.T.: 'Wyndham Lewis', *3 Aug.*

Character, Nature of: Special number, *27 July*

Chauvel, Jean: 'Commentaire', *5 Oct.*

Chesterton, G.K.: Biography (Barker), *17 Aug.*

Child rearing, Schreber family and, *13 July*

Children's Books: Special numbers, *6 April, 15 June, 28 Sept., 23 Nov.*

China:
Art, *21 Dec.*
Colour prints, *21 Sept. (p. 1077)*
History, *17 Aug.*
3,000 years of, *28 Dec.*

Chissell, Joan: 'Schumann Piano Music', *27 April*

Chomsky, Noam: 'For Reasons of State', 'The Backroom Boys', *21 Dec.*

Churchill, Winston S.: Biographies (Gilbert), *9 March;* (Thompson), *26 Oct.*

Cirlot, J.-E.: 'Picasso: Birth of a Genius', *2 Feb.*

Civility, Ideal of, *26 Jan., (p. 93)*

Clare, John: 'The Critical Heritage', *27 July*

Clark, G.K.: 'Churchmen and the Condition of England 1832–1885', *5 Oct.*

Classicist, Changed focus of the, *15 June (p. 691)*

Clive, John: 'Thomas Babington Macaulay', *29 June*

Clough, Arthur Hugh, *12 Jan.*

Cohen, John (ed.): 'The Essential Lenny Bruce', *26 Oct.*

Coke, Van Deren: 'The Painter and the Photograph from Delacroix to Warhol', *9 March*

Cole, H. S. D. (and others) (ed.): 'Thinking About the Future', *14 Sept.*

Coleridge, S. T.: Voyage to Malta and Italy, *2 Nov.*

Collingwood, R. G.: Philosophy of, *30 March*

Communist intellectuals, *17 Aug. (p. 949)*

Connolly, James: Biography (Levenson), *27 July*

Conrad, Joseph, *15 June*

Conrad, Peter: 'The Victorian Treasure-House', *6 July*

Constantine Porphyrogenitus: Study of (Toynbee), *11 May*

Corrigan, Felicitas: 'Siegfried Sassoon: Poet's Pilgrimage', *7 Dec.*

Cortazar, Julio: 'Libro de Manuel', *12 Oct.*

Costes, Alain: 'Albert Camus et la parole manquante', *12 Oct.*

Courbet, Gustave: 'The Studio of the Painter', *6 July*

Crabbe, George: Criticism (ed. A. Pollard), *2 Feb.*

Crathorne, Nancy: 'Tennant's Stalk', *8 June*

Crime, Organized and unorganized, *26 Jan.*

Criminology, New, *24 Aug.*

Cromwell, Oliver: Biographies (Fraser and Wedgwood), 20 *July*

Cromwell, Thomas: Biography (Elton) 20 *April*

Crowley, Aleister: 'White Stains', 'Magick', 27 *July*

Crozier, Brian: 'De Gaulle', 5 *Oct.*

Crummey, Donald: 'Priests and Politicians', 1 *June*

Cuba: and the United States, 12 *Jan.*

Cuyler, Louise: 'The Emperor Maximilian I and Music', 7 *Dec.*

D'Annunzio, Gabriele: Biography (Jullian), 23 *Feb.*

D'Arblay, Madame: see Burney, Fanny

Darwin, Charles: Criticism (Hull), 9 *Nov.*

Davie, Donald: 'Thomas Hardy and British Poetry', 13 *July*

Davies, J. K.: 'Athenian Propertied Families 600–300 B.C.', 23 *Feb.*

Davison, Dennis (ed.): 'The Penguin Book of Eighteenth-Century English Verse', 5 *Oct.*

Defoe, Daniel: 'A General History of the Pyrates', 26 *Jan.*

Deleuze, Gilles: 'Capitalisme et schizophrenie', 16 *March*

Del Mar, Norman: 'Richard Strauss', 18 *May*

Deutscher, Tamara (ed.): 'Not by Politics Alone', 26 *Oct.*

Deviance, 16 *Feb.*, 2 *March* (*p. 242*), 24 *Aug.* (*p. 970*)

de Vries, Peter: 'Forever Panting', 10 *Aug.*

Dictionaries:
Harrap's New Standard French and English, 6 *April*
'Supplement to the O.E.D.', 26 *Jan.*

Dodds, E. R.: 'The Ancient Concept of Progress', 15 *June*

Doderer, Heimito von: 'Die Erzählungen', 20 *April*

Donleavy, J.P.: 'A Fairy Tale of New York', 7 *Sept.*

Donoughue, Bernard and Jones, G.: 'Herbert Morrison', 19 *Oct.*

Dortu, M. G.: 'Toulouse-Lautrec et son Oeuvre', 15 *June*

Drama: see Theatre and drama

Dresden Codex, 5 *Oct.* (*p. 1194*)

Dryden, John: and the Jacobites, 16 *March*

Duby, Georges: 'Guerriers et paysans VII-XIIe siècle', 'Hommes et structures du moyen âge', 94

Dummett, Michael: 'Frege', 217

Durkheim, Émile: Biography (Lukes), 16 *March*

Durrell, Lawrence: 'The Black Book', 27 *April*

Economists, Boom in, 27 *July*

Economy:
Medieval, 94
Prices and incomes, 13 *July* (*p. 807*)

Eliot, George: Dorothea's husbands: some biographical speculations, 16 *Feb.*, correspondence, 2, 9, 16, 23, 30 *March*, 4, 11, 18, 25 *May*, 1, 15, 22 *June;* 'Felix Holt, The Radical', 20 *April*

Eliot, T. S.: 'The Waste Land' as a Buddhist poem, 4 *May*

Ellmann, Richard: 'Golden Codgers', 26 *Oct.*

Elton, G. R.: 'Reform and Renewal', 20 *April*

Elvin, Mark: 'The Pattern of the Chinese Past', 17 *Aug.*

English, Survival of, 7 *Sept.* (*p. 1027*)

English history:
George III's reign, 20 *July* (*p. 833*)
Henry II's reign, 85
Revolution of 1688, 19 *Oct.*

English language: 'The Complete Plain Words', 22 *June* (*p. 719*)

English literature: Oxford Anthology, 2 *Nov.*

Erskine-Hill, Howard: 'Pope: The Dunciad', 5 *Jan.*

Ethiopia:
Church and State 1270–1527, 19 *Jan.*
Emperor's Autobiography, 1 *June*

Europe:
Britain and, 23 *Feb.* (*p. 196*)
Immigrant workers and class structure, 46

Eversley, David: 'The Planner in Society', 7 *Dec.*

Expressionist periodicals, Indexing of, *23 March* (*p. 332*)

Eysenck, H. J.: 'Psychology is about People', *2 March*

Fairlie, Henry: 'The Kennedy Promise', *8 June*

Family life, *4 May* (*p. 485*), *26 Oct.* (*p. 1307*)

Fantasy literature for children, *23 Nov.* (*p. 1427*)

Farwell, Byron: 'Queen Victoria's Little Wars', *15 June*

Faulk, O.B.: 'Tombstone', *6 April*

Felix, David: 'Walther Rathenau and the Weimar Republic', *19 Jan.*

Fellow-travelling, *6 July*

Ferguson, Sarah: 'A Guard Within', *23 Nov.*

Fiedler, L. A.: 'The Stranger in Shakespeare', *30 March*

Finberg, H. P. R. (ed) : 'The Agrarian History of England and Wales', *25 May*

Finlay, Ian: 'Celtic Art', *21 Dec.*

Firbank, Ronald: Biography (Brophy), *30 March*

Fischer, F. W.: 'Max Beckmann', *24 Aug.*

Fisher, Nigel: 'Iain Macleod', *11 May*

Flaubert, Gustave: 'Correspondance', *3 Aug.*

Flew, Antony: 'Crime or Disease?', *2 March*

Floto, Inga: 'Colonel House in Paris', *10 Aug.*

Foot, Michael: 'Aneurin Bevan', *12 Oct.*

Foreign Field, The: Special number, *25 May*

Forster, E. M.: 'Arctic Summer', *21 Sept.*

Frame, Janet: 'Daughter Buffalo', *26 Jan.*

France:
Art and Architecture in Eighteenth Century, *11 May* (*p. 527*)
Present-day, *21 Dec.*
Rise of the Writer, *5 Oct.*

Frankfurt Book Fair, *19 Oct.*

'Frankfurt School', *14 Dec.* (*p. 1539*)

Fraser, Antonia: 'Cromwell', *20 July*

Fraser, P. M.: 'Ptolemaic Alexandria', *9 Nov.*

Frayn, Michael: 'Sweet Dreams', *10 Aug.*

Frege, Gottlob: Biography (Dummett) 217; 'Conceptual Notation and related articles', *2 Feb.*

French and English Dictionary, Harrap's New Standard, *6 April*

Frend, W. H. C.: 'The Rise of the Monophysite Movement', *19 Jan.*

Freud, Sigmund; *23 March* (*p. 317*); and Lou Andreas-Salomé letters, *26 Jan.*

Friedman, Isaiah: 'The Question of Palestine 1914–1918', *2 Nov.*

Frost, Robert and Elinor: 'Family Letters', *26 Jan.*

Fruton, J.S.: 'Molecules and Life', *9 March*

Fuller, Roy: 'Professors and Gods' (Oxford lecture), *9 March, 14 Dec.*

Gadda, C. E.: 'Novella seconda', *27 April*

Galdós, Benito Perez, *12 Oct.*

Gamble, Andrew: 'From Alienation to Surplus Value', *9 Feb.*

Gardner, Helen (ed.): 'The New Oxford Book of English Verse', *16 Feb.*

Gauguin, Paul: in Brittany, *25 May*

Gaulle, General Charles de, *5 Oct.*

Gazley, J. G.: 'The Life of Arthur Young 1741–1820', *28 Dec.*

Geach, P. T.: 'Logic Matters', *2 Feb.*

Genetics and education, 154

George III, *20 July*

Germany:
Biedermeier literature, *19 Jan.*
Weimar Republic, *19 Jan.*

Giannaris, George: 'Mikis Theodorakis', *17 Aug.*

Gilbert, Martin: 'Winston S. Churchill', *9 March*

Giovene, Andrea: 'The Dilemma of Love', *26 Jan.*

Gitelman, Z. Y.: 'Jewish Nationality and Soviet Politics', *3 Aug.*

Glendinning, Nigel: 'Literary History of Spain: The Eighteenth Century' *23 March*

God as the absolute Thou, *28 Dec.*
Goethe: as Scientist, *3 Aug.*
Gopaleen, Myles na: *see* O'Brien, Flann
Gowers, Sir Ernest: 'The Complete Plain Words', *22 June*
Grabar, Oleg: 'The Formation of Islamic Art', *28 Dec.*
Grammar of contemporary English, *2 Feb.* (*p. 123*)
Grammaticus, The Great, 210
Greece:
  Music and social change, *17 Aug.* (*p. 951*)
  Theodorakis and the Colonels, *30 March*
Greek Anthology, *29 June*
Greek medicine, *4 May* (*p. 506*)
Greenberg, Clement: 'Art and Culture' *14 Sept.*
Greene, Graham: 'The Honorary Consul', 200
Greig, Ian: 'Subversion', *26 Oct,*
Grigg, John: 'The Young Lloyd George', *10 Aug.*
Grogan, Emmett: 'Ringolevio', *26 Jan.*
Growth, Limits to, *14 Sept.* (*p. 1041*)
Guattari, Félix: 'Capitalisme et schizophrénie', 'Psychanalyse et transversalité', *16 March*
Guillemin, Henri: 'La liaison Musset-Sand', *30 Nov.*

Haile Selassie I, Emperor: Autobiography, *1 June*
Halberstam, David: 'The Best and the Brightest', *18 May*
Haldane, A. R. B.: 'New Ways Through the Glens', *31 Aug.*
Halsband, Robert: 'Lord Hervey', *2 Nov.*
Hammarskjöld, Dag, *20 April*
Hanley, James: 'A Woman in the Sky', *5 Oct.*
Hardy, Thomas: and Tryphena Sparks *27 April;* 'Thomas Hardy and British Poetry' (Davie), *13 July*
Hare, R. M.: 'Essays on the Moral Concepts', 'Applications of Moral Philosophy', *19 Jan.*
Harlan, L. R.: 'Booker T. Washington' *13 April*

Harris, C. R. S.: 'The Heart and the Vascular System in Ancient Greek Medicine', *4 May*
Harris, José: 'Unemployment and Politics', *9 March*
Hartley, L. P.: 'The Will and the Way', *13 April*
Hašek, Jaroslav: 'The Good Soldier Švejk', *21 Sept.*
Hatton, Ragnhild: 'Louis XIV and his World', *8 June*
Hayter, Alethea: 'A Voyage in Vain', *2 Nov.*
Hayward, Jack: 'The One and Indivisible French Republic', *21 Dec.*
Hazzard, Shirley: 'Defeat of an Ideal', *20 April*
Hegel, Georg W.F., *12 Oct.*
Hegelian Jesus, 115
Heinesen, William: 'Panorama med Regnbue', *2 March*
Helfferich, Karl: Biography (Williamson), *19 Jan.*
Henry II: Biography (Warren), 85
Henry VIII: Florence's musical gift to, *29 June*
Herrmann, Wolfgang: 'The Theory of Claude Perrault', *12 Oct.*
Hervey, Lord: Biography (Halsband), *2 Nov.*
Hesse, Hermann, 175
Hilen, Andrew (ed.): 'The Letters of Henry Wadsworth Longfellow', *9 Nov.*
Hindemith, Paul, *16 March*
History: 'Fiction in History', 'History in Fiction' (articles), *23 March*
Hobsbawm, E. J.: 'Revolutionaries', *17 Aug.*
Hodes, Aubrey: 'Encounter with Martin Buber', *28 Dec.*
Holmes, C. S.: 'The Clocks of Columbus', *1 June*
Homberger, Eric (ed.): 'Ezra Pound: The Critical Heritage', *16 March*
Homer: through Pope, *5 Jan.* (*p. 8*)
Hough, Richard: 'Captain Bligh and Mr. Christian', *26 Jan.*
House, Colonel E. M.: at 1919 Peace Conference, *10 Aug.*
Housman, A. E.: 'Classical Papers', 137

Howard, Dick: 'The Development of the Marxian Dialectic', *9 Feb.*

Howard, Sir Robert: Copy of 'The Country Gentleman' found, *28 Sept.*

Hughes, Richard: 'The Wooden Shepherdess', *6 April*

Hull, D. L.: 'Darwin and His Critics', *9 Nov.*

Hundred Best Books List (article), *16 Feb.* (*p. 189*)

Huxley, Julian: 'Memories II', *5 Oct.*

Ianni, F. A. J.: 'A Family Business', *26 Jan.*

Imagist poetry, *2 Feb.*

Immigrant workers in Western Europe, 46

Inalcik, Halil: 'The Ottoman Empire', *13 April*

Industrial archaeology, *31 Aug.*

Inglis, Brian: 'Roger Casement', 12

IQ, Race and, 154

Ireland:
    Casement and, 12
    Distilling and the spirit trade, *20 April*
    and its Historians, *16 Nov.*
    History, *27 July* (*p. 857*)

Ireland, Northern: *see* Ulster

Islamic art, *28 Dec.*

Islamic history, *16 Nov.*

Italy:
    Allied invasion of, *14 Dec.* (*p. 1543*)
    History since the War, *16 Feb.*
    Poetry, *5 Oct.* (*p. 1176*)
    Politics, *21 Dec.* (*p. 1569*)
    Resistible rise of the Duce, *2 March*

Itard, Jean: 'The Wild Boy of Aveyron, *9 Feb.*

Ives, C. E.: 'Memos', *7 Sept.*

Jackson, Bruce (ed.) 'Wake Up Dead Man', *27 July*

Jackson, Laura: *see* Riding, Laura

Jacobson, Dan: 'The Wonder-Worker' 64; 'Inklings', *16 March*

Jakobson, Roman: 'Questions de poétique', *25 May*

James, Henry, *30 Nov.*

Jameson, Fredric: 'Marxism and Form', *27 April*

Janik, Allan: 'Wittgenstein's Vienna', *17 Aug.*

Javogues, Claude, *26 Oct.* (*p. 1320*)

Jaworska, Wladyslawa: 'Gauguin and the Pont-Aven School', *25 May*

Jay, Peter (ed.): 'The Greek Anthology and Other Ancient Greek Epigrams', *29 June*

Jens, Inge: 'Dichter zwischen rechts und links', *22 June*

Jensen, A. R.: 'Genetics and Education', 'Educability and Group Differences', 154

Jerusalem, *2 Nov.* (*p. 1344*)

Jesus of the Hegelians, 115

Jews:
    'Encyclopaedia Judaica', *23 March*
    Soviet Union and, *3 Aug.*

Johnston, Jennifer: 'The Gates', *26 Jan.*

Jones, Aubrey: 'The New Inflation', *13 July*

Jones, J. R.: 'The Revolution of 1688 in England', *19 Oct.*

Jones, Peter (ed.): 'Imagist Poetry', *2 Feb.*

Joyce, James: Language of (Burgess), *15 June*

Judaica, Encyclopaedia, *23 March*

Jullian, Philippe: 'D'Annunzio', *23 Feb.*

Jung, C. G.: 'Letters', *19 Oct.*

Kaiser, Georg: 'Werke', *1 June*

Kalnein, Wend Graf: 'Art and Architecture of the Eighteenth Century in France', *11 May*

Keneally, Thomas: 'Bring Larks and Heroes', *26 Oct.*

Kennedy Brothers, *8 June*

Kenny, A. J. P. (and others): 'The Nature of Mind', *22 June*

Kenny, Anthony: 'Wittgenstein', *1 June*

Kerenyi, Karl: Hesse's correspondence with, 184

Kerouac, Jack: 'Visions of Cody', *2 Nov.*

Keynes, John Maynard: 'Collected Writings', *27 July*

King, Cecil: 'On Ireland', *16 Nov.*

King, Francis: 'Flights', *19 Oct.*

Kipling, Rudyard: 'Barrack-Room Ballads', *14 Dec.*

Klein, Barbara: 'Gauguin's Paradise Lost', *25 May*

Klemperer, Klemens von: 'Ignaz Seipel', *24 Aug.*

Kline, Morris: 'Mathematical Thought from Ancient to Modern Times', 224

Kocher, P. H.: 'Master of Middle-Earth', *8 June*

Kollman, E. C.: 'Theodor Körner', *24 Aug.*

Körner, Theodor: Biography (Kollman), *24 Aug.*

Kortepeter, C. M.: 'Ottoman Imperialism during the Reformation', *16 Nov.*

Koyré, Alexandre, *31 Aug.*

Kozakiewicz, Stefan: 'Bernardo Bellotto', *5 Jan.*

Krausz, Michael (ed.): 'Critical Essays on the Philosophy of R. G. Collingwood', *30 March*

Kriegel, Annie: 'The French Communists', *21 Dec.*

Lacouture, Jean: 'André Malraux', *7 Dec.*

Lancaster, Osbert: 'The Littlehampton Bequest', *28 Dec.*

Langford, P.: 'The First Rockingham Administration', *20 July*

Languages and Literature, Modern: Special number, *25 May*

Lanier, Emilia, 131

Larkin, Philip (ed.): 'The Oxford Book of Twentieth-Century English Verse', 36

Laslett, Peter (ed.): 'Household and Family in Past Time', *4 May*

Lawrence, D. H.: Three versions of 'Lady Chatterley's Lover', 103

Lee, Joseph: 'The Modernisation of Irish Society 1848–1918', *16 Nov.*

Lenin, V. I.: 'The Other Lenin' (ed. Deutscher), *26 Oct.*

Lenz, Siegfried: 'Das Vorbild', *14 Dec.*

Lessing, Doris: 'The Summer before the Dark', *4 May*

Lessing, Gotthold Ephraim, *6 July*

Letters as Literature: Special number, *26 Jan.*

Levenson, Samuel: 'James Connolly', *27 July*

Levey, Michael: 'Art and Architecture of the Eighteenth Century in France', *11 May* (*p. 527*)

Levin, Harry: 'Grounds for Comparison', *25 May*

Lewis, John: 'The Marxism of Marx', *9 Feb.*

Lewis, Wyndham, *3 Aug.*

Linguistics, *25 May*, *29 June* (*p. 745*)

Linton, William James: Biography (Smith), *23 Nov.* (*p. 1420*)

Lister, Raymond: 'British Romantic Art', *4 May*

Littlehampton Bequest, *28 Dec.*

Livermore, H. V.: 'Portugal', *27 July*

Llosa, M. V.: 'Pantaleón y las visitadoras', *12 Oct.*

Lloyd George, David: 'The Young Lloyd George' (Grigg), *10 Aug.*

Logic, Refoundation of, *2 Feb.*

Loire, Terror in the, *26 Oct.* (*p. 1320*)

Lombard, Maurice: 'Espaces et réseaux du haut moyen âge', 94

London School of Economics Library (article), *2 Feb.*

Longfellow, Henry Wadsworth: 'Letters', *9 Nov.*

Louis XIV, *8 June*

Lowell, Robert: 'The Dolphin', 'For Lizzie and Harriet', 'History', *10 Aug.*

Lucas, Colin: 'The Structure of the Terror', *26 Oct.*

Lukács, Georg: 'Political Writings', *5 Oct.*

Lukes, Steven: 'Émile Durkheim: His Life and Work', *16 March*

Macaulay, Lord: Biography (Clive), *29 June*

MacDonnell, Kevin: 'Eadweard Muybridge', *9 March*

McGuire, E. B.: 'Irish Whiskey', *20 April*

McKelvey, J. L.: 'George III and Lord Bute', *20 July*

Mackenzie, Norman and Jeanne: 'The Time Traveller: The Life of H. G. Wells', *29 June*

McLellan, David: 'Karl Marx', *19 Oct.*

Macleod, Iain: Biography (Fisher), *11 May*

Macmillan, Harold: 'At the End of the Day 1961–1963', 1

MacNeill, Éoin, *16 Nov. (p. 1399)*

McWeiss, Charles (ed.): 'Boswell in Extremes', *23 March*

Madge, Charles: 'Art Students Observed', *21 Sept.*

Maguire, John: 'Marx's Paris Writings' *9 Feb.*

Malamud, Bernard: 'Rembrandt's Hat', *5 Oct.*

Malaparte, Curzio: 'Il ballo al Cremlino e altri inediti di romanzo', *12 Jan.*

Malefakis, E. E.: 'Agrarian Reform and Peasant Revolution in Spain', *16 March*

Malraux, André: Biography (Lacouture), *7 Dec.*

Malson, Lucien: 'Wolf Children', *9 Feb.*

Mandrou, Robert: 'Louis XIIV en son Temps', *8 June*

Manuel, F. E.: 'A Portrait of Isaac Newton', *1 June*

Marchand, L. A. (ed.): 'Byron's Letters and Journals', 122

Martin, Kingsley: Biography (Rolph), *13 April*

Marx and Marxism, *9 Feb.*, *27 April*, *19 Oct (pp. 1283, 1284)*

Mary, William and: Biography (Van der Zee), *19 Oct.*

Mason, H. A.: 'To Homer through Pope', *5 Jan.*

Mathematical heritage, 224

Matisse, Henri: 'Ecrits et propos sur l'art', Biography (Aragon), *16 Feb.*

Maximilian's motets, *7 Dec.*

Maya, Glyphs of the, *5 Oct.*

Medieval economy, 94

Meiggs, Russell: 'The Athenian Empire', *18 May*

Meredith, George: Meeting with the Carlyles, *9 Nov.*

Meslier, Jean: 'Oeuvres complètes', *5 Jan.*

Mexico: Agrarian struggle, *20 July (p. 839)*

Michelangelo, Poetry of, *8 June*

Michels, Volker (ed.): 'Materialien zu Hermann Hesses "Der Steppenwolf"', 176

Mill, John Stuart: New Political Economy of (Schwartz), *9 March;* 'Later Letters', *14 Sept.*

Milton, John: Elitist politics of, *1 June*

Mind, Nature of (Kenny and others), *22 June*

Mishima, Yukio: 'Runaway Horses', 206

Molony, C. J. C. (and others): 'History of the Second World War', *14 Dec.*

Monophysites, *19 Jan.*

Monroe, Elizabeth: 'Philby of Arabia', *7 Dec.*

Monter, B. H.: 'Koz'ma Prutkov', *25 May*

Montesinos, J. F.: 'Galdós', *12 Oct.*

Montgomery, Field Marshal Lord: Biography (Brian Montgomery), *26 Oct.*

Montherlant, Henry de, 165

Moral philosophy, *19 Jan. (p. 65)*

Morgan-Witts, Max: 'The Strange Fate of the Morro Castle', *12 Jan. (p. 49)*

Morrison, Herbert: Biography (Donoughue and Jones), *19 Oct.*

Morro Castle, Fate of the, *12 Jan. (p. 49)*

Muggeridge, Malcolm: 'Chronicles of Wasted Time', *28 Sept.*

Murdoch, Iris: 'The Black Prince', 57

Music:
  Black music and ragtime, *26 Oct.*
  Gift of madrigals and motets, *29 June (p. 751)*
  Greek, *17 Aug. (p. 951)*
  Maximilian's motets, *7 Dec.*
  Stockhausen, *2 March (p. 239)*
  Worksongs from Texas prisons, *27 July*

Mussolini, Benito, *2 March*

Muybridge, Eadweard: and the Zoopraxiscope, *9 March*

Nabokov, Vladimir: 'Transparent Things', 190; 'A Russian Beauty', *12 Oct.*

Naipaul, Shiva: 'The Chip-Chip Gatherers', *13 April*

Newby, P. H.: 'A Lot to Ask', *11 May*

Newman, John Henry: 'Letters and Diaries', *27 July*

Newton, Isaac: the Maths and the man, *1 June*; as Theologian, *29 June;* and Russia, *24 Aug.*

Nicoll, Allardyce: 'English Drama 1900–1930', *29 June*

Nicolson, Benedict: 'Courbet', *6 July*

Nicolson, Nigel: 'Alex', *30 March;* 'Portrait of a Marriage', *2 Nov.*

Nizan, Paul: 'Antoine Bloyé', *24 Aug.*

Novels:
Epistolary novels, *26 Jan.*
'History in Fiction', 'Fiction in History' (articles), *23 March*
Novelist's creation of character, *27 July*
Novels of 1973, 57, 190
Science fiction, 144; Special pages, *9 Nov.*

Nowell, C. E.: 'Portugal', *27 July*

O'Brien, Flann (Myles na Gopaleen) (ed.): 'The Poor Mouth', *7 Dec.*

Oliveira Marques, A. H. de: 'History of Portugal', *27 July*

Omdurman, Battle of, *26 Oct.*

O'Neill, J. P.: 'Workable Design', *30 Nov.*

Opera: Whose 'Carmen'?, *24 Aug.*

Ottoman Empire, 1300–1600, *13 April*

Owen, Wilfred: 'War Poems and Others', *21 Dec.*

Oxford English Dictionary: 'Supplement', *26 Jan.*

Painting and photography, *9 March* (*p. 275*)

Pala, Alberto: 'Isaac Newton, Scienza e filosofia', *1 June*

Palestine, 1914–1918, *2 Nov.*

Paperbacks for children, *15 June* (*p. 671*)

Paris Peace Conference (1919), *10 Aug.* (*p. 929*)

Parkinson, Roger: 'Blood, Toil, Tears and Sweat', *2 March*

Parody, Art of, *25 May* (*p. 595*)

Pasolini, Pier Paolo, *12 Oct.*

Passmore, John: 'The Perfectibility of Man', *12 Jan.*

Pearson, Lester B.: 'Through Diplomacy to Politics', *24 Aug.*

Peloponnesian War, *18 May*

Perrault, Claude: Biography (Herrmann), *12 Oct.*

Peters, Margot: 'Charlotte Brontë', *3 Aug.*

Phelps, Gilbert: 'The Old Believer', *31 Aug.*

Philby, St. John: Biography (Monroe), *7 Dec.*

Phillips, E. D.: 'Greek Medicine', *4 May*

Philology: Politian's 'Miscellaneorum Centuria Secunda', 210

Philosophy of language, 217

Photography:
Painting and, *9 March* (*p. 275*)
Victorian and Edwardian, *21 Dec.* (*p. 1573*)

Picasso: from ten to twenty-two (Cirlot), *2 Feb.*

Pickles, Dorothy: 'The Government and Politics of France', *21 Dec.*

Plant, Raymond: 'Hegel', *12 Oct.*

Poetry:
Children's Verse, Oxford Book of, *15 June*
Eighteenth-Century English Verse, Penguin Book of, *5 Oct.*
English Verse, New Oxford Book of, *16 Feb.*
Imagist, *2 Feb.*
Poetry of 1973, 19
Twentieth-Century English Verse, Oxford Book of, 36

Police, World view of the, *2 March* (*p. 242*)

Politian (Angelo Poliziano): 'Miscellaneorum Centuria Secunda', 210

Pollard, Arthur (ed.): 'Crabbe: The Critical Heritage', *2 Feb.*

Pope, Alexander: 'Dunciad' (Sitter and Erskine-Hill), *5 Jan.* (*p. 6*); and Homer, *5 Jan.* (*p. 8*); as Landscape gardener, *22 June*; Family scandal (articles), *31 Aug.*, *7 Sept.*

Popper, K. R.: 'Objective Knowledge', *16 Feb.*

Portugal, England and, *27 July*

Posner, Donald: 'Watteau: A Lady at her Toilet', *6 July*

Postan, M. M.: 'Essays on Medieval Agriculture and General Problems of the Medieval Economy', 'Medieval Trade and Finance', 94

Pottle, F. A. (ed.): 'Boswell in Extremes', *23 March*

Pouget, Jean: 'Un certain capitaine de Gaulle', *5 Oct.*

Pound, Ezra: 'Selected Prose 1909–1965', 'The Critical Heritage' (ed. Homberger), *16 March*

Powell, Anthony: 'Temporary Kings', 192

Pre-Raphaelite landscape, *10 Aug.*

Printing:
  Special number, *7 Dec.*
  Ten years of new typefaces, *7 Dec.*

Pritchett, V.S.: 'Balzac', *14 Sept.*

Privacy and the numinous, *25 May*

Proust, Marcel: Invisible vocation, *13 April;* Biography (Sansom), *14 Sept.;* Housekeeper's story, *21 Dec.*

Prussian Academy of Arts: 'Poetry Section', *22 June*

'Prutkov, Koz'ma', *25 May* (*p. 595*)

Psychoanalysis, *16 March* (*p. 295*)

Pynchon, Thomas: 'Gravity's Rainbow', 70

Quercia, Jacopo della, *30 Nov.*

Quinton, Anthony: 'The Nature of Things', *23 March*

Quirk, Randolph (and others): 'A Grammar of Contemporary English', *2 Feb.*

Race and IQ, 154

Rackett family, Pope and (articles), *31 Aug.* (*p. 1005*), *7 Sept.* (*p. 1031*)

Rackstraw, S. J.: 'A Question of Answers', *29 June* (*p. 745*)

Ramthun, Hertha (ed.) 'Bertolt-Brecht-Archiv Bestandsverzeichnis', *23 Nov.*

Rathenau, Walter: and the Weimar Republic, *19 Jan.*

Read, P. P.: 'The Upstart', *7 Sept.*

Realism, *9 Feb.*

Religion: Victorian Church and the poor, *5 Oct.*

Religious language, *10 Aug.*

Reprints: Special pages, *26 Jan.*, *30 March*, *22 June*, *28 Sept.*

Reuss-Ianni, Elizabeth: 'A Family Business', *26 Jan.*

Rhodes, P. J.: 'The Athenian Boule', *23 Feb.*

Richards, D. H. (ed.): 'Islamic Civilisation', *16 Nov.*

Richardson, Joanna: 'Enid Starkie', *31 Aug.*

Richardson, Samuel: 'The History of Sir Charles Grandison', *26 Jan.*

Richelieu, Cardinal, *27 July*

Riding, Laura, *9 Feb.*

Riedel, Johannes: 'The Art of Ragtime', *26 Oct.*

Roberts, J. S.: 'Black Music of Two Worlds', *26 Oct.*

Robinson, Ian: 'The Survival of English', *7 Sept.*

Robinson, J. A. T.: 'The Human Face of God', *6 April*

Robinson, W. P.: 'A Question of Answers', *29 June*

Rockingham, Marquis of, *20 July* (*p. 833*)

Rolland, Romain: Hesse's Correspondence with, 184

Rolph, C. H.: 'Kingsley', *13 April*

Romanticism, *4 May* (*p. 499*), *8 June*

Rondfeldt, David: 'Atencingo', *20 July*

Roosevelt, Franklin D.: Essays on (Tugwell), *27 July*

Rosicrucian Movement, *20 April* (*p. 445*)

Roth, Philip: 'The Breast', *23 March*: 'The Great American Novel', *21 Sept.*

Rousseau, Jean-Jacques: as Musician, *20 July*

Rowse, A. L.: 'Shakespeare the Man', 130

Royal Anthropological Institute Library (article), *6 July*

Rubens, Peter Paul: Before 1620, *6 July*

Rule, J. B.: 'Private Lives and Public Surveillance', *25 May*

Ruskin Family Letters, *14 Dec.*

Russia (*see also* Soviet Union): Newton and, *24 Aug.*

Sachs, Albie: 'Justice in South Africa', 7 *Sept.*

Ste Croix, G. E. M. de: 'The Origins of the Peloponnesian War', *18 May*

St. John of the Cross: His Life and Poetry (Brenan), *24 Aug.*

Salzinger, Helmut: 'Swinging Benjamin', *14 Dec.*

Sampson, Anthony: 'Sovereign State: The Secret History of ITT', *3 Aug.*

Sand, George: 'Correspondance', *30 Nov.*

Sansom, William: 'Proust and his World', *14 Sept.*

Sassoon, Siegfried: 'Poet's Pilgrimage' (Corrigan), *7 Dec.*

Satirist, Art of the, *5 Jan.*

Schafer, W. J.: 'The Art of Ragtime', *26 Oct.*

Schatzman, Morton: 'Soul Murder', *13 July*

Schlesinger, A. M. (ed.): 'History of U.S. Political Parties', *2 Nov.*

Schoenberg, Arnold: as Painter, *13 July*

School Library Association conference *28 Sept.* (*p. 1111*)

Schreber family, *13 July*

Schumann, Robert, *27 April*

Schwartz, Pedro: 'The New Political Economy of J. S. Mill', *9 March*

Sciascia, Leonardo: 'Il mare colore del vino', *5 Oct.*

Science, History of, *31 Aug.* (*p. 994*)

Science fiction, History of, 144; Special pages, *9 Nov.*

Scotland: Helping the Highlands, *31 Aug.*

Scott, Sir Walter: 'Journal', *5 Jan.*

Second Strings (articles), *1, 8, 15, 22, 29 June, 13, 20 July, 3 Aug.*

Seipel, Ignaz: Biography (Klemperer), *24 Aug.*

Semiotics, Survey of: Special numbers, *5, 12 Oct.*

Sengle, Friedrich: 'Biedermeierzeit', *19 Jan.*

Seymour, Charles (jr): 'Jacopo della Quercia, Sculptor', *30 Nov.*

Shakespeare:
Biography (Rowse), 130

Birmingham Shakespeare Library Catalogue, *14 Dec.*
German translation, *2 Feb.* (*p. 126*)
New light on a dark lady, 130
Riddle of the Sonnets, *30 March* (*p. 346*)

Shaw, D. E.: 'Literary History of Spain: The Nineteenth Century', *23 March*

Shaw, George Bernard: Study of plays (Valency), *26 Oct.*

Shelley, P. B.: 'Complete Poetical Works', *2 March*

Shils, Edward: 'The Intellectuals and the Powers and other Essays', *26 Jan.*

Shipping: Fate of the Morro Castle, *12 Jan.*

Short Title Catalogue 1641–1700, *26 Jan.*

Shulman, Milton: 'The Least Worst Television in the World', *13 April*

Sillitoe, Alan: 'Men Women and Children', *19 Oct.*

Simon, Claude: 'Triptyque', 198

Sithole, Ndabaningi: 'The Polygamist', *31 Aug.*

Sitter, J. E.: 'The Poetry of Pope's "Dunciad" ', *5 Jan.*

Sitwell, Sacheverell: 'For Want of the Golden City', *10 Aug.*

Škvorecký, Josef: 'Mirákl', *13 April*

Slim, H. Colin: 'A Gift of Madrigals and Motets', *29 June*

Smith, Anthony: 'The Shadow in the Cave', *16 Nov.*

Smith, F. B.: 'Radical Artisan', *23 Nov.*

Smollett, Tobias, *26 Jan.*

Sonnino, Sidney: 'Diario', *21 Dec.*

South Africa: Justice in, *7 Sept.*

Soviet Union:
'Bulletin of the Opposition', *23 Nov.*
Jews in, *3 Aug.*
Protest and conformism in, *19 Oct.* (*p. 1267*)

Spain:
End of the Republic, *16 March*
Literary history, *23 March*

Sparks, Tryphena: Thomas Hardy and, *27 April*

Staley, Allen: 'The Pre-Raphaelite Landscape', *10 Aug.*

Starkie, Enid: Biography (Richardson), *31 Aug.*

Stern, J. P.: 'On Realism', *9 Feb.*

Stevens, Joan (ed.): 'Mary Taylor, Friend of Charlotte Brontë', *3 Aug.*

Stevens, Wallace, *6 April*

Stocchi, M. P. (ed.): 'Politian's Miscellaneorum Centuria Secunda', 210

Stockhausen, Karlheinz, *2 March*

Stone, Lawrence: 'Family and Fortune', *13 July*

Storey, David: 'A Temporary Life', 196

Storey, Mark (ed.): 'Clare: The Critical Heritage', *27 July*

Strachey, John: Biography (Thomas), *11 May*

Strauss, D. F.: 'The Life of Jesus Critically Examined', 115

Strauss, Richard: Biography (Del Mar), *18 May*

Subversion, *26 Oct.*

Tamrat, Taddesse: 'Church and State in Ethiopia', *19 Jan.*

Taylor, Ian (and others): 'The New Criminology', *24 Aug.*

Taylor, Mary: Friend of Charlotte Brontë, *3 Aug.* (*p. 903*)

Television:
British, *13 April*
Children's books and, *6 April*

Témime, Emile: 'The Revolution and Civil War in Spain', *16 March*

Tennants of the Glen, *8 June*

Theatre and drama:
Actors and character (article), *27 July*
English drama 1900–1930, *29 June*
Georg Kaiser, *1 June*
Lost Restoration comedy found, *28 Sept.*
'Theatre of War' (Bentley), *25 May*

Theodorakis, Mikis: 'Journals of Resistance', *30 March:* Biography (Giannaris), *17 Aug.*

Thomas, Gordon: 'The Strange Fate of the Morro Castle', *12 Jan.*

Thomas, Hugh: 'Europe: The Radical Challenge', *23 Feb.; 'John Strachey', *11 May*

Thompson, H. A.: 'The Athenian Agora', *11 May*

Thompson, J. E. S. (ed.): 'The Dresden Codex', *5 Oct.*

Thompson, R. W.: 'Generalissimo Churchill', *26 Oct.*

Thought in Western and non-Western Societies, Modes of, *15 Sept.*

Thurber, James: Biography (Holmes), *1 June*

Tolkien, J. R. R., *8 June* (*p. 629*)

Tolstoy, Count Aleksei, *25 May* (*p. 595*)

Tombstone: Myth and reality, *6 April*

Tomory, Peter: 'The Life and Art of Henry Fuseli', *4 May*

Toulmin, Stephen: 'Wittgenstein's Vienna', *17 Aug.*

Toulouse-Lautrec, Henri de: *Catalogue raisonné* (Dortu), *15 June*

Toynbee, Arnold: 'Constantine Porphyrogenitus and His World', *11 May*

Trevor, William: 'Elizabeth Alone', *26 Oct.*

Trollope, Anthony: Palliser Novels, *20 April*

Trotsky's 'Bulletin of the Opposition', *23 Nov.*

Truman, Harry S.: Biography (by Margaret Truman), *7 Sept.*

Tschichold, Jan: 'Chinese Colour Prints', *21 Sept.*

Tugwell, R. G.: 'In Search of Roosevelt', *27 July*

Turner, Merfyn: 'Dealing with Deviants', *16 Feb.*

Ulam, Adam: 'The Fall of the American University', *2 Feb.*

Ulster, *7 Sept.* (*p. 1029*)

Unemployment, *9 March* (*p. 267*)

United Nations: Secretaries-General, *20 April*

United States:
Art, *9 Nov.*
Bibliographica, *9 March* (*p. 276*)
Book production, *7 Dec.* (*p. 1511*)
Cuba, and, *12 Jan.*
Dawn of the New Deal, *27 July*
Foreign policy, *19 Oct.* (*p. 1267*)
ITT scandals, *3 Aug.*
Political parties, *2 Nov.*

United States (*cont.*):
Truman, President, *7 Sept.*
Universities, *2 Feb.* (*p. 115*)
Updike, John: 'Museums and Women',
4 May
Urbanism, *23 Feb.* (*p. 204*), *7 Sept.*,
7 Dec. (*p. 1520*)
Urquhart, Brian: 'Hammarskjöld',
20 April
Ustinov, N. B.: 'Klop and the Ustinov
Family', *1 June*

Vaculík, Ludvík: 'The Axe', 'The
Guinea Pigs', 66
Valency, Maurice: 'The Cart and the
Trumpet', *26 Oct.*
Vandalism, *26 Oct.*
Van der Zee, Henri and Barbara:
'William and Mary', *19 Oct.*
Viallaneix, Paul: 'Le premier Camus',
12 Oct.
Victorian Church and the poor, *5 Oct.*
Victorian city, The, *7 Sept.*
Victorian periodicals, Wellesley Index
to (1824–1900), *9 Feb.*
Victorian studies, *11 May* (*p. 530*)
Victorian Treasure-House (Conrad),
6 July
Vietnam, *18 May*, *21 Dec.* (*p. 1565*)
Volker, Klaus (ed.): 'Brecht-Chronik',
23 Nov.
Voltaire, Studies on, *20 April*, *4 May*,
13 July, *21 Sept.*
Vonnegut, Kurt (jr.): 'Breakfast of
Champions', 'Happy Birthday,
Wanda June', *20 July*

Waddington, C. H. (ed.): 'Towards a
Theoretical Biology', *18 May*
Wait, R. J. C.: 'The Background to
Shakespeare's Sonnets', *30 March*
Waldheim, Kurt: 'The Austrian Ex-
ample', *24 Aug.*
Walton, Paul: 'From Alienation to
Surplus Value', *9 Feb.*
War, For and against, *15 June*
War, Second World:
Dunkirk to Alamein, *2 March* (*p.
231*)
History, *14 Dec.*
Warren, W. L.: 'Henry II', 85
Washington, Booker T., *13 April*
Watteau, J. A.: 'La Toilette', *6 July*

Wedgwood, C. V.: 'Oliver Cromwell',
20 July
Weightman, John: 'The Concept of
the Avant-Garde', *25 May*
Weinberger, Barbara: 'Art Students
Observed', *21 Sept.*
Welch, Denton: 'Maiden Voyage',
'Journals', *28 Sept.*
Wellesley Index to Victorian Periodic-
als, *9 Feb.*
Wells, H. G.: Biography (Mackenzie),
29 June
West, Rebecca: Criticism (Wolfe),
74
Westfall, R. S.: 'Force in Newton's
Physics', *1 June*
Whiskey, Irish, *20 April* (*p. 441*)
White, Patrick: 'The Eye of the
Storm', *21 Sept.*
Whiteley, Stuart: 'Dealing with
Deviants', *16 Feb.*
William and Mary: Biography (Van
der Zee) *19 Oct.*
Williams, Bernard: 'Problems of the
Self', *14 Dec.*
Williams, Raymond: 'The Country and
the City', *7 Sept.*
Williamson, J. G.: 'Karl Helfferich',
19 Jan.
Willmott, Peter: 'The Symmetrical
Family', *26 Oct.*
Wilson, Angus: 'As If By Magic', 60
Wilson, John: 'CB. A life of Sir
Henry Campbell-Bannerman', *2
Feb.*
Wilson, Woodrow, *10 Aug.* (*p. 929*)
Winchester Psalter, *28 Sept.* (*p. 1140*)
Wing, D. G.: 'Short Title Catalogue . . .
1641–1700', *26 Jan.*
Winnifrith, Tom: 'The Brontës and
Their Background', *3 Aug.*
Wiskemann, Elizabeth: 'Italy since
1945', *16 Feb.*
Wittgenstein, Ludwig: Biography
(Kenny), *1 June*; Austrian back-
ground, *17 Aug.*
Wodehouse, P. G.: 'The Little Nugget',
'Sam the Sudden', 'Pearls, Girls
and Monty Bodkin', *26 Jan.*
Wolf children, *9 Feb.* (*p. 145*)
Wolfe, Peter: 'Rebecca West: Artist
and Thinker', 74
Workers abroad, 46

Wormald, Francis: 'The Winchester Psalter', *28 Sept.*

Wörner, K. H.: 'Stockhausen', *2 March*

Wycherley, R. E.: 'The Athenian Agora', *11 May*

Yates, F. A.: 'The Rosicrucian Enlightenment', *20 April*

Yeats, W. B., *19 Jan.*

Young, Arthur: Biography (Gazley), *28 Dec.*

Young, Michael: 'The Symmetrical Family', *26 Oct.*

Youngson, A. J.: 'After the Forty-Five', *31 Aug.*

Zeller, Bernhard: 'Hermann Hesse', 188

Zhemchuzhnikov Brothers, *25 May* (*p. 595*)

Ziegler, Philip: 'Omdurman', *26 Oct.*